T5-BPY-606

BETJEMAN

The Making of the Christian Imagination

Stephen Prickett
general editor

OTHER BOOKS IN THIS SERIES

Rowan Williams, *Dostoevsky*

BETJEMAN
Writing the Public Life

Kevin J. Gardner

BAYLOR UNIVERSITY PRESS

PR
6003
.E77
Z676
2010

© 2010 by Baylor University Press
Waco, Texas 76798-7363

All Rights Reserved. No part of this publication may be reproduced, stored in a retrieval system, or transmitted, in any form or by any means, electronic, mechanical, photocopying, recording or otherwise, without the prior permission in writing of Baylor University Press.

Jacket Design by Andrew Brozyna, AJB Design, Inc.
Cover Art: Martin Jennings' sculpture of John Betjeman, St. Pancras Station, London, UK. Photograph © Troika Photos Ltd., 2010. Used by permission. Background image © iStockPhoto.com/Linda Steward

The work of Sir John Betjeman is reproduced here by kind permission of the Estate of John Betjeman.

Library of Congress Cataloging-in-Publication Data

Gardner, Kevin J.
  Betjeman : writing the public life / Kevin J. Gardner.
      p. cm. -- (Making of the Christian imagination)
  Includes bibliographical references (p.   ) and index.
  ISBN 978-1-60258-254-5 (hardback : alk. paper)
  1. Betjeman, John, 1906-1984--Criticism and interpretation. 2. Betjeman, John, 1906-1984--Religion. 3. Religion in literature. I. Title.
  PR6003.E77Z676 2010
  823'.912--dc22

                                    2010007763

Printed in the United States of America on acid-free paper with a minimum of 30% pcw recycled content.

To Hilary

and

to Graham

Contents

"What I don't relish is the feeling that I have become the object of envy and—what's much worse—of professional inquiry for Eng. Lit., which is the death of literature."

John Betjeman
Daily Herald, 1961

PREFACE

This book began its life with an essay, "Anglicanism and the Poetry of John Betjeman," which I published in *Christianity and Literature* in 2004. Expanding that article into the present book has been a delightful experience. I could hardly imagine a more congenial subject than Sir John Betjeman, nor could I ask for the processes of research, writing, and production to have gone more smoothly. As a result, there are many to whom I will remain deeply grateful and profoundly indebted.

Foremost among these is my editor, Stephen Prickett, who encouraged me to write this book, who patiently offered advice on my writing, and who steadily guided this project through to publication. Without Stephen this book would not have been written. I am grateful as well to Carey Newman, director of the Baylor University Press, for his support of this project, and to Bob Banning, Caroline Gear, Cassandra Nelson, Peter Rice, Diane Smith, and Elisabeth Wolfe for their help with the production. My continuing thanks are due as well to Robin Baird-Smith and Ben Hayes of Continuum Books, who were the first in the publishing world to support and encourage my work on Betjeman.

This project would also not have been possible without the groundbreaking work of Bevis Hillier and Bill Peterson. Few biographers have accomplished for their subjects what Hillier has for Betjeman in his magisterial trilogy. No one can write about Betjeman without first dining at the great feast laid out so generously by Hillier. My thanks are due to Bevis as well for his careful and generous reading of the first draft of this manuscript and for his thoughtful criticism and helpful suggestions for improvement. Bill Peterson's new catalogue of Betjeman's writings—itself a monument to bibliographic scholarship—has now joined Bevis Hillier's biographies as an indispensable aid to Betjeman scholars. It proved vital and essential in my research, and I am grateful to Bill as well for his helpful and patient responses to my many queries. I owe an unpayable debt to both Bevis Hillier and Bill Peterson.

I am thankful as well to have made the acquaintance of, and to have shared ideas with, other scholars passionate about Betjeman, including Roger Pringle, Philip Payton, John Bale, Greg Morse, and especially Stephen Games, who shares my deep commitment to broadening an understanding of Betjeman and to showing the world the rich complexity of his thinking and writing. Without Games' anthologies of Betjeman's radio and film scripts, my book would have been a significantly less substantial account of the influence of Anglicanism on Betjeman's thinking. Games' work has been not only an invaluable aid to my own understanding of Betjeman but a delight to thousands of readers.

I am grateful to a number of people at Baylor University, whose assistance was invaluable as well. Dr. Lee Nordt, Dean of the College of Arts and Sciences, and the Research Leave Committee awarded me a research leave for the spring semester in 2008 that gave me the time away from teaching that was essential to writing the bulk of this manuscript. Andrew Armond, who served as my research assistant in 2006, helped to make much of my initial historical research such a delight. I am especially appreciative of Ken Carriveau and his staff in interlibrary services at Moody Memorial Library, who tirelessly filled my seemingly endless requests for obscure publications. Dr. Dianna Vitanza, chair of the English department, gave invaluable support to this project in its final stages, and I owe her a debt of gratitude.

Following is a list of permissions granted for the use of excerpts from secondary material: *John Betjeman: Reading the Victorians* by Greg Morse (Sussex, 2008), used by permission of Sussex Academic Press; *John Betjeman Letters, vols. 1 & 2*, edited and introduced by Candida Lycett Green (London, 2006), used by permission of Methuen; *The Letters of Evelyn Waugh*, edited by Mark Amory (London: Weidenfeld and Nicolson, 1980), used by permission of The Wylie Agency and the Orion Publishing Group; *The Essays, Articles and Reviews of Evelyn Waugh*, edited by Donat Gallagher (London: Methuen/Boston: Little,

Brown, 1983), used by permission of The Wylie Agency and Little, Brown & Co.; *John Betjeman: A Bibliography* by William S. Peterson (Oxford: Oxford University Press, 2006), used by permission of Oxford University Press.

Lastly, I must acknowledge my gratitude to the estate of the late Sir John Betjeman, who have granted me permission to quote from his works. Unless otherwise noted, quotations from Betjeman's poems are from the most recent edition of his *Collected Poems* (London: John Murray, 2006), which includes *Uncollected Poems*. Citations are made parenthetically by page number preceded with the abbreviation *CP*. The date of initial publication of individual poems is provided parenthetically upon first citation. I have used the first edition for quotations from his autobiographical poem *Summoned by Bells* (London: John Murray, 1960), with citations in endnotes. Quotations from other poems not published in *Collected Poems* and from all of his prose works and broadcasts are cited individually in endnotes.

Introduction

A man's religion colours his work.[1]

Mention the name of John Betjeman (1906–1984) in the United States and you will likely elicit little more than a shrug of unfamiliarity, even from a literary scholar. The response in the United Kingdom, however, could hardly be more antipodal. More than twenty years after his death he is still widely remembered: as a poet of suburbia and nostalgic Englishness, as a radio and television personality and the beloved teddy bear to a nation,[2] and as a devotee of causes that at one time must have seemed amusingly quaint or even eccentric. Victorian architecture, abandoned churches, gas lamps, and London's early suburbs were among the threatened hallmarks of English culture whose preservation he pioneered. The 2006 centenary of his birth, which went unnoticed in the United States, occasioned in the United Kingdom innumerable publications, exhibitions, broadcasts, and retrospective celebrations.[3] Even now, hardly a week passes without Betjeman's name cropping up in British newspapers, usually without recourse to his actual words or ideas, often used as shorthand for a particular and narrow idea of Englishness. Allusions to Betjeman in the popular press typically and unfortunately diminish the complexity of his vision in order to promote a nostalgic, middlebrow fantasy or bourgeois political agenda that has little to do with who this man truly was and what he represented. John Betjeman was in fact a complex of contradictions: a retiring poet who enjoyed being a public figure; a modernist in a traditionalist's garb who could write glibly of a "Jacobean wireless set" and a "Perpendicular gramophone"[4]; a lover of steam engines and narrow-gauge branch lines and all things archaic who adroitly used radio and television to advance his causes; a loather of automobiles and traffic congestion who launched and edited a series of motorists' guidebooks for Shell Petroleum; and a lifelong Anglican and preserver of churches who struggled mightily to believe the faith.

It is this aspect of Betjeman and his religion that is the occasion of this book. For this very public figure, faith was no private matter. He openly declared his Christian faith, using poetry, newspapers and magazines, and radio and television broadcasts to address issues ranging from articles of faith to the relationship between religion and culture. He celebrated the social and aesthetic joys of Anglicanism, describing the intersection of architecture and faith, of beauty and the spirit: the physical and spatial splendor of its churches, the joy of its liturgy and worship, and its role in providing a cultural identity for the English people. However, he was no simple propagandist for the Church of England or for Christianity. He demonstrated the social and spiritual failings of Christianity in general as well as his own spiritual failures. He wrote of the perils of a life of faith and described the anxiety of death without the certainty of Christian consolation. And yet, despite such doubts and frustrations, he wrote unapologetically of his commitment to Anglicanism. Through his own journey of faith and doubt, Betjeman was able not only to describe the parabola of his own religious belief but also to illumine the nature of belief for all his readers. Since doubts were so weighty for him, he relied on the traditions of the Church of England to offer spiritual sustenance, and quite naturally its essence infuses his poetry and prose. Because so much of his work is constructed with the stuff of English Christianity, it is my contention that his poetry is specifically "Anglican" in nature and a vital part of a living tradition of Anglican poetry and worship.

But what exactly is meant by "Anglican"? It has often been noted that the Church of England, along with the entire Anglican Communion, resists definition, that it can only be described. As Bishop Stephen Neill admits, "There is an Anglican attitude and an Anglican atmosphere that defies analysis."[5] A central paradox concerns the place of Anglicanism in time: its doctrine of apostolic succession suggests a quality of timelessness, yet the denomination was clearly born in the historical moment of King Henry VIII's break with Rome in November 1534. The result of this paradox is that the Church of England is both Catholic and Protestant. Since it is a liturgical church, its prayer book and its common rites, along with other ritual displays of formal worship, are certainly among its defining qualities. Beyond its unusual history and its marked aesthetics of worship, Anglicanism has several characteristics that clearly imbue the church, its adherents, and Betjeman's writings. Not least among these is an acceptance, a celebration even, of spiritual mystery, accompanied by a suspicion of rigid or dogmatic theological positions. Related to this is the tendency for Anglicans, even (or especially) among the clergy, to experience their faith ranging between belief and doubt; the Anglican spiritual life is tolerant of unbelief, for in the struggle with doubt the believer may at last discover the presence of God. Because of the profound emphasis Anglicanism places on the doctrine of the incarnation, according to which God not only took on human form but remains incarnate in the created world, encounters with the divine are thus possible when one remains open to God's surprising if unlikely manifestations. It is its social position, however, that may be most distinct. As an established church, enjoying an officially sanctioned status by the government, the Church of England has cultural significance well beyond its religious role. Its emphasis on history and tradition means that it has (or at least once had) a vital and irreducible place in the community—for example, the parish church as the center of village life. Betjeman's poetry embodies this intrinsic, constitutional weaving of religion and culture: if faith provides cultural identity, then being an Englishman means being an Anglican. This is the romanticized version of Anglicanism at the heart of Betjeman's imagination.

Such openness among modern writers about the vital and essential nature of religion is rare, especially for such a public figure. Of all Betjeman's achievements perhaps his most significant was becoming the great poet of the church in his time. My claim is undoubtedly a bold one and thus demands explanation. A number of his contemporaries were also accomplished poets who embraced the Church of England: such were T. S. Eliot, W. H. Auden, and R. S. Thomas. To be the great poet of the church, however, is to be the poetic *sine qua non* of Anglicanism. Thomas, Auden, and Eliot were poets and Anglicans, but Betjeman was the poet of Anglicanism. It was Betjeman who most dramatically intoned the culture of the church, who most consistently celebrated its beauty and mystery, and who unfailingly voiced its potency as the unifying source of English culture. This is not to claim that his was the greatest voice of Christian belief; certainly his poetic concerns were remote from theology. Rather it is the material culture of Anglicanism that comprises so much of his verse; no poet since George Herbert has made such a fetish of the Church of England, and no poet ever has made such an unequivocal connection between Anglicanism and Englishness. In a 1943 radio address to a nation besieged by continuing threats of Nazi invasion, Betjeman described the things he treasured most about England—the sense memory of its churches: "My eyes, my nose, my ears all strain for England when I am away: oil lamps on bold Gothic mouldings at Evensong in a country church; tattered copies of *Hymns Ancient and Modern*; the crackle of the slow-combustion stove."[6] His idea of Englishness is imbedded in ecclesial imagery: "For me, at any rate, England stands for the Church of England, eccentric incumbents, oil-lit churches, Women's Institutes, modest village inns, arguments about cow parsley on the altar."[7] What is most significant when he enumerates the threatened hallmarks of Englishness is that he defines England foremost by the stuff of Anglican culture.

Yet what unites Betjeman with his fellow twentieth-century Anglican poets—beyond his friendship with each—is well worth considering.[8] Like Eliot, he believed that religion was the primary source of culture, and therefore that the decline of religion in the West was responsible for the cultural fragmentation that each perceived in the twentieth century. Both poets were drawn to Anglicanism for its symbolic role: the national church was (potentially) a unifying cultural and spiritual force. Betjeman would certainly have agreed with Eliot's pronouncement: "The religious sense, and the sense of community, cannot be finally divorced from each other."[9] Auden's embrace of Anglicanism had less to do with an obsession with cultural unity than with the simple pleasures to be found in high Anglican worship. Like Betjeman, he delighted in liturgy, ritual, and the almost magical quality of both the ceremonies and the spaces in which they were conducted. Theologically for Auden, however, Anglicanism was merely one proper way of worshipping. What he appreciated about the correctness in Anglican worship was "that it is first and foremost a community in action, a thing done together, and only secondarily a matter of individual feeling or thinking."[10] Auden recognized the fundamental goal of unity within Anglicanism, yet he did not place great value on it himself. More than either Eliot or Betjeman, Auden was a theologically minded poet, though heterodox, and in most ways he should be considered more broadly as a Christian poet, rather than an Anglican poet. The example of R. S. Thomas strays considerably from the Anglican experiences of Eliot, Auden, and Betjeman. Thomas was a lifelong Anglican priest as well as a poet, though he shared Betjeman's and Auden's natural propensity toward theological doubt. In fact, his faith in poetry was always stronger than his faith in Christianity: "my whole vocation as priest and preacher . . . ," he once said, "is to present poetry."[11] If Thomas' commitment to Christianity was tenuous, his commitment to Anglicanism was even more so: he was a priest in the Church in Wales, the Welsh branch of Anglicanism that enjoys the political privileges of establishment but endures the indignity of its minority status in a country wherein nonconformity (i.e., Protestant dissent) enjoys a paradoxical majority. Anglicanism could therefore never suggest cultural unity to a poet in Thomas' position, even if his poetry is rife with musings on faith and worship.

Though Betjeman clearly stands among those poets who have contributed to the making of the Christian imagination, it is fair to ask how much influence Betjeman had (or has) as a writer and to question the extent to which the works of his Christian imagination have rooted themselves into English culture, or into Christian culture as a whole. To a great degree, the sales figures of his books—more than three million volumes of his poetry sold to date—together with the public accolades he received attest to the fact that he is one of the most influential of twentieth-century writers. In Great Britain, if not in the rest of the world, Betjeman remains a household name, as his centenary celebrations revealed. His fame is attributable to more than his poems, however; he is equally famous for his numerous and diverse writings on architecture and topography (including the Shell Guides to English counties, a series which he developed and edited, and for which he wrote a number of the volumes), for his many documentary films commemorating England's vanishing heritage, for his tireless campaigns to save threatened architectural landmarks and natural landscapes, for his service on national commissions along with his countless appearances on radio and television panels to promote the preservation of English culture, and also for the public awards and honors he collected (a CBE, a knighthood, the laureateship, a governorship in Oxford's Pusey House, and so forth). By the time of his death, a mystique had already grown about him, suffusing and labeling his interests as "Betjemanesque."[12] Even by Betjeman's middle age, a reviewer could claim that "He has created an attitude, a myth perhaps, almost a dialect."[13] An extended study of Betjeman's careers as poet, journalist, and radio and television writer and broadcaster will reveal just how extensive was his contribution to modern culture and to the Christian imagination. His poetry and prose alike show a way of thinking about Anglicanism, about the Church of England, about English Christianity, and about Englishness itself.[14]

To many readers familiar with Betjeman, his idea of Englishness is a celebration of middle-class suburbia, what he once called the "illegitimate child" of town and country.[15] These were the settings that inspired Betjeman in countless poems, essays, and films, and almost certainly no other poet of the twentieth century has gained such inspiration from the seemingly uninspiring. As his friend Osbert Lancaster observed, "In a predominantly middle-class civilisation he is the only writer who has succeeded in wringing poetry out of the middle classes."[16] From his first published volume of poetry to his final television films, Betjeman sang the praises of a world at which other poets turned up their noses. "The Outer Suburbs" (1931), an early poem thus far excluded from his *Collected Poems*, describes endless lines of faux Tudor brick boxes stretching deep into London's home counties; the result is a mélange of beauty and pathos tinged with a touch of amusement:

> The weary walk from Oakleigh Park
> Through the soft suburban dark
> Bedizened with electric lights
> Which stream across these Northern Heights.
> In blackened blocks against the view
> Stands gabled Rosslyn Avenue,

And bright within each kitchenette
The things for morning tea are set.
A stained-glass window, red and green,
Shines, hiding what should not be seen
While wifie knits through hubbie's gloom
Safe in the Drage-way drawing-room.
Oh how expectant for the bed
All "Jacobethan" overhead![17]

Despite the tackiness and dreariness of the suburban setting, Betjeman has wrought a unique poetic vision from this scene. The barest hint of a spiritual life is hinted at here in the modern, domestic stained-glass window, whose cheapness implies a shallowness in contemporary faith. If there is condescension toward the world of the middle class in this early poem, it would give way to deeper appreciations and more potent concerns. By 1946, despairing that "all England will soon be one great suburb," he wrote nonetheless in praise of the suburb: "Here are the roots of a young London and of the new mechanical England. They are firm in the only fruitful earth for human beings, the earth of family life." He would conclude this piece with an artistic manifesto suggesting the possibilities of poetic inspiration in these very suburbs. "God has given to artists and poets the gift of making beauty out of chaos," he wrote, and if these "new suburbs are still chaos," the poets and artists will nevertheless reveal the beauty inherent in suburbia.[18] Betjeman may have been the only artist to respond to his own manifesto, but he did so wholeheartedly, finding in suburbia not only the beautiful but the spiritual as well. In 1973 he made his great television film, *Metro-land*, a tribute to the suburbs that developed along the rail lines leading out of London:

Over the points by electrical traction,
Out of the chimney-pots into the openness,
'Til we come to the suburb that's thought to be commonplace,
Home of the gnome and the average citizen.[19]

There was nothing commonplace about Betjeman's treatment of suburbia: *Metro-land* was a tribute to real people and their lives and homes, and the film has been widely praised for its celebration of Englishness.[20]

Why then has a poet so cherished as a national icon generated so little light or heat from the community of academic scholars? Critical snobbery against Betjeman's sources of poetic inspiration has something to do with it, but his success is also to blame. Based on sales figures, Betjeman is arguably the most popular of twentieth-century poets. His work endures the dubious distinction of being enjoyed by millions of readers, many of whom never otherwise read poetry. This is, as Dennis Brown so aptly observed, "a fact worth taking seriously in a democratic society."[21] And yet academic scholars have by and large ignored him.[22] The surprising paucity of critical attention to Betjeman from the light industry of academia is attributable in part to his popularity; it is an ugly truth, alas, and one most critics prefer to hide, that academic criticism is inveterately prejudiced against a poet who enjoys widespread acclaim and popularity. If the masses approve, the poetry must be inferior—or so goes a standard of critical thinking since T. S. Eliot. For poet and critic John Wain, for example, Betjeman's popularity was proof not only of his "pathetic inadequacy" but also of the bad judgment of "the mass middle-brow public."[23] Fortunately, there has been much sound resistance to this critical snobbery over the years.[24] Nevertheless, misunderstandings of Betjeman are rife. To dismiss him as "a purveyor of nostalgic, middle-class greetings-card whimsy" or as "a weird light-entertainment act" whose "stock was retrospective sentimentality," as critic A. A. Gill wrote in the *Sunday Times* during the centenary hype in 2006, is entirely to misread him and perhaps to reject him solely on the basis that he remains popular with middlebrow readers.[25] That he is lionized outside intellectual circles does not mean his works lack serious, intelligent, and psychologically complex ideas as well as rich poetic structure. Reading Betjeman's writings sensitively, particularly within the context of his faith, will effectively counter the neglect from obscurantist literary critics as well as the knee-jerk outbursts and snobbish hostility from ill-tempered media critics.[26]

Prejudice also exists against modern poets who so openly eschew the tenets of modernism, and Betjeman's verse is certainly traditional. Instead of innovating with meter and form, he preferred to cast his poems in molds successfully employed by Victorian poets and hymnodists, giving himself a unique if untenable position among twentieth-century poets.[27] Early in Betjeman's poetic career, his friend and editor John Sparrow noted that Betjeman's poetry is "a pleasant change from the shapeless and unarticulated matter, the 'fluid puddings,' offered us by so many of his contemporaries. He delights the ear by the sound of his words, the run of his lines, the shape of his stanzas."[28] Although in structure Betjeman appears to be an antimodernist, he was clearly engaged with his culture, and his language is immersed in the sensibility of modernism.[29] In fact, Betjeman was not nearly so opposed to the edifice of modernism as is often claimed; instead, he was quite open-minded about the modern world.[30] In tone Betjeman was often a prophet of doom; like many of his fellow poets he rejected the popular fantasy of endless progress and social advancement for humanity, using poetry as a vehicle to excoriate society for its cultural, spiritual, political, and aesthetic failures. However, Betjeman could just as often resist the cynical despair that typifies twentieth-century poetry; contrasting the modernisms of Eliot and Betjeman, Timothy Mowl notes succinctly that "one poet neurotically writhes; the other cheerfully embraces modernity."[31] In any case, to be easily understood—as Betjeman always aimed to be in verse—did not create respect in the hostile climate of modernism. Faulting him for rejecting the principles of literary modernism and for resuscitating a poetic tradition believed to be properly dead and buried, Betjeman's early critics refused to engage his verse on its own terms and unfairly attacked him with those of Pound and Eliot.[32] Such tactics did not dissuade the numerous reviewers and fellow poets who praised Betjeman's publications through the decades, and eventually his critics drifted into silence.[33] Hostile criticism of him has all but disappeared, and the void of silence is gradually filling with measured evaluations, in part due to the magisterial biographical trilogy published to great acclaim by Bevis Hillier.[34]

A further explanation for Betjeman's rejection by academic scholars may be his deeply held Christian beliefs. Betjeman was quite forthright about his faith, writing in 1948, "It's never easy, the Christian life, and the more effort it demands, the more worth keeping up it is."[35] Critics have little trouble coping with the religious poems of seventeenth-century writers, poets who lived in what was still an age of faith; but what should we do with a troublesome twentieth-century poet who persisted in believing the tenets of Christianity despite the overwhelming counterclaims of science and philosophy? For Betjeman, the church provided a faith system, a cultural identity, and a set of images with which to stock his verse. As Evelyn Waugh sagely observed to his old friend Betjeman as early as 1947, "you have built your life & learning & art round the Church of England."[36] Indeed, Anglicanism occupied Betjeman's thought and imagination more than any other subject. In prose and poetry alike, the church was an ever-present concern, something that defined the nation and its subjects and something he defined as well. "Our Church of England," he wrote in 1951, "is a sacramental Church. We claim that it has Apostolic succession. We stress the sacraments of Baptism and Holy Communion. Many of us use the other sacraments which are available in our church. We are a unity in ourselves. We have Protestants and Catholics among us. Our teaching is in our catechism and Prayer Book. Many millions have died in it."[37] The remarkable fact of Betjeman's studied faith in an age of skepticism, his sentimentality in a time of jaundiced cynicism, makes him interesting and worthy of serious attention.

The study that follows centers on the most significant influence in the development of Betjeman's poetic imagination and that element of his life that he took most seriously: the Church of England. In chapter 1, I discuss the various manifestations, meanings, and paradoxes of Betjeman's Anglicanism, exploring his numerous and often contradictory statements on and evocations of faith and doubt. Using texts as various as poems, letters, journalism, and broadcasts, I show the unflagging centrality of Anglicanism in his life and imagination. In chapter 2, I focus on the obsessive role of doubt in Betjeman's life, particularly his recurring anxieties about death and the absence of God. These anxieties I place within an Anglican context, showing how belief demands a dialogue with doubt within the Anglican tradition. Whereas this chapter dwells on Betjeman's doubt, chapter 3 explores the manifestations of belief in his writings. Although belief was rarely secure for Betjeman, it nevertheless ran deep in his thinking and writing, as he was forever perceiving a profound spiritual mystery that expressed itself in sexuality and nature. Chapter 4 turns to Betjeman's public life as a leading campaigner for the preservation of England's natural and built heritage to show that his Anglican faith informed and guided his social conscience. For him, faith was not compartmentalized but infused into all thought and action. Having established the public role that faith could play in his life, in chapter 5 I explore the implications of a social faith. For Betjeman, Anglicanism was not merely the spiritual center of life but the cultural center as well, and he embraced the Church of England for its communal spirit and its capability of uniting a diverse and disparate nation into one. In Betjeman's writings, Anglicanism is indeed paradoxical, embracing a dialectic of faith and doubt, spirit and culture. In the end, his Anglicanism infused essentially all that he wrote, thought, and accomplished.

This is an Anglicanism that is at times romanticized and at times historicized, but always spiritual. His poetry in particular is part of a living tradition rooted in Anglican spirituality that includes such poets as Donne, Herbert, and Vaughan, as well as Eliot, Auden, and Thomas.[38] Betjeman clearly belongs to this poetic tradition characterized by, in the words of A. M. Allchin, a "persistent capacity to stimulate the creation of works of art directly linked to the prayer of the Church."[39] Throughout his *Collected Poems* are poems whose titles are highly evocative of the church, including "In Westminster Abbey," "St. Saviour's, Aberdeen Park, Highbury, London, N.," and "Lenten Thoughts of a High Anglican." In fact, at least a third of his poems are specifically about matters of his faith and his church, while countless others allude to Anglicanism and employ ecclesial imagery. Not just in his poetry but throughout his very public life Betjeman devoted his energies to celebrating the architecture, the ritual, and the history of the church. For many years he supported his family as a journalist, writing for daily as well as weekly and monthly presses, and as often as his editors permitted he turned to ecclesial topics.[40] But especially through his numerous BBC radio talks, and later through his documentary films for BBC television, he spread the gospel of life in the Church of England to the public. In the 1950s, he also read on the radio a popular series of original poems called "Poems in the Porch," using his typical blend of humor and sentiment to explore church life and matters of faith.[41] At the same time, he was occupied with his magnum opus of English ecclesiastical architecture, publishing in 1958 his *Collins Guide to English Parish Churches*, considered by many to be the most authoritative architectural guidebook to churches and for which Betjeman's introductory essay is a masterpiece in scope and style. Further illustrating the relationship between his work and his faith, in addition to a host of minor prose works, are *Altar and Pew: Church of England Verses* (1959), an anthology of Anglican poems he edited; *The City of London Churches* (1965), a guidebook he wrote for the immensely popular Pitkin Pictorials series, still sold at tourist sites; and the 1981 collection of his own verse, *Church Poems*, accompanied by line drawings done by his friend John Piper.[42] Together, Betjeman's diverse works of poetry, history, and architectural criticism establish the centrality of the Church of England in his imagination.

Undoubtedly, he dedicated his life not only to advancing an appreciation of the Anglican manifestation of Christianity but also to agitating the nation out of its spiritual indolence. For Betjeman, England's ever-ringing church bells, with their magnificently varied clangs, chimes, peals, and tings, summon a lax nation to a common faith and a sense of community. Clearly his favored Anglican symbol, the church bell is associated in his mind with the muse of poetry, as he even titled his verse autobiography, an account of his poetic and spiritual awakening, *Summoned by Bells* (1960). For Betjeman, church bells summon the believer to worship and to a communal tradition, but they also embody the essence of the English landscape by way of a metaphysical experience of nature and eternity. All this he describes in his marvelous BBC film *A Passion for Churches* (1974):

> I hear a deep, sad undertone in bells—
> Which calls the Middle Ages back to me.
> From prime to compline, the monastic hours
> Echo in bells along the windy marsh
> And fade away. They leave me to the ghosts
> Which seem to look from this enormous sky
> Upon the ruins of a grandeur gone.[43]

Here the resonating bells, the changes ringing across the land to fill all space, embody Betjeman's concept of the spirit of God. The poet's faith in a Christian eternity is challenged by his sense of isolation in the universe, while his hope for the renewal of England is rutted by anxiety caused by cultural decay. In the words of Stephen Games, "A cloud hangs over almost everything he cherishes."[44] For Betjeman, hope and despair were never far apart, especially when faced with England's growing indifference to religion. As the nation waited for a new cathedral in Coventry to be built out of the ruin and rubble left by the Luftwaffe, Betjeman insisted that such a design could "only come from a man of sincere belief," for the idea was not to produce a masterpiece of ecclesial architecture but to "shake the populace around it out of its indifference."[45] Shaking the people out of their spiritual indifference was Betjeman's primary obligation as a writer, and it was rooted in his lifelong faith. This was a public faith; it was not merely about how God worked in his life but about how God worked in the lives of the people of England.

Although Betjeman was an influential apologist for the Church of England and for Christianity, personal questions of belief run throughout his work. He wrote scathingly and satirically of ecclesiastical and spiritual corruption, smugness, and complacency. He posed questions about faith and the struggle to believe in Christianity's promise of salvation, exploring the uncertainty of eternity beyond the inevitability of death as well as his own recurring terror of dying. Despite such doubts and frustrations he wrote unapologetically about his faith, celebrating the wonders and mysteries of God incarnate in the world. This idea is central in his 1950 letter about religious doubt to his friend Alan Pryce-Jones. Though he confesses to doubting at times the divinity of Christ, Betjeman insists that the world about him provides all the evidence he needs in order to believe: "And I have only to look round me at various spires, towns, domes, hospitals, and ways of doing things to know that other people have known He was God too. And I know I have to go on practising the Faith by receiving the Sacraments."[46] Betjeman's evidence of God's existence lies not just in the natural world but in the things people have done and have built that illustrate godly principles and the enduring faith of humanity in God's love. Perhaps because of the recurrence of doubt, Betjeman knew that truth cannot be determined absolutely; when mystery and ambiguity are embraced, one can sense the incarnate God even in the most extraordinary of situations. As he depicts it, amid mundane human activity God became incarnate at the nativity, but an even greater mystery resides in the fact of God's real presence, his immanence within the Communion elements. For Betjeman, there may be no stronger statement of his faith in the incarnational nature of God than in the mysterious symbolism of the Eucharist. Throughout his writings, eucharistic motifs reveal humanity persisting in its obsessive preoccupation with self and with technological advancement, all but obliterating the capability of perceiving God. Nevertheless, Betjeman sensed that God is immanent, still present in our world for anyone who dares to be still, to look, and to listen. It is this idea that he uses to conclude "St. Saviour's, Aberdeen Park, Highbury, London, N." (1946):

> Wonder beyond Time's wonders, that Bread so white and small
>   Veiled in golden curtains, too mighty for men to see,
> Is the Power which sends the shadows up this polychrome wall,
>   Is God who created the present, the chain-smoking millions and me;
> Beyond the throb of the engines is the throbbing heart of all—
>   Christ, at this Highbury altar, I offer myself To Thee. (*CP* 127)

ETERNITY CONTAINED IN TIME
The Paradoxes of Betjeman's Anglicanism

> Perhaps a religious history should come first. It is interwoven into my
> life more than anything else. I have rarely fully believed & equally rarely
> fully disbelieved.[1]

John Betjeman's profession of the centrality of religion in his life
should not be underestimated. For all his love of writing and reading poetry, his passion for visiting old railway stations and mouldy
churches, and his commitment to the preservation of human and
natural landscapes threatened by thoughtless development, it was a
mature Anglican faith that held the most import and value in his life.
As he avowed in 1947 to poet William Plomer, "I am a Church of England Catholic. I *love* the Church of England."[2] The meaning of Betjeman's Anglicanism has surely been a point of significant disagreement
among the legions of his readers and fans, however. Those who require
that he be an exemplary Christian believer find plenty of evidence in
his writings to support this position, but those who need him to be a
doubter find ample cause as well. It does not help matters that he could
think of himself as an "Agnostic Christian."[3] Betjeman certainly made
numerous public confessions of his faith, yet he also admitted candidly
to suffering surfeits of doubt. For Betjeman faith was not a private cir-
cumstance. He openly declared his Christian belief, using not only his
poetry but also radio and television to address issues ranging from articles of faith to the relationship between religion and culture. Although

his devotion to the Church of England was well known to the public, faith was not an easy matter for Betjeman in the quiet of his own spirituality. As his friend Auberon Waugh (son of the novelist Evelyn Waugh) eulogized him, "I am almost certain he decided to affect a cosy certainty in religion which he was never within miles of feeling."[4] His poems reveal little such affectation, however, as he was often plagued by nagging spiritual doubts: a fear that he was unfit for heaven, a terror of dying, and an anxiety that Christianity's promises might all be empty. Still, he sustained his faith, partly by devoting so much of his writing to his faith and to the spiritual and social roles of the English church, but especially by committing his own life to a devout observance of Anglican worship.

Betjeman's public and private commitment to the Church of England, so apparent through his poems, journalism, broadcasts, and correspondence, could thus be taken as a sign either of a committed faith or of a façade masking spiritual anxiety. Those who doubt the sincerity of his public claims of faith typically argue that Betjeman could not believe in any aspect of the church other than the symbolic cohesion it provided the English people, that he loved the church because it was so old, so unchanging, and so very English. Patrick Taylor-Martin, for instance, insisted that the "Englishness" of his religion was more important to him than its catholicity; Betjeman's church was "a social and spiritual entity rooted in the English soil. . . . It was the national religion and, as such, demanded his allegiance and loyalty."[5] At times Betjeman himself seemed to substantiate this opinion, as in *London on Sunday*, a popular 1972 television film:

> Church remains the same:
> A reminiscence of the good old days
> Our parents lived in and of Sunday roasts.
> Church is a change from lonely sitting rooms,
> For rich or poor the aches of age come on.
> Church is a chance once more of making friends
> And meeting the Eternal here on earth.[6]

Here the appeal of a church lies in the temporal fellowship of Englishness, not in its religiosity. The Englishness of Anglicanism was indeed vital to him (though, as I shall argue, no less vital than its catholicity).

For one of Britain's most beloved icons of Englishness, however, there likely were undercurrents of self-doubt concerning his own identity. Philip Payton has noted that Betjeman was "never confident of his English credentials" and that he "remained convinced that at root he was an outsider in England."[7] His verse autobiography, *Summoned by Bells* (1960), makes clear that his Dutch (or German) surname caused him anxiety about his Englishness. Childhood insecurity created by anti-German sentiment in the Great War was a likely contributor to his lifelong obsession with Englishness, and despite his mother's attempt at reassurance ("Thank God you're English on your mother's side"[8]), Betjeman reached for external symbols of Englishness as psychological security and to convince himself of his national identity. The most reliable of these symbols was perhaps the church:

> Safe were those evenings of the pre-war world
> When firelight shone on green linoleum;
> I heard the church bells hollowing out the sky,
> Deep beyond deep, like never-ending stars.[9]

It may not thus surprise that his friend and fellow poet Philip Larkin should observe that Betjeman's faith seemed "dependent not only on actual churches . . . but on England itself."[10]

Beginning with this early perception of the church as the basic symbol of his English identity, Betjeman would come to see the church as the primary source and symbol of Englishness for the entire nation. In a 1938 radio address, he averred that "the old churches of England are the story of England. They alone remain islands of calm in the seething roar of what we now call civilisation."[11] In 1953 he lamented the increasing scarcity of unblemished churches: "There are few things more beautiful than a candle-lit church and few things in modern England that are rarer."[12] The preservation of the church and its traditions was tantamount to the preservation of society. Betjeman wrote to novelist Oliver Stonor in 1948 that one should attend the closest Anglican church even if one does not care for the local vicar and parish because it helps to sustain village life: "I go on going to church because I know that however awful my church is, it is Christ's body in this village and I can't rend it apart by leaving it."[13] Though the pronoun referent here is vague, I think it likely that Betjeman was referring to disintegrating the village in a social way more than a theological one. And Betjeman's poems often celebrate the church for its symbolic role in uniting a disparate people. "To Uffington Ringers" (1942), written during a bout of homesickness while he was working in Dublin during the war, notes the emotional consolations of the church but excludes any spiritual consolation:

> And here is Ireland, hemisphered in stars:
>   High, lucky stars! you hang on Berkshire too,
>   On brittle Christmas grass of Berkshire ground.
> And fierce, above the moonlight, blazes Mars.
> Would, Berkshire ringers, I could wait with you
>   To swing your starlit belfries into sound.[14]

Despite his frequent attendance at church and his partaking of the sacrament of the Eucharist, faith did at times leave him, and in its absence Betjeman was able to find spiritual resonance in the cultural traditions embodied in the English church. He admitted to Evelyn Waugh in 1947 that "upbringing, habit, environment, connections—all sorts of worldly things" caused him to love the Church of England. Nevertheless, it is important to note that he went on in this letter to insist that those cultural valuations would not matter at all "if I *knew*, in the Pauline sense, that Our Lord was not present at an Anglican Mass."[15]

Some have argued that essentially all Betjeman cared for in the church was its aesthetics: the pleasure that came from church crawling and from his scholar's knowledge of ecclesiastical architecture, and the delight he found in the indulgent rituals and fashions of high church worship. After all, Betjeman himself wrote, "Churchgoing is one of London's greatest and least-tasted pleasures."[16] Dennis Brown claims that Betjeman's "key religious perception" is less about theology "than about a sacred *caritas* revealed in hallowed places and buildings, consecrated customs and rituals, dedicated music making, flower arranging, days of special observance or celebration, and reverence for time-honoured 'petits récits'—most particularly from the Bible and Prayer Book."[17] Indeed there is a measure of truth here. In 1938 Betjeman wrote to the future Anglican priest Gerard Irvine about the aesthetic delectation of Anglo-Catholicism: "I think I am a Catholic in a low way. Red velvet and a couple of candles for illumination. Prayer book version of the Mass. In fact Georgian 'High' Church. Frequent mass, celebrated in a long surplice and black scarf at a red velvet covered communion table. Clear glass. Box pews."[18] Betjeman's tastes were certainly refined, and undoubtedly one aspect of his interest in religion was a superficial attachment to the trappings of Anglo-Catholicism; however, there was much more to his experience of church than aesthetic delights. In the poem "Anglo-Catholic Congresses" (1966), the voice of an aging poet recalls with excitement his youthful discovery of the beauty and pageantry of Anglo-Catholicism in the 1920s: the incense, the bells, the "fiddle-back vestments," the candles, the banner-led processions. In this movement Betjeman recalls witnessing the revitalization of faith and a rebirth of devotion, "the waking days / When Faith was taught and fanned to a golden blaze" (*CP* 265). Indeed Betjeman tried to emphasize that the splendors of Anglo-Catholicism were meaningless unless they directed worshippers to a stronger faith. As he wrote to church architect Ninian Comper in 1939, "I wonder how many hundreds have been instructed in Catholicism by your planning, delicacy of proportion, texture and colour? Many, I suspect—me for one. . . . So long as you go on doing what only you in England can do, you will be doing God's will."[19] In a 1943 book called *English Cities and Small Towns*, Betjeman described how visiting a poorly restored church indeed diminished his aesthetic appreciation of the place but added that worshipping there created an altogether different experience. Then, aesthetic pleasures (or disappointments) were no longer an issue: "Only by worshipping in the church, at an early Communion service, do I forget the restoration and learn to love the building."[20] Even in a church whose beauty he adored, the worship was of greater import; as he said of Blisland parish church, one of his favorites in Cornwall, "I think I like the look of this church best of all when it is being used—when, as here, you see human figures giving scale and purpose to the glorious decoration designed for the service of God."[21] It is clearly the act of worship rather than the aesthetic experience that matters.

Betjeman's writings reveal that an interpretation of his faith as merely aesthetic or social is only a partial truth at best. The national decline of faith and churchgoing was of paramount concern to him. In fact, Betjeman insisted that aesthetic concerns in liturgy were now displaced by more pressing matters: "What bothers a young clergyman is not how many candles he is to be allowed on the altar, but the apathy of his parish to any form of divine worship whatsoever."[22] Indeed the spiritual apathy of the nation and the emptiness of churches, especially in the cities, was an ongoing concern for Betjeman. At the same time that he was assailing the bishop of London for selling off its withering city churches, he found himself fascinated with Billy Graham's Greater London Crusade in the spring of 1954. Writing in the *Spectator* "as an Anglo-Catholic to whom the revivalistic approach is unattractive," Betjeman found nonetheless a deep attraction to Graham's message and an appreciation for his accomplishments. According to Betjeman's report, Graham "has the great Evangelical love of Our Lord as Man. Jesus as a person is vivid to him. . . . He is genuinely above religious differences and . . . his message is that people should return to their particular churches." This was very open-minded in an Anglo-Catholic, wedded to set prayer-book formulae rather than to fervent, extempore preaching. Betjeman's hope seemed to be that Graham's evangelism would help to fill not only England's Nonconformist churches but also its Anglican churches. "Let the Church go on saying its offices, administering the sacraments," Betjeman concluded with gratitude to Billy Graham, and "Let it not sell all its old churches in the cities to build new ones in the suburbs."[23] This was the theme of his next column in the *Spectator*, less than a month later. He argued that the doomed Church of St. Peter, Windmill Street, sited in "the most used and depraved part of London," was of value not for its architecture but as a mission outpost. "How many prostitutes or people lost in London, of all ages and races, might not have found sanctuary and advice here, had this church been kept open . . . by a community of mission priests?" Alas, Betjeman concludes, "the Bishop has been advised by keen young business efficiency experts who, for all their sincerity, have let money and population statistics argue their case for closing the church. But imagination and a little more Faith, Hope and Charity would have kept it open."[24]

In other contexts, Betjeman would insist that an empty church was not empty at all. This is a paradox that he learned through the mysteries of Anglican theology. For instance, he insisted that "an empty church is full, especially one in which the Consecrated Host is reserved in a tabernacle or cupboard in the wall with a light before it. Such a building may be alarming. One may feel oneself elbowed out by angels but the emptiness is awe-inspiring, not desolate. . . . Churches are built on reality in the mystical sense of that word."[25] If paradoxes characterize Betjeman's faith, so does humility. In a 1944 radio broadcast, he asserted that his own faith lacked an intellectual underpinning but argued effectively that a rational pursuit of faith could easily lead to doubt and despair:

> I fancy that few are even convinced intellectually of the mysteries of the true faith. Indeed, the intellect is a stumbling block to belief. Speaking as a non-intellectual and as a believing member of the Church of England, I can well understand the bewilderment of someone who has lapsed from it, who is of another faith or who has never considered the importance of religious belief when they read the Church catechism in the prayer book. It requires as big a surrender of pride to accept those few but inspirational demands as it does to accept the demands of any defined faith, even Nazism. It involves taking a lot on trust from the centuries.[26]

Despite his anti-intellectual assertion, this is a carefully reasoned argument. (One can find such carefully crafted poses throughout his writings.) He understands that the intellect is likely to lead one away from faith, and he therefore models his thinking after the New Testament gospel, appropriating not only Christ's humility but also the concept of surrender. Ever the typical Anglican, he emphasizes the vitality of tradition as a source of belief and inspiration, and, perhaps most effectively of all, he confesses his personal history of a lapsed faith, implying that the tendency to doubt is a strong and recurring one indeed.

These ideas are central to the sermon Betjeman preached at Evensong in St. Matthew's Church, Northhampton, on 5 May 1946, a sermon filled with rhetorical echoes of such poems as "Christmas," "A Lincolnshire Church," and "St. Saviour's, Aberdeen Park, Highbury, London, N."[27] Betjeman began with praise for the architectural beauty and mystery of St. Matthew's but insisted that it was the spiritual life of the church, not its aesthetics, that brought him to his knees: "For this is a building which has been loved and prayed in. Your prayers, particularly at the Holy Communion, have soaked its stones in worship and have made St. Matthew's a place where it is easy for a stranger to humble himself before God, to ask Him questions and to wait, in the reverent stillness of the congregation at the beautiful singing of '*O Lamb of God*,' for His answer." Betjeman then confessed his personal difficulty in believing in God, the incarnation, the resurrection, and God's continuing immanence in the Church. He asks, then answers this difficult question: "And there, where that light is twinkling through the iron screen in the Lady Chapel, nearly 2,000 years later, is that where He is Himself present in the form of consecrated bread and wine? When I worship with you at the Mass I *know* it is true. And those moments when I *know* this is true remain in the memory so that doubt is dispelled." He concludes his sermon with a call to a life of prayer, to pray not merely at home but here in the church, "before the altar or before the Blessed Sacrament where our Lord lives more intensely than anywhere else." His advice is to "Wait and listen." This will not be easy, for there are many distractions, ranging from one's own thoughts to the noises of life in a technological age; however, "gradually a silence will be caverned out of the noise and you are in the Presence of God." This active life of prayer, he insists, will grant us the spiritual rest we crave, "the real calm sense of proportion in this roaring world. . . . God's time is not our time. . . . He will settle your problems for you, if you listen to Him and pray."[28] In the honest confessions of this sermon Betjeman reveals a deep and personal faith and an intellectual and spiritual commitment to God that could survive the onslaught of doubts both rational and emotional.

It is nonetheless true that Betjeman frequently experienced and acknowledged a difficulty in believing, true also that he was frequently dogged by spiritual lapses. However, he tried to quell his theological fears and to maintain his faith by participating in the timeless traditions of Christian worship. As he wrote in the *Spectator* in 1954, "frequent confession and communion have proved to me, unwilling though I sometimes am to believe, that prayer works, that Christ is God, and that He is present in the Sacraments of the Church of England."[29] Later that year, again in the *Spectator*, he wrote that "the only practical way to face the dreaded lonely journey into Eternity seems to me the Christian one. I therefore try to believe that Christ was God, made Man and gives Eternal Life, and that I may be confirmed in this belief by clinging to the sacraments and by prayer."[30] Indeed Betjeman put great stock in the power of prayer, especially those prayers of committed believers such as the Anglican nuns of the Society of the Precious Blood: "This place has in my own experience caused what seemed like miracles to happen when I have asked for its prayers about particular personal problems," he claimed in the pages of the *Spectator*.[31] Elsewhere he described his own experience of prayer in metaphors redolent of both danger and comfort: "Willing to pray, the mind waits on the edge of a sliding stream. The prayers push the boat off out into the current. Once in the stream, the prayer is effortless compulsion carrying the mind along and sometimes swerving close to the presence of the Creator."[32] Betjeman's private admissions were somewhat less overt and assured than what he published, and he was more willing to confess to doubts in private than in public. To his old friend Evelyn Waugh, Betjeman confessed in 1947 that he was "assailed by doubt," yet he insisted, "I do know for certain that there is nothing else I want to believe but that our Lord was the Son of God and all He said is true."[33] Here he admits not that he *does* believe but that he *desires* to believe. All his life he tried to rid himself of uncertainty, but the difficulty in believing persisted. Though he loved the Church of England and its rituals, it is clear that he often struggled mightily to embrace the central Christian tenets of God's forgiveness and eternal life. What Betjeman's desire to believe suggests, however, is not precisely an anxiety that Christianity's promise is a myth or that God does not exist. Instead, what he craves is a confirming sense of God's presence, when what he is too often left with is a sensation of God's absence. Though he would give voice to this spiritual emptiness time and again in his poetry, it is balanced with an insistence that living the Christian's life is more important than consistently believing in the finer points of its doctrines.

This is a central idea in Betjeman's 1939 letter to the economist Roy Harrod, in which Betjeman had described himself to be, like Harrod, "an Agnostic Christian."[34] Harrod had written to disparage religion for failing to solve either the world's problems or an individual's. Though Betjeman claims that he is no philosopher and that he does not have the intellectual gifts to engage in Christian apologetics, he nonetheless undertakes a remarkable if unlikely response that functions as a brief and rare Christian apologetic. (Indeed Betjeman was not a Christian apologist in the sense in which we commonly understand that term and was happy to let C. S. Lewis monopolize that title. Though he never indulged in the sorts of Christian writing in which Lewis specialized, like Lewis he used the radio to advance his own stamp of Christianity.[35]) In this letter Betjeman addresses both the social and the spiritual strengths of the religion. He agrees with Harrod that the church has flaws and that it cannot easily solve social problems—poverty, brutality, madness, and so forth—due to human frailty. Betjeman deflects Harrod's charge that religion fails to provide solutions to these ageless problems by showing how social ills are rooted in the fundamental imperfection of humanity and the etiological problem of good and evil. Though he fears his letter may come across as "arrogant, proselytising and smug," he continues to defend Christianity on the basis that—this was 1939 after all—it was capable of "immunising people against worse creeds, such as Fascism."

However, it is Betjeman's defense of Christianity on a personal rather than social level that gives this letter its great power. Christianity may be hard to believe in, but Betjeman turns its dubiety to great effect in his surprising suggestion that atheists have chosen the easier intellectual path: "It boils down to the alternative: materialist or Christian. For intellectuals the materialist standpoint is the obvious one and the easiest. The second is harder, but I hold that it is the most satisfactory, especially when one comes up against injustice, birth and death." To Betjeman, the Christian standpoint is obviously difficult and demanding, and embracing Christianity does not—and need not—exempt one from doubt:

> I choose the Christian's way (and completely fail to live up to it) because I believe it true and because I believe—for possibly a split second in six months, but that's enough—that Christ is really the incarnate son of God and that Sacraments are a means of grace and that grace alone gives one the power to do what one ought to do. And once I have accepted that, the questions of atonement, the Trinity, Heaven and Hell become logical and correct.

Two points in this passage seem significant. One is Betjeman's offhand remark that Christianity is first a choice before it is a belief; acting as a Christian—or trying sincerely to do so—is much more important than the abstractions of belief. Doing precedes believing. The other is that one need not believe—at least not consistently—in order to consider oneself a Christian. And so he ends by suggesting that he and Roy really are quite alike in their shared abhorrence of vice. Thus, Betjeman concludes, "I know that you are an Agnostic Christian. So am I for most of the time." What allowed Betjeman to accept and even embrace the doubt within his spiritual life was the great tolerance for ambiguity within his particular stamp of Christianity, the Church of England.

Because Anglicanism played such a vital role in Betjeman's life and imagination, it is worth recounting his tortuous journey through the church. This journey is marked by distinct and recurring motifs, the first of which was a regular observance of the sacraments and a devotion to the life of the church. Born 28 August 1906, he was baptized on 25 November 1906 at St. Anne Brookfield, a Victorian church near the family home in Parliament Hill Mansions in the north London suburb of Highgate. (Betjeman would later recall his Highgate parish church as ominous and foreboding: the "bells from sad St. Anne's" and the "awe and mystery . . . in the purple dark of thin St. Anne's."[36]) Following an adolescent affectation of atheism at Marlborough, where he refused the sacrament of confirmation, he was at last confirmed at Oxford's Pusey House when he was an undergraduate at Magdalen. In 1933, he eloped with Penelope Chetwode, the ceremony kept secret in order to postpone the wrath of her aristocratic father and to prevent her losing her annual allowance. Though the union was sealed in a London register office, at Betjeman's insistence the sacrament was solemnized afterwards in a nearby church, St. Anselm's, Davies Street.[37] Except for a brief period of worshipping with the Quakers in the 1930s, Betjeman was a committed Anglican throughout his adult life, making every effort to receive the sacrament of Holy Communion as frequently as possible and worshipping regularly in his parish church, wherever he was living. Following his death on 19 May 1984, he was buried according to Anglican rites in the churchyard of St. Enodoc, a beloved old church near his seaside home in Trebetherick, Cornwall.

In addition to observing the sacraments, Betjeman's religious life was also characterized by an abiding commitment to the life of the Church of England. During his and Penelope's years in Berkshire, and then in London when his work in journalism and broadcasting (together with a failing marriage) necessitated that he take a flat in the City,[38] Betjeman was constantly active in a series of parishes. In 1934 the Betjemans moved to Uffington, where they involved themselves in the parish church

famed now as then
The perfect Parker's Glossary specimen
Of purest Early English, tall and pale,
—To tourists the Cathedral of the Vale,
To us the church. (*CP* 391)[39]

Here at Uffington St. Mary, Betjeman learned the art of bell ringing, which would become such an important symbol in his poetry, and served as people's warden. Also at Uffington John and Penelope organized a Parochial Youth Fellowship, and their efforts, though largely of a secular entertainment nature, were much appreciated by the villagers. In 1939 he yielded to the blandishments of T. S. Eliot and attended and lectured at a Student Christian Movement summer camp in Swanwick, Derbyshire.[40] Following their move to Farnborough in 1945, the Betjemans were still active in their local parish. At Farnborough All Saints, where Betjeman is memorialized in a window by John Piper, he saw himself and Penelope as the chief supporters of the parish. In a 1947 letter to Evelyn Waugh, he wrote:

> If we were to desert it, there would be no one to whip up people to attend the services, to run the church organisations, to keep the dilatory and woolly-minded incumbent (who lives in another village) to the celebration of Communion services any Sunday. It is just because it is so disheartening and so difficult and so easy to betray, that we must keep this Christian witness going. In villages people still follow a lead and we are the only people here who will give a lead. I know that to desert this wounded and neglected church would be to betray Our Lord.[41]

Eventually, John was left to lead the parish by himself, as Penelope—partly from the influence of Waugh, as we shall shortly see—renounced Anglicanism in favor of Roman Catholicism. When the family moved to Wantage in 1951, Betjeman was again involved in the parish church. At Ss. Peter and Paul he participated in a restoration appeal, lent the growing fame of his name to such mundane events as church bazaars, and wrote a history of the church. When he took up residence in London in 1954, he attended services at St. Bartholomew the Great in West Smithfield and served on its parochial church council. There he met the chaplain of St. Bartholomew's Hospital, through whose influence he took up a ministry of hospital visitation to terminal patients.

Betjeman's lay ministry to the dying suggests a second motif in his spiritual journey: an anxiety about death. "I think about death every day of my life," he wrote in 1958. "I do not think it is morbid to do so but natural." Yet these "natural" thoughts often took a "morbid" turn as Betjeman dwelled obsessively on what would follow death. In early childhood, he was troubled by fears of damnation that in adulthood were supplanted by panicky anxieties of extinction: "And then I think perhaps there is no life beyond the grave and no God and the promises of Christ are not true and I think I would rather hell than extinction and anyhow I am going away alone, as alone as I came into the world."[42] He first heard of hell from his "hateful nurse," Maud; tormented by Calvinistic demons, she was convinced she would be consumed by eternal flames and expressed her anxiety by abusing the boy. As he recounted in his poetic autobiography, *Summoned by Bells* (1960), she would punish him by

> Thrusting me back to babyhood with threats
> Of nappies, dummies and the feeding bottle.
> She rubbed my face in messes I had made
> And was the first to tell me about Hell,
> Admitting she was going there herself.[43]

Maud's fears taught him to dread God's wrath and to doubt himself—anxieties he would never outgrow, as he wrote in "N.W.5 & N.6" (1957):

> It was not what she'd do
> That frightened me so much as did her fear
> And guilt at endlessness. I caught them too,
> Hating to think of sphere succeeding sphere
> Into eternity and God's dread will.
> I caught her terror then. I have it still. (*CP* 232)

His childhood fear of dying did indeed stay with him, which may explain the comfort the adult Betjeman would find in the poetry of William Blake, whose *Songs of Innocence* and *Songs of Experience* are marvelous palliatives against the miseries and torments of childhood; it might even explain his choice of Blake—a preference he stated late in his life—as England's greatest religious poet.[44]

Despite the psychological torture of his early spiritual experience, the young Betjeman embraced the church, even writing his earliest verses in imitation of the Anglican hymnal, *Hymns Ancient and Modern*. Indeed, he continued to be fascinated by the church and all that went with it. A third motif in his Anglican journey appears in his love of the aesthetics of English churches. This began to take hold of him during his prep-school days at the Dragon School in Oxford, where he developed a scholarly knowledge of English ecclesiastical architecture. He described in *Summoned by Bells* how he would cycle around Oxford on weekends, carefully exploring its churches and absorbing as much of its history and aesthetics as he could apprehend:

> Who knew what undiscovered glories hung
>
> Waiting in locked-up churches—vaulting shafts,
>
> Pillar-piscinas, floreated caps,
>
> Squints, squinches, low side windows, quoins and groins—
>
> Till I had roused the Vicar, found the key,
>
> And made a quick inspection of the church?[45]

Cursory inspections gave way to detailed examinations as an adult, when Betjeman became well known for his writings on church architecture, a lifetime pursuit crowned by his *Collins Guide to English Parish Churches* and the BBC film *A Passion for Churches*.[46] Of the two hundred or more civic and ecclesiastical organizations that he served or supported during his lifetime, the diocesan advisory committees of London and Oxford were among his strongest commitments. He served the Oxford Diocesan Advisory Committee for thirty-two years as an advisor on matters of ecclesiastical architecture, and he was also active on both the Council for the Care of Churches and the Historic Churches Preservation Trust.[47] Yet this architectural commitment, he believed, deeply enhanced his faith. In 1948 he wrote:

> Some learn their faith from books, some from relations, some (a very few) learn it at school. I learned mine from church-crawling. Indeed it was through looking at churches that I came to believe in the reason why churches were built and why, despite neglect and contempt, innovation and business bishops, they still survive and continue to grow and prosper, especially in our industrial towns.[48]

Eventually Betjeman grew to love the ritual of the church as much as its architecture—a love that would evolve into the fourth and final motif of his spiritual journey. All things liturgical—aumbry and thurible, cassock and alb, canticle and versicle—appealed deeply to Betjeman's growing fascination with the mystery of the Church of England. One of his favorite boyhood activities was attending services of Evening Prayer on his Sundays in London. In a 1941 radio address extolling London's ruined and surviving churches, Betjeman recalled this pleasure:

> One of the most moving experiences London had to offer before this war was the City on a fine summer evening of a Sunday. Offices were shut, underground trains were infrequent, the sharks had floated away in their limousines on Friday, the streets were empty and the City became the ancient capital of a Christian country. In the late evening light it was easy to imagine that the winding alleys and footpaths between high Victorian office blocks were flanked by overhanging medieval houses, and to add to the illusion there were church bells ringing round every corner. Here and there one saw a few choirboys racing towards the one building that was awake, a neighbouring City church. A single ting-ting from St. Alban, Wood Street, at six, and there was that green gas-lit interior, dusted for evensong. By a quarter to seven Christ Church, Newgate Street, nearby had started ringing for service while the fuller peals—St. Andrew Holborn, St. Clement Danes, St. Mary-le-Bow—provided deeper and more distant music beneath the single tinkles. And in the streets and from the bridges Sunday reasserted the forest of chiming towers and steeples, white Portland stone or black, tapering lead, with St. Paul's, a mother hen brooding among them, just as before 1666 many more towers and spires were seen from Clerkenwell marshes, gathered round old St. Paul's in Rembrandt's drawing.[49]

This was a pleasure he had sought out since the age of twelve. In *Summoned by Bells* he fondly describes intentionally seeking out obscure and quiet churches in the City, listening for a single bell, looking for an empty nave—"St. Botolph this, St. Mary that." What drew Betjeman to these services was not a well-defined faith, however, but "a longing for the past, / With a slight sense of something unfulfilled."[50] It would be years before this longing and seeking turned into something more closely resembling mature faith. For the time being, Anglican tradition meant little more to him than English tradition; these City churches embodied England's fading past, to which the budding poet was instinctively drawn. Betjeman continued his ruin-bibbing ambles during family seaside holidays in Cornwall. The rector of St. Ervan's Church drew his attention from the humble and cozy Evensong to grander notions of Celtic mysticism, which encouraged him to reject dogma and to search for the divine in nature. Although "No mystical experience was vouchsafed" for him in Cornish holy sites,[51] he continued to seek and to feel, and he often drew upon Celtic mysticism in his poetry. He averred that his encounter with the priest in St. Ervan's was life changing.[52] If so, it must be that it opened his heart to prepare it for something new and different—something that would make a much greater impact on him than either Celtic mysticism or the familiar language and liturgy of *The Book of Common Prayer*.

That something different was Anglo-Catholicism, which he first encountered while a university student at Oxford. High Mass at Pusey House was not merely an aesthetic experience; as he related in *Summoned by Bells*, it was also theological. It was not Christian truth that he discovered, however, but the quest for that truth, a quest he would sustain all his life. For him, Christianity was never merely the trappings of Anglo-Catholicism, yet those elements served as the lintel of his faith: "The steps to truth were made by sculptured stone, / Stained glass and vestments, holy-water stoups, / Incense and crossings of myself."[53] Indeed he believed that faith began with observing the conventions of religion. As he wrote in 1950 to Gerard Irvine, who was by now in Anglican orders and beginning his parish ministry, "My experience is that there is no Faith in English villages at all, only convention, but that the convention can be turned into Faith."[54] Although Anglo-Catholicism did provide a theological awakening for Betjeman, it is likely that at Oxford he remained a little too much attached to the aesthetic experience, for he neglected to apply himself to his studies. When his master, the Magdalen don C. S. Lewis, failed him in his required examination in Divinity, Betjeman left Oxford without a degree:

> Failed in Divinity! Oh count the hours
> Spent on my knees in Cowley, Pusey House,
> St. Barnabas', St. Mary Mag's, St. Paul's,
> Revering chasubles and copes and albs![55]

High church Anglicanism was to guide Betjeman in the struggles of his faith throughout his adult life. When doubts arose, the timelessness of Anglo-Catholicism was a reliable support on which to lean. It was a bastion of Anglo-Catholicism that was his last church affiliation. In his final years he was a regular member of the congregation at Grosvenor Chapel in South Audley Street in Mayfair; when he grew too frail to attend services, he received Communion from Gerard Irvine at home in Chelsea, an ironing board serving as a makeshift altar. Despite the frail health that kept him homebound, he kept his humor. Bevis Hillier suggests that this may have been Betjeman's last couplet of poetry: "Of all the things within this house that are by me possessed / I love, oh yes, I love by far, my ironing board the best."[56]

Whatever doubts he suffered, his spiritual journey was directed by something more profound than the aesthetics of Anglo-Catholicism. In his public expressions he may have emphasized his love for churches and for the outward forms of Anglican worship, but in private his spiritual life was rooted in theological orthodoxy. Although he did not express theological profundities with any frequency, particularly in his poetry, it is nonetheless true that he was deeply informed and guided by Anglican theology. If C. S. Lewis was perhaps the twentieth century's most influential Anglican, for Betjeman it was Francis Harton, Vicar of Baulking (a village about four miles from his home in Uffington) and future dean of Wells Cathedral. Harton became to the Betjemans, as Bevis Hillier puts it, both "confessor" and "marriage guidance counsellor," and they in turn became his "devoted disciples."[57] The Betjemans' daughter, Candida Lycett Green, affirms that Harton's selfless and holy life profoundly affected both her parents.[58] Not long after meeting them in 1936, Father Folky, as John and Penelope styled him, gave them a copy of his book, *The Elements of the Spiritual Life: A Study in Ascetical Theology*, and, according to Hillier, Betjeman "felt his faith renewed by it."[59] Harton's book is no mere devotional tract but a learned and lengthy study of the Christian life, divided into five sections dealing with grace, sin, the sacraments, prayer, and holiness. What must have really impressed itself on Betjeman, who before this experience was caught up in the external expressions of the Christian religion, was Harton's insistence that the Christian life should be understood as "essentially spiritual and supernatural, a life whose real inwardness will never be known to those who neglect these levels."[60] When he first read the book, it awakened within him an excitement and a desire to lead a more reflective and spiritual life. By coincidence he had just begun a correspondence with T. S. Eliot, and without reservation he unabashedly recommended the book to the older poet, himself a recent convert to Christianity. "It has caused me to take more than an academic interest in ecclesiastical matters," he wrote in only his second letter to Eliot, "and you, as a sincere Catholic, will admire it very much if you have not read it already."[61] *The Elements of the Spiritual Life* proved to be a significant influence on Betjeman's development of a mature faith. For him, this would mean establishing a life of prayer, embracing the spiritual workings of the sacraments as acts of grace, and a steady awareness that his nature and actions were sinful. Though he would never lead a holy or ascetic life, Betjeman now began to sense the movement of divine grace and would thereafter attempt a more spiritual life of faith.

Although some debate over the nature of Betjeman's faith may continue, the central place that religion occupied in his life cannot be overlooked. The year 1947, as we have already witnessed in several of his letters, was an especially remarkable year in his development of a mature faith, and an examination of a number of texts written that year—poems, radio broadcasts, letters—will reveal a faith that was mature enough to resist the occasional onslaught of doubt. His particular commitment to Anglicanism is manifest in a range of tones that can best be appreciated by a consideration of both private and public discourses—illusory distinctions, no doubt, but useful ones nonetheless. In a letter to John Sparrow, fellow (and future warden) of All Souls College, Oxford, written on Christmas Day, 1947, Betjeman confessed Christianity's influence on his poetry: "Also my view of the world is that man is born to fulfil the purposes of his Creator i.e. to Praise his Creator, to stand in awe of Him and to dread Him. In this way I differ from most modern poets, who are agnostics and have an idea that Man is the centre of the Universe or is a helpless bubble blown about by uncontrolled forces."[62] Betjeman had for some time been dwelling on the image of God, not man, as the center of all things and on the purpose of humanity as worship. During this time he was suffering marital distress and personal anxiety, and a visit to Cambridge in November had

donc much to renew his faith and to lift his spirits. He was especially
moved by King's College Chapel, the beauty of which seemed to give
him hope that God would make things right and which he would insist
in other contexts was the single finest English medieval or Renaissance
structure.[63]

A return visit a month later to stay with Kenneth Harrison, the
dean of King's College, reinforced the effect of the beauty of the architecture of King's on his faith. By the time he made this second visit,
Betjeman had already drafted a poem in celebration of the college's
magnificent chapel, a copy of which he included in the letter to Harrison. Ironically, Betjeman wrote to the dean that "words cannot express
the wonder of my visit. . . . My mind is still dizzy." Betjeman then, with
typical humility, downplayed his verses on the chapel as "bombastic
and inadequate," insisting that "the building, music and glass are so
much too great to be effable in verse or prose."[64] The ineffable, however, is exactly what Betjeman captures in "Sunday Morning, King's
Cambridge" (*CP* 152), which is both a celebration of the physical splendor of Anglican worship and itself an act of worship. Like the great fifteenth-century chapel, the poem is ablaze with color. The first stanza
describes the procession of the world-renowned choir of the chapel of
King's College, Cambridge, and the spiritually overwhelming aesthetics of the building: its stalls, its stained glass, and especially its stunning
fan-vaulted ceiling, "a shower that never falls." In stanza two, the poet's
mind wanders away from the service, and he imagines being outside
among the "windy Cambridge courts," though this too is the dwelling
place of the divine. Again there is a great emphasis on the vast variety
of color, but all the colors are transformed into "waves of pearly light"
reflected off the Cambridge stone. The image suggests that the incarnation of God is not to be found easily or exclusively in the chapel, but
in the world, the space that contains both God's works and man's: not
just the fens and trees of Cambridgeshire but the colleges and streets
of the town as well; all are embraced by God's light.

Stanza three expands these images both geographically and historically, reaching beyond the college and town and out into the county, and
reaching as well beyond the past and present and out into the future:

> In far East Anglian churches, the clasped hands lying long
>   Recumbent on sepulchral slabs or effigied in brass

> Buttress with prayer this vaulted roof so white and light and strong
>   And countless congregations as the generations pass
> Join choir and great crowned organ case, in centuries of song
>   To praise Eternity contained in Time and coloured glass.

Here the poet imagines the tombs that fill churches throughout East Anglia, the effigies of the deceased captured for eternity in postures of prayer. The prayers of these dead are a "Buttress" for the light and airy fan-vaulted ceiling of the chapel at King's, which, built near the end of the Gothic period, needs no architectural buttresses.[65] In this image, Christianity exists because of prayer, not because of aesthetics. The church is supported by a tradition of faith, not because of the marvels of fifteenth-century engineering and design. In "Sunday Morning, King's Cambridge," the moment of worship exists out of time, as the living and the dead, the choir and the poet join in the eternal praise of God; through the seeming timelessness of Anglican worship, they approximate eternity itself. The poem has no irony, except perhaps in the last line: "To praise Eternity contained in Time and coloured glass." Here Betjeman illustrates the futility of humanity's desire to share in God's timelessness; all human efforts are confounded by our foolish need to contain and control God and time. Nevertheless, his tone in this poem is consistent; there is no ambivalence or ambiguity about faith, and thus perhaps we ought to read his praising "Eternity contained in Time" as celebrating the incarnation of Christ: God-made-man is the living theology of Timelessness contained ever so briefly by Time, of the Divine in human form. In the end, however, imagery is more vital than doctrine, and "Sunday Morning, King's Cambridge" is most memorable for the way it captures a joyful and spontaneous expression—albeit emotionally restrained in the proper Anglican manner—and a sense of wonder in the celebration of Anglican worship.[66]

The chapel of King's College was also a topic of Betjeman's BBC radio talk, "Christmas Nostalgia," broadcast on Christmas Day, 1947.[67] Attending the Festival of Nine Lessons and Carols (an Anglican tradition started at King's in 1918) had triggered in him some memories of boyhood Christmases. One of these was accidentally breaking a cherished gift from his beloved nurse, Hannah Wallis. He had attempted to hide the evidence, but she found it; unable to express himself, he was burdened with guilt that she thought he loathed the gift and had broken it on purpose. "I think that cracked glass was the first crack in my heart, the first time I lost ignorance and the first time I realised the overwhelmingly unpleasant things of the world," he confessed to his listeners.[68] This incident and other memories made Betjeman acutely aware of humanity's need for redemption, and he confessed his desire to believe that the birth of Christ is the first chapter in this story of redemption. It is a story that Betjeman knows many of his listeners also find difficult to fathom: "But can I believe this most fantastic story of all, that the Maker of the stars and of the centipedes, became a Baby in Bethlehem not so long ago?" He would argue that all our Christmas traditions and customs—observed by believers and doubters alike—"bear witness to its truth."[69] For Betjeman, admitting that "architecture is, with poetry, my chief interest," the truth of the story is manifest in his experience at the chapel at King's. Here in this "forest glade of old coloured glass," as the poet puts it, or the "superbly proportioned" "swansong of Perpendicular architecture," as the architectural critic puts it, he is vouchsafed a vision of eternal truth:

> All the schoolchildren of Cambridge had filed into a carol service and there they were in the candlelight of the dark oak stalls. We stood waiting for the choir to come in and as we stood there the first verse of the opening carol was sung beyond us, behind the screen, away in the mighty splendour of the nave. A treble solo fluted up to the distant vaulting. Once in Royal David's City . . . It was clear, pure, distinct. And as I heard it I knew once more—knew despite myself—that this story was the Truth. And knowing it I knew that because of the Birth of Christ, the world could not touch me, and that between me and the time I smashed Mrs Wallis's Christmas present, the figure of God became man, crucified in the great East Window, hanging there.[70]

And so ends this superb radio broadcast, not just with a declaration that the Christmas story is true, that Jesus was God-made-man, but with a confession of its personal relevance, that the poet himself is restored by this incarnation.

This was also the year in which Betjeman wrote his poem "Christmas" (*CP* 153–54). First published in *Harper's Bazaar* in December 1947, and now one of the most recited of all his poems, these verses would be introduced by Betjeman to a much wider audience when he read them on the radio in December 1953. The poem begins with familiar and comforting images of Christmas ("The bells of waiting Advent ring," "many a stained-glass window sheen") before dislocating this sentiment with anxiety about spiritual superficiality. The second stanza draws the reader in with pleasant imagery of a church decorated with Christmas greens but ends with a sense of human banality:

> The holly in the windy hedge
>   And round the Manor House the yew
> Will soon be stripped to deck the ledge,
>   The altar, font and arch and pew,
> So that the villagers can say
> "The church looks nice" on Christmas Day.

Betjeman attempts to inject anxiety into the reader here with the sense of the shallowness of the human response not just to the decorations but to the real wonder of Christmas: the metaphysical reality of God becoming man, of the divine presenting itself to humanity. Amidst our embarrassing "paper decorations" and "bunting" is the profundity of the nativity, "The Maker of the stars and sea / Become a Child on earth for me." Though believers try symbolically to reenact this gift of God by exchanging gifts with our loved ones, these gifts of ours are often ludicrous and embarrassing:

> Around those tissued fripperies,
>   The sweet and silly Christmas things,
> Bath salts and inexpensive scent
> And hideous tie so kindly meant.

However base human gifts are, it is not just our bad gifts that do not compare with God's gift of Christ. Even the best efforts of humanity to replicate God's love fall short:

> No love that in a family dwells,
>   No carolling in frosty air,
> Nor all the steeple-shaking bells
>   Can with this single Truth compare—
> That God was Man in Palestine
> And lives to-day in Bread and Wine.

"Christmas" works so well because it reminds believers of the mystery and wonder at the center of the story of the nativity and of humanity's utter failure either to deserve or to replicate this gift. Despite this assertion of belief, however, the poem exemplifies the paradox in Betjeman's faith, for the assertion begins with a question, "And is it true?" asked three times as if in echo of Peter's three denials of Christ, and the answer is prefaced with the conditional phrase, "For if it is. . . ." This is belief that cannot escape doubt.

A touching irony can be found in the line, "No love that in a family dwells." When Betjeman penned that line in 1947, his marriage was beginning to break apart, and Christmas 1947 would be the last time that he and Penelope and their two children attended church together. Although their marriage was always volatile, one thing that had kept them together was their shared devotion to the Church of England, witnessed in their activities in Farnborough parish that I noted earlier. According to A. N. Wilson, Anglicanism was "a form of marital glue."[71] When both John and Penelope were assailed by doubts, however, they responded quite differently. John, though he disliked the suffering that came with his doubts, had little trouble living with them. Penelope, on the other hand, had no stomach for doubt and demanded a church that would replace doubt with dogma. Ever tolerant of difference and ambiguity, the Church of England could no longer provide her with the religious certainties her own spirit now required. And so in 1947 she began receiving instruction in the Roman Catholic faith. Anticipating the marital divisions this would cause, in March 1947 Betjeman wrote to Gerard Irvine requesting prayer and advice. Though Penelope was becoming serious about conversion to Rome, John felt "it would be *wrong* for me to go over, mainly betraying the Church of God. But it will not be at all wise to live in a divided family, as I shall, I suppose, have to do. For P will want the children over too."[72] According to their daughter, Candida Lycett Green, John "felt hurt that she could have forgone something as strong as the physical side of the Church of England for the sake of such a small difference in beliefs."[73] The tolerance usually associated with Anglicanism did not in any way assist John to accept her conversion, and he began to perceive her desertion of their church as a kind of infidelity. If their marriage was already rocky, and their devotion to the Church of England the primary bond holding them together, then it was quite likely that John could think of her abandonment of the church as in effect a betrayal of their marriage.[74]

All the spiritual and connubial pain Betjeman poured into a sonnet he titled "Easter MCMXLVII," not published until 1994.[75]

> In the perspective of Eternity
>   The pain is nothing, now you go away
>   Above the steaming thatch how silver-grey
> Our chiming church tower, calling "Come to me
>
> My Sunday-sleeping villagers!" And she,
>   Still half my life, kneels now with those who say
>   "Take courage, daughter. Never cease to pray
> God's grace will break him of his heresy."
>
> I, present with our Church of England few
>   At the dear words of Consecration see
>   The chalice lifted, hear the sanctus chime
> And glance across to that deserted pew.
>   In the Perspective of Eternity
>   The pain is nothing—but, ah God, in Time.

Here we sense the poet's initial pain of attending his church alone, of seeing the empty pew, and of imagining her prayers for him in her new church. The irritation of being prayed for as a heretic was not nearly so searing as the pain of his loneliness, but the poem emphasizes the power of God's love to heal him of his suffering, even if it takes an eternity. The poem's strength is in the contrast of "Time" and "Eternity"; as long as Betjeman is in Time the pain is searing, but he hopes that in Eternity the pain will be nothing. Betjeman situates a poignant ambiguity in the first two and final two lines. There he implies not merely that his pain will be gone when he joins Eternity; there he personifies God with the name of Eternity, indicating that to God—in God's "perspective"—the pain is insignificant. Perhaps he even wonders whether God can feel his pain. The structure of this poem is also significant, as a sonnet is a form appropriate to the tradition of a yearning lover mourning a lost love. Perhaps not surprisingly, he portrays his passion in a deeply religious demeanor. This poem reveals what so many of his poems do, that no matter the proper subject of his poem, his perspective is profoundly spiritual, for Betjeman is a poet who imbues human emotion and experience with a religious sensibility.

The aftermath of Penelope's conversion can be witnessed in a long letter John wrote to her on 2 June 1949. By this point the couple were temporarily separated and contemplating the future of their marriage. Penelope had written to him to say that "it would be idiotic to separate, we would neither of us be any happier and the children would be very *un*happy."[76] John was less certain about the likelihood of a successful reconciliation. In reply he reflected earnestly and truthfully on himself, on her, on the state of their marriage, and on the effects of her conversion. While he may not have appreciated her convictions, he at least was apologetic for his inability to be supportive and for having blamed her new church for driving a wedge between them: "Of course it is God's will and we must leave it at that. But I was jealous of Rome and RC . . . for further pulling us apart. That is really why I have an 'obsession' about Rome, because I love you so much."[77] The sticking point for John was Penelope's deep desire to bring up their daughter as a Roman Catholic. To him this abandonment of the Church of England was a reiteration of Christ's crucifixion as well as a rejection of the traditional life of an English village, and so he embarked upon an attempt to explain his basic religious position:

> I long for Jesus as a Man, I long to see Him, to be lifted up to Him, to love Him, not to injure Him as much as I do all the time. I try to long for Him when I don't long for Him. Jesus is the centre of my faith and the Sacraments are one of the ways by which I try to know Him. I have never doubted our Sacraments in the C of E and I see in Farnborough that the only witness to Jesus is our church there. I see Jesus on the Cross there, very much more crucified and suffering than, say at Wantage (C of E or RC). Each person who leaves Jesus here in Farnborough drives another nail in His Cross. That was how I felt (and I hope you won't mind my saying it) first when you left Farnborough for Rome. But now I know that it is God's will for you to go there, and so I must say I'm sorry I felt like that. But you do see, don't you, that if I let Wubz [a pet name for their daughter Candida] go I personally think I would be further wounding Our Lord in our feeble church in Farnborough, which one day may be a great one and a full one. It's just when things seem quite hopeless, as they do now, that they brighten. To let Wubz leave the C of E at present would, I think, be your will not God's will.[78]

Sadly, there would be no permanent rapprochement. Penelope's rigid adherence to Catholicism may have precluded divorce, but in 1954, after several years of itinerant living, John obtained a permanent residence in London. Though he and Penelope would remain close throughout their lives, John was soon to embark on a lifelong relationship with another woman that would bring Penelope immeasurable pain and himself immeasurable guilt.

Betjeman's adulterous life began as early as 1951 when he met Elizabeth Cavendish, daughter of the tenth duke of Devonshire. They fell in love almost immediately and soon became lifelong companions, living together from 1972 until his death. In 1952 Betjeman was asked to contribute a devotional reflection to a question-and-answer book called *Moral Problems: Questions on Christianity with Answers by Prominent Churchmen.* He addressed the difficulty of trying to be a Christian when it was impossible to live up to Christ's ideal standard. In what could only have been a painful irony, Betjeman was asked to respond to this question from the angle of marriage and adultery. Speaking (though at this time secretly) from personal experience, Betjeman agonizingly wrote, "Heaven knows it is difficult for many people to remain faithful. . . . I do not see how, without sacramental grace, it is possible for many people to remain married in middle life. But they *do* remain married and, in many households this is a miracle for which one can thank God." For this "miracle" to happen, Betjeman notes, at least one partner must be a practicing Christian who receives God's grace from the sacrament of the Eucharist. Tellingly, he admits that marriages may survive even where adultery occurs: "Despite lapses, a man may continue married even if he is not happily married, by grace given to him in the sacraments and in moments of stress by counsel of a priest and use of the sacrament of penance." Though Betjeman did not render his advice as an autobiographical admission, it was in essence a privately coded confession based on personal experience. He concludes with the paradoxical consolation that although no one should ever expect perfection we should nevertheless try: "The very fact of wanting to follow Christ is something. One is given the strength to follow Him in the sacraments."[79]

Although Betjeman's writings in the late 1940s and early 1950s reveal a strongly pronounced Christian faith, he still had undercurrents of skepticism that would surface in expressions of disbelief. One such confession of doubt about the resurrection resulted in a volatile epistolary exchange between Evelyn Waugh and the Betjemans. Waugh, who had converted to Catholicism in 1930, commenced his infamous series of letters to the poet innocently enough with concern over his theological state. Soon, however, Waugh resorted to hectoring and bullying with sincerely held if somewhat ludicrous charges of heresy. In one letter, for instance, Waugh wrote, "Awful about your obduracy in schism and heresy. Hell hell hell. Eternal damnation." In another he wrote, "I wouldnt give a thrushs egg for your chances of salvation at the moment." In yet another he wrote to Betjeman that if he continued to "luxuriate in sentimental raptures, you will naturally break out in boils & carbuncles & question the authenticity of the incarnation."[80] When Waugh learned that Penelope was seeking instruction toward conversion, he began writing to her as well, manipulating her anxieties until it strengthened her conviction to convert.[81] To Penelope he apologized for "persecuting" John but still insisted to her that "there is very clearly a devil at work in him" evident in his "preposterous theory that Our Lord founded two churches—Roman & Anglican," which is not "a harmless & amusing speculation" but "a denial & perversion of God's truth."[82] In her edition of her father's letters, Lycett Green discusses what she considers Waugh's "interference" in her parents' lives; in her account, Waugh merely "confirmed" Penelope's decision to convert on her own, though he also "manag[ed] to exacerbate the wounds on both sides."[83] Waugh's letter to Penelope in March 1948, coming several months after her reception into the Roman Catholic church (and following several months of marital decay), is a clear effort to dissuade her from a lingering sense of guilt over what following her religious convictions may have done to her family. Waugh tells her that, having now joined a more important "Household," she should treasure the knowledge of always "having your chair at the table, a place laid, the bed turned down, of the love & trust, whatever their family bickerings, of all Christendom. . . . It is a particular joy for me to be able to welcome you home."[84] It is not known whether John read this letter, but it is nonetheless a clear betrayal of their friendship.

The amity between John Betjeman and Evelyn Waugh had been a long and close one, beginning in the 1930s and rooted in their similar tastes in books, the arts, politics, and even religion. Their mutual interest in the latter may have hindered Waugh from seeing just how inappropriate his interference was, for religion was something he and the Betjemans had discussed for years and in which they had found much common ground. In 1945, for instance, when he was asked by the *Daily Herald* to review Waugh's latest novel, *Brideshead Revisited* (he had been churning out voluminous reviews for the *Herald* since 1943), Betjeman wrote to Waugh:

> It will get a spanking good notice. To me it is a great treat to read a book with a standard of values behind it, Christian values what is more. I shall have somehow to hint this fact to readers without letting it be apparent to the Editors, since recently I had a letter from them to say that I was using this paper for Roman Catholic propaganda. . . . I was also accused of "Jesuitry." This made me rather proud. Of course, I have not altered my tactics.[85]

This letter would indicate then a close relationship between Waugh and Betjeman concerning religion and especially a sensitivity of Betjeman toward Roman Catholicism. Moreover, Betjeman made it clear to Waugh how much his respect for him was based in the novelist's propensity for drawing faith into his art; in 1946 he described to Waugh how his "admiration is so wholly engaged as it is with your writings," and again that year how he confirmed that Waugh was "the greatest living English novelist." A key reason for this, in Betjeman's mind, was Waugh's "sense that people are only complete when considered in relation to God."[86] Betjeman did not keep his appreciation of Waugh private, writing and delivering a BBC broadcast in December 1946 on Waugh's merits as "the one English novelist of my own generation . . . who is certain to be remembered while English novels are read." Waugh will last, Betjeman effused, because "he is a consummate user" of the English language as well as "an accurate and learned observer, a born storyteller and possessed of a faultless ear for dialogue, finally because he is a whole person with a complete philosophy of life." That system of thought involved the relationship between humans and God, and according to Betjeman what really set Waugh apart from other novelists was his concern "with the human mind and soul as part of Divine creation" and the undercurrent of Roman Catholicism in Waugh's novels which Betjeman referred to as "a fully worked-out philosophical system."[87]

Despite the respect for Waugh's faith apparent in Betjeman's public and private critical assessments of the novelist, however, an April 1947 letter from Waugh to Betjeman indicates his growing frustration toward the poet over what he perceived as slights, jokes, and general condescension toward Roman Catholicism, asking, "why do you persist in cutting down my Catholic life[?]"[88] Waugh's reputation for paranoia, which manifested itself later in his life, has here a basis in fact. Betjeman had a tendency to joke about things that made him uncomfortable, including Roman Catholicism, which he may very well have done in person to Waugh; however, Waugh was responding particularly to something Betjeman had just printed. When Waugh's short story "Tactical Exercise" was published in the *Strand* in March 1947, it was prefaced with an introductory essay by John Betjeman. There Betjeman connected the righteous anger against society so prevalent in Waugh's books to his religion. Here was a man, he wrote, who "demanded a logical framework for existence, a consolation for the loss of an ordered world which he saw collapsing round him, and armour against the oncoming darkness of the slave state." So far, nothing objectionable. However, Betjeman implies, whether intentionally or not, that Waugh's mind and faith were somewhat weaker and therefore needed an authoritarian system, a "full solution," to prop them up, something Anglicans seemed not to require. Thus Waugh "was received into the Roman Catholic Church, which supplied the logical framework he needed . . . once the postulant surrendered his will, his faith, to its demands."[89] Though the essay is filled with praise for Waugh's vision and gifts as a writer, a touch of condescension mars Betjeman's remarks on Waugh's religion. Betjeman's insult may have been subtle, especially in comparison with Waugh's subsequent contumely. However, Waugh felt traduced, and it must have been especially galling to be teased in this manner when the focus should have been on celebrating his story. My point here is not to excuse Waugh for his malicious interfering in the Betjemans' marriage and in their spiritual lives, but merely to show that it was not unprovoked as is sometimes assumed.

At the root of the Waugh-Betjeman conflict, however, is more than Waugh's feeling insulted by Betjeman's japes against Catholics, and more, even, than the personal taunts of Waugh. Underneath Waugh's unwarranted assault lies a theological conflict. Betjeman had a firm sense of himself as a Catholic, Anglicans being, in his mind, Catholics of an equal but English stripe; to Alan Pryce-Jones, who was soon to convert briefly to Roman Catholicism before return-ing to Anglicanism, he wrote in 1950, "I don't think it matters a bit whether you are RC or not. So long as you are C[atholic] and have the Sacraments."[90] To Waugh, however, this was heresy: Anglicans were apostate, and there could be only one sort of Catholicism. (Ironically, Penelope may have agreed with her husband on this point, confessing to John in 1949 that she had been "completely converted to Catholi-cism by Fr Folky's book."[91]) Although the general thrust of Waugh's assault has been effectively summarized by Betjeman's biographers, it will be helpful to recapitulate some of his arguments in order to place Betjeman's replies in a clear context that illustrates the extent of his Christian thought and action.[92] Waugh's arguments are typi-cally offensive. He reduces the Church of England to "a handful of homosexual curates" and Betjeman's commitment to Anglicanism to mere taste, connecting faith to his "literary & aesthetic predilection" and "the source of pleasurable emotions & sensations."[93] Waugh's problem with the Church of England is that in his mind it fosters illogical thinking and tolerates doubt. He makes an argument by anal-ogy meant to appeal to Betjeman's knowledge of architectural history and his impatience with decorative fakery: "You must not suppose that there is anything more than the most superficial resemblance between Catholics & Anglo-Catholics. They may look alike to you. An Australian, however well-informed, simply cannot distinguish between a piece of Trust House timbering and a genuine Tudor Build-ing; an Englishman however uncultured knows at once."[94] Waugh's argument, though specious, distinguishes not just between the gen-uine and the fraudulent but also between the native and the alien. Waugh definitely knew that Betjeman was apt to speak of Roman Catholicism as Roman and therefore foreign; indeed Betjeman wrote of "our dear old C of E" as "the true Catholic church in this coun-try."[95] Thus, in response to Betjeman's distaste for a "foreign" religion setting up camp in England, Waugh reverses the terms to insist that the native church is the historic one and that the newer Anglican church should no more be considered genuine English than should an English colony be taken for England itself.

Although Bctjcman and Waugh had been close friends for a long time, it was not the longevity of their friendship that allowed it to survive; its survival was basically a measure of Betjeman's patience, tolerance, and generosity of spirit. After their debate had ended, Betjeman wrote to Waugh in February 1948 to tell him he had just finished reading *The Loved One* and that it "is the BEST THING YOU HAVE WRITTEN and this is the highest praise I can give since I think you the best living writer of English prose."[96] Nevertheless, the friendship cooled and correspondence between them abated to general pleasantries. Though there would be the occasional invitation to visit, Waugh was aware that he had gone too far, telling Penelope in 1950 that "I dont think John likes me." This was probably true not just because of what had passed between them but also because Waugh had not changed. Waugh made it clear that a visit would not go well, as "I detest all talk about the varying fads of heretics. I can stomach a traditional, sceptical, formal, Barchester Towers protestantism of the sort my father & grandfathers professed but the nearer these people ape the ways of Catholics the nearer they approach flat blasphemy and it turns me sick."[97] Despite the tension, Betjeman would write again in 1950 to congratulate Waugh on his novel *Helena*, a life of the saint modeled after and dedicated to Penelope Betjeman.[98] Making this compliment must have been especially difficult, since Waugh enjoyed implying that an affair had occurred between himself and Penelope, and though evidence for such a liaison was unconvincing, Waugh's claims were still galling.[99] By this point John and Penelope's marriage was deteriorating rapidly, so Betjeman's generosity toward Waugh, who had done his best to undermine them both, is laudable for its apparent spirit of forgiveness. Betjeman's friend A. L. Rowse, a historian and Shakespearean scholar who shared the poet's delight in Anglican churchiness, wrote to Lycett Green about this theological and psychological battle between her father and Waugh: "Though I was not a religious believer, I always respected John's religion, he was a true Christian and had Christian charity and compassion—as did not Evelyn Waugh who was a bad Catholic for being so very uncharitable and *unChristian*."[100]

On Waugh's death in 1966, Betjeman wrote to Evelyn's son Auberon: "Your father was one of the only great people I ever knew— loyal, secretly very kind, generous, and oh my goodness how piercingly funny." The hatchet was not buried so deeply as it might appear, how-ever. Betjeman concluded his letter with a final dig at the faith of Auberon's father: "I'll remember you all in my Anglican prayers."[101] Either Betjeman effectively masked his feelings behind a façade of good manners, or perhaps the passing of time reopened an unhealed wound.[102] According to Reg Read, bookseller and amanuensis to Betje-man, in 1977 the poet erupted in rage at Read's discovery of a stack of books by Waugh inscribed to the Betjemans: "He was furious, because he considered—rightly or wrongly—that Evelyn Waugh had been responsible for the breakdown of his marriage. 'He was cruel,' he was this, he was that—John went berserk."[103] Betjeman may have fulfilled his Christian obligation of turning the other cheek, but underneath there were wounds festering and seething from unresolved vendet-tas.[104] That aggression eventually needed to find a release valve. One such valve was his poem "An Ecumenical Invitation" (1982), a dramatic monologue that satirizes Roman Catholic prejudice against Angli-cans (*CP* 380–81). The speaker, ensconced in a velvety smugness and a sense of spiritual superiority, claims to disavow the Catholic use of the term "non-Catholic" for other Christians yet utters it anyway because she cannot think of another term to use, and then she further widens the ecumenical gulf by referring to Betjeman as a "rank outsider." To Betjeman this indicates an unwillingness on the part of Roman Catho-lics to see other Christians as having a legitimate expression of their faith. The poem's title is ironic, for ecumenical dialogue is impossi-ble when one group sees other believers as simply "not us." Moreover, the speaker cannot resist the urge to gloat about differences in church attendance. Anglican cathedrals may be beautiful but they are empty; Roman cathedrals may be "brash and cheap" but are always full of wor-shippers. In fact she patronizingly pities both Anglican and Roman, demanding that the Church of England complete its Anglo-Catholic metamorphosis by returning their churches back to the Holy Father, the rightful owner dispossessed of his ecclesial property since the six-teenth century.

Waugh's missives may have failed to convert Betjeman (if that was even their intent) and may very well have further undermined the Betjemans' marriage. However, they had the unintended effect of forc-ing him to think and write theologically for the first time in his life. For all his ecclesial obsessions, he rarely delved into theology; matters of doctrine and specifics of belief held little interest for him, even though he could be quite impatient with the church when he perceived it to be wishy-washy on theological matters.[105] Faced with Waugh's Catholic assaults, however, he had little choice but to think seriously and soundly about his beliefs, and his letters of the late 1940s (some of which were quoted at the beginning of this chapter) are rife with genuine theological questioning. The theological conflict between Waugh and Betjeman is of course in part political. Fundamental to Betjeman's thinking is his belief that the Church of England is part of the Catholic church, for there are no key distinctions he can find concerning either creed or ritual: "The teaching on Sacraments, the Scriptures, Incarnation, Virgin Birth, even on the Immaculate Conception is the same in the church to which I go."[106] Betjeman adhered to the theory of the church architect Ninian Comper: "There is no such thing as a Protestant church. The church is of its very nature Catholic, embracing all things."[107] If Waugh was correct, though, in his belief that the schismatic Anglican church was apostate and that to adhere to it was therefore heretical, why should Betjeman not go over to Rome if there were no doctrinal distinctions? For Betjeman, it would be tantamount to abandoning one's neighbor and the work of Christ in the local community; to him the sin was not remaining in a possibly schismatic church but leaving a church in which he believed Christ to be immanent. Betjeman had no argument with one born into the Roman Catholic Church, but he felt strongly that those born in the Anglican fold had a spiritual obligation to remain in the Church of England to do God's work there: "And if Our Lord is present in the Anglican Church, it is my duty not to leave a sinking ship, but to go on in it until, in God's time, the Anglican Church is wholly Catholic and can be received in Communion with your church."[108]

While Waugh believed that only his church was right, Betjeman believed that both churches could be right (excepting the Roman Catholic positions concerning the supremacy of the pope and the heresy of Anglicans). Betjeman pointed out that "the strength of the C of E is the diversity of opinion which can be held in it."[109] Waugh's arguments have the force of Roman dogma behind them, and in response, Betjeman notes, "All I can do now is to read, pray and study the life of Our Lord. That I am doing. I feel that it is not so much a matter of which church, as of loving God."[110] Like many another Anglican, he relies on personal experience when tradition, Scripture, and reason fail his belief that Anglicans will not go to hell: "Surely the evidence of one's own spiritual experience and that of other Anglican Catholics is not false."[111] If Betjeman bristled at Waugh's insistence that Anglicans were bound for hell, he was even more irritated with Waugh's assertions that Betjeman's attachment to the Church of England was based on aesthetic pleasure. In response, Betjeman insisted that there was no pleasure at all in an English village church and that remaining in Farnborough parish "requires a great act of Faith," in light of which "it would be far *easier* (but against my conscience) to become RC."[112] Though pleasurable emotions first brought him into the church as an undergraduate at Oxford, as he readily admits to Waugh, "it has been a stern struggle for the last fourteen years."[113] Though some readers have been convinced that Betjeman's loyalty to the Church of England is symptomatic of his Anglophilia, I think it evident to anyone who reads his letters to Waugh that his commitment to Anglicanism is a Christian conviction, not merely a nationalistic one. In his biography, A. N. Wilson substantiates this, arguing convincingly that for Betjeman to abandon his church, as his wife did, was tantamount to "turning his back on Christ Himself," not on England.[114]

However, Betjeman concludes his letter—the final one to Waugh on the subject of religion—with a subtle dig at Waugh's embracing a foreign religion. After stating that he prays daily for "the Catholic Church," by which of course he means Catholicism broadly to include Anglicans and Romans, he changes his course suddenly and urges him not to move to Ireland despite that nation's charms and allure: "But you will always find yourself a *foreigner* there. Do you mind being a foreigner?"[115] The argument about religion was ended with an appeal to Waugh's sense of English identity. In the end, it is true that Betjeman's Anglicanism is nearly inseparable from his Englishness. This idea neither impugns his faith nor diminishes my assertion of the genuine depth of his faith. However, his sense of himself as an Englishman informs his identity as an Anglican Christian just as his firmly held Christian and Anglican beliefs bolster his identity as an Englishman. Simply put, Christianity was as fundamental to Betjeman's identity as

was his nationality. If doubts about the validity of key Christian doctrines (the incarnation, the virgin birth, the resurrection, and even life
eternal) were at times difficult for him to shake off, Betjeman was able
to compensate for his loss of Christian belief with Christian action.
Though his was a faith underscored by doubt, that dichotomy marked
his intellect, heightened the ambiguity of his verse, and even strengthened his Anglican identity. As he wrote to Mary Wilson, wife of prime
minister Harold Wilson, in 1974, "we are seeds planted here and
become roots of Eternity on earth but Eternity is when we blossom
and flower. . . . Certainly time is a dreadful pit to be landed in" for "we
are all little bits of immortality—little bits of 'God.'"[116] Only Eternity
would explain what Time could not.

2

DOUBT INSERTS THE KNIFE
The Absence of God and the Anxiety of Eternity

I force my will to make me believe that God became Man nearly two
thousand years ago. Lord, I believe. Help Thou mine unbelief.[1]

John Betjeman's imagination was sufficiently capacious to embrace
both a love of life and a horror at life. His friend the Reverend
Harry Williams, fellow and dean of Chapel at Trinity College, Cambridge, remarked, "That's the doubt and the faith. It's expressed in his
poetry. I mean, the way he loves life—that's the faith. And when he
feels the terror and horror—that's the doubt."[2] Despite his devotion to
the Church of England, he enjoyed no certainty in his faith. In a 1949
radio broadcast, Betjeman confessed: "I am a practising Christian like
a good many people are but of course, like all practising Christians,
these moments of doubt in one's faith keep coming along and to me
it's an eternal struggle whether there's an afterlife."[3] To A. N. Wilson,
the ambiguity in Betjeman's faith is a product of his psychology: "[He]
lived on cycles of mood swings from elation, when he loved clown-
ing and showing off, to deep melancholy and self-doubt. Like many
melancholics, he was of a very religious temperament. The churchgoing was no mere outward form; it was his bedrock and strength.
But churchgoing did not prevent appalling consciousness of his own
inadequacies, a morbid near-revelling in sin, and a deep, almost total
doubt."[4] Throughout his life he endured ambiguity in spiritual matters, and his meditations on guilt, judgment, damnation, and death—

doubts and fears that he found in both his adult experiences and his early childhood memories—became a pervasive motif in his poetry. Betjeman describes endless variations on this theme, but a common thread is always there: that neither he himself nor the church nor God can save him from his emotional and spiritual torment, whether the torment is a fear of hell's flames or the anxiety of extinction into nothingness. Anxious thoughts along these lines are precisely the stuff from which he constructed his poetry. Some of the most satisfying of his poems are those typified by a healthy respect for the role doubt plays in the process of faith, but as the epigraph to this chapter suggests, willing oneself to believe is an unlikely event.

To Betjeman, then, doubt was a fundamental quality of his faith and his poetry. As Geoffrey Harvey has written, Betjeman's "poetry of doubt rests on a foundation of Christian faith and draws its restless energy from the perpetual tension between these two poles of experience."[5] One of the central themes of *Summoned by Bells*, Betjeman's blank-verse account of his poetic and spiritual awakening, is the tension between faith and doubt against which the budding poet struggled as an adolescent. He recalled sitting in chapel during school at Marlborough and experiencing a deep frustration at the gulf that separates the human and divine: "Oh, who is God? O tell me, who is God? / Perhaps He hides behind the reredos . . . / Give me a God whom I can touch and see."[6] The lament he describes here—a sensation of God's absence—is one that he would voice again and again, yet the religious struggle of his adolescence would eventually give way to a quiescent resignation in the face of lifelong doubt. Though he was diffident in admitting his doubts, interviewers were often able to induce the truth. To Kenneth Allsop he admitted in 1960, "I dread the idea of extinction and think about death every day."[7] In 1983, nearing the end of his life, Betjeman spoke with Jonathan Stedall in a series of films about his life and beliefs. When asked by Stedall whether any of his religious convictions were "unshakable," Betjeman asserted, "No. No, I don't think there is anything. I don't think I'd ever lay down the law . . . I hope 'The Management' is benign and in charge of us. I do very much hope that." Seeking clarification, Stedall asked, "Hope rather than belief?" To which Betjeman replied, "Yes, certainly hope. Hope's my chief virtue."[8] Despite the irony this implies, even Betjeman's darkest poems reveal a desire to believe, a desire for God's immanence, a yearning for the Eucharist to reveal God's love for him. Truly agnostic expressions in his poetry are accompanied by an appalling sense of emptiness that suggests an underlying Christian hope.

What interviewers were able to coax from Betjeman about his doubts came flooding out in his poetry, and a brief look at two poems will illustrate the fluctuation of God's presence in his thinking. When God is absent from Betjeman's spiritual perception, the void is filled with an anxiety that manifests itself in a fear of dying and a concomitant fear of eternity. In "Good-bye" (1966), the poet imagines those final days before he dies, "When food's tasting sour on my tongue, / . . . And lust has gone out." The anticipation of death brings no relief, only hopelessness: "More worthless than ever / Will seem all the songs I have sung." The apparent meaninglessness of his life is heightened by an existential angst, "With Judgement or nothingness waiting me, / Lonely and chill." Despite the despair, despite the absence of any hope of spiritual reward, the poem still lacks certainty even in unbelief: death may bring oblivion, or it may bring hell. "Good-bye" reveals the tiniest measure of acceptance in Betjeman's mind of the likelihood of death bringing oblivion. It is no happy thought, but it is one he has no energy to oppose, finding a passive acquiescence in having merely struggled to live and to accomplish a few small achievements (*CP* 275). A greater sense of closure is manifest in "The Last Laugh" (1974), a poem whose brevity symbolizes the sudden onset of death as well as a stronger sense of certainty in the presence of God:

> I made hay while the sun shone.
> My work sold.
> Now, if the harvest is over
> And the world cold,
> Give me the bonus of laughter
> As I lose hold. (*CP* 341)

In this poem Betjeman feels he has come to terms with his life and at last seems at peace with how he has lived it. Now he has one more request to make of Life before he departs it. "Give me the bonus of laughter" is his plea for equanimity and joy in the face of Death, for release from the burden of anxiety in the waning days of his life. The title suggests then that the last laugh will be his and not Death's; however, the poem still embodies doubt. Phrased as a plea or prayer for laughter, it suggests that he cannot feel certain that he will be able to laugh.

For a man who tried so very hard to believe and to observe the sacraments, his poetry is quite simply characterized by uncertainty. Betjeman's doubting faith might seem frail and uninspiring to readers perhaps more accustomed to the firm expressions of belief from that other well-known twentieth-century Anglican apologist, the one whom Betjeman sarcastically referred to as "St. C. S. Lewis."[9] However, the ambiguity in belief that Betjeman expresses is not proof of a melancholic disposition, as A. N. Wilson demands. In fact such ambiguity is not altogether uncommon among Anglicans; it seems accepted, encouraged even, by its theologians. As Sibyl Harton, widow of the dean of Wells Cathedral and a spiritual advisor and friend to Betjeman for more than forty years, wrote, having just heard his poem "Christmas" read on the radio on Christmas Day, 1980, "flung high into the air over Great Britain is your affirmation of faith (requiring doubt), hope (resting on despair), love, love which is the final resolution of life."[10] L. William Countryman refers to this paradox as a "dialectic of absence and presence" and argues that it is a central characteristic of Anglicanism.[11] The Anglican adherent often finds his or her faith on a spectrum of doubt and belief wherein consistency or certainty is neither expected nor perhaps even possible. Anglicanism can have a marked tendency toward skepticism, especially within the context of the search for God. The difficulty in sustaining faith may be caused by a heightened awareness of human limitations, especially sin and death, although in the midst of this depressing awareness a spiritual encounter sometimes occurs.[12] Because at times Betjeman would intensely feel God's presence while at others he would only sense God's absence, his poetry occupies a spectrum between belief and doubt that is reflected in his expressions of a relationship with God. Though he is by no means a confessional poet, he is a personal poet, one who uses poetry to explore his emotions and thoughts in an honest fashion. He rarely distances himself with an ironic persona (excepting the occasional dramatic monologue), preferring to express himself through his poetry simply as John Betjeman. The origins and development of his spiritual dialectic are thus fodder for his muse, and autobiographical explorations of his doubting faith are common.

In "N.W.5 & N.6" (1957), a poem whose title alludes to the postal codes of the North London suburbs of Betjeman's early childhood, the adult poet journeys back in memory to recall how his spiritual fears began in child abuse at the hands of his nanny. Betjeman's memories of his "cheap nursery-maid" are vivid and fearful: he recalls being "Forcibly fed" and "Lock'd into cupboards, left alone all day." Although there was physical abuse, it was her psychological abuse that most disturbed him, particularly her tales of the gaping maw of hell, licking its chops in anticipation of her own certain and imminent arrival. But a worse memory for him is the echo of the *Gloria Patri* that she prays: "'World without end.'"[13] His childhood misunderstanding makes "World without end" not a promise of eternal bliss for those of Christian hope but a threat of certain eternal damnation for children everywhere. Of this incident Betjeman wrote in 1950, "That was the first phrase I can remember which really struck amazed terror to my heart. Something without an end. It was an appalling idea. And stars going on without stopping for millions of miles behind one another."[14] The poet recalls the child being most afraid of "her fear / And guilt at endlessness." It is little wonder that he would recall her spiritual abuse of him as more terrifying than the physical. Betjeman remembers his five-year-old self asking his nurse if he will go to heaven when he dies. The nurse— "Sadist and puritan as now I see"—replies, "'You will. I won't,'" and her thoughtless answer exposes him to the fear and uncertainty that will plague him all his life. While she never told Betjeman that he would spend eternity in hell, her certainty that she would was sufficient to plant an ineradicable anxiety in his mind. Her anxieties about death are also a contagion for him:

> I caught them too,
> Hating to think of sphere succeeding sphere
> Into eternity and God's dread will.
> I caught her terror then. I have it still.

Over this entire scene in Betjeman's memory ring the "bells from sad St. Anne's," the very church in which he was baptized, a reminder that the church and its rituals cannot always fill the spiritual void (*CP* 231–32).[15]

Two additional poems about childhood memories suggest that the terror of sin and judgment were rooted deeply. This melancholy note would become a leitmotif in his descriptions of childhood: "And over all there brooded the loneliness of Eternity."[16] "Original Sin on the Sussex Coast" (1951) is constructed, like "N.W.5 & N.6," around Proustian memories as the adult Betjeman is led by sensory impressions into the recollection of a painful childhood experience of bullying. Being beaten up by other children is for Betjeman no mere rite of passage but evidence of a central tenet of Christian doctrine.[17] Not only does the title supply this interpretation, however. Parents can launder their bullying children's clothes, but they cannot scrub clean their souls from original sin:

> Does Mum, the Persil-user, still believe
> That there's no Devil and that youth is bliss?
> As certain as the sun behind the Downs
> And quite as plain to see, the Devil walks.[18]

The contrast between the boys' actions and their appearances reveals the darkness we all hide in our souls, symbolized by the falling light Betjeman describes in the poem: outwardly we are like the boys with their innocent satchels of homework heading happily home for a snack of "Post Toasties mixed with Golden Shred," but the encroaching darkness of the sunset on the Sussex downs hides our lurking sins (*CP* 175–76). In "Norfolk" (1953), Betjeman laments the inevitable loss of childhood innocence while insistently suggesting that this loss has a theological explanation. With echoes of Blake, Betjeman juxtaposes images of innocence and experience onto a memory of a barge holiday with his father along the River Bure in Norfolk. An obscure allusion to the architect James Fowler[19] implies an analogy between church restoration and our psychological efforts to restore ourselves to some version of childhood innocence: "How did the Devil come? When first attack? / The church is just the same, though now I know / Fowler of Louth restored it." Betjeman's implication seems to be that we will inevitably fail at restoring our own innocence, as Fowler surely failed in the eyes of Betjeman, the architectural critic and purist. However, most people are fooled by Fowler's work—and by themselves, blinding themselves to the failure of their own self-restorations. The poem concludes with something like a prayer: Betjeman petitions Time to restore "The rapturous ignorance of long ago, / The peace, before the dreadful daylight starts, / Of unkept promises and broken hearts." Betjeman's plea for prelapsarian innocence and grace will go unanswered (*CP* 168).

The tenderness that Betjeman expresses for his father in this memory is unusual. More common is the fear of parental judgment and wrath that precedes the poet's overwhelming sense of personal shame and worthlessness, accompanied by a sense of spiritual doom. "Narcissus" (1965) presents us with the perspectives of both adulthood and childhood on the painful experience of his forced separation from a treasured friend. As a child, Betjeman suffered confusion over this separation and a desire to do anything to be restored to his friend. Perhaps their behavior was an innocent sexual exploration, but to the adults it must have been shameful. Here Betjeman apostrophizes his friend Bobby, recalling their games that now have overtones of sexual play:

> For I know hide-and-seek's most secret places
>   More than your sisters do. And you and I
> Can scramble into them and leave no traces,
>   Nothing above us but the twigs and sky,
> Nothing below us but the leaf-mould chilly
> Where we can warm and hug each other silly.

Whether or not their play is innocent, it occurs, significantly, in a deathly setting of barren branches and decaying leaves. Notably, his mother, murmuring things about "a man called Oscar Wilde," reinforces the fear that he is doomed to hell, telling him that "a fate far worse than death awaited / People who did the things we didn't know," while Archibald, his teddy bear, remains his sole comfort (*CP* 280–81). The poem "Archibald" (1982), composed in stanzas exactly like those of "Narcissus" and probably written about the same time, further explores the comfort of a childhood toy in a house of isolation and anger:

> The dreaded evening keyhole scratch
>   Announcing some return below,
> The nursery landing's lifted latch,
>   The punishment to undergo—
> Still I could smooth those half-moon ears
> And wet that forehead with my tears.

Reading "Archibald" in conjunction with "Narcissus," it appears that Archie the bear has become Bobby's surrogate. When Betjeman is an adult, the sight of the bear which he has kept all these years fills him with a sense of dread and despair that are adult enhancements of his childhood anxieties. The harsh and judgmental voices of his parents are transferred to the bear, which he now imagines telling him, in echo of his nanny, that he is going to hell: "He has no mouth, but seems to say: / 'They'll burn you on the Judgment Day.'" Still he cannot part with the toy. Despite the bear's mockery of his immortal soul, to contemplate its loss is to contemplate venturing into a "dreadful void" of dark and echoing emptiness: "Its draughty darkness could but be / Eternity, Eternity" (*CP* 349–50).

The childhood terror instilled in Betjeman by his nanny and by his parents he kept throughout his life. As he grew old and infirm, the anxiety of his spiritual worthlessness increased, manifesting itself in a bizarre conflation of sin, guilt, damnation, and suffering. Near the end of his life he suffered badly from Parkinson's disease, which his doctor, Jill Parker, referred to as a "soul-destroying" affliction.[20] Betjeman's body and soul were both wracked with nervous spasms, and on one occasion he rushed into Dr. Parker's office to seek treatment for a sudden and uncontrollable sense that he was damned to hell for a life of wickedness.[21] Through most of his life, however, Betjeman was able to exorcise these psychological demons through his poetry. "Guilt" (1982), for instance, addresses the same sense of wickedness. Though the specific sin is not addressed, it is fair to assume that Betjeman had in mind his failure as a husband, having left his wife Penelope long before to live permanently with Elizabeth Cavendish. The poem begins with the symbolism of a soot-blanketed London rendered as an urban hell. The speaker has abandoned faith and hope, but confessing to himself his dishonesty he hides his faithlessness behind a "breastplate of self-righteousness." Because he dwells in an archetypal landscape, the hypocrisy of the poem's speaker may represent the hypocrisy of Englishmen in general, a fault of which they were often accused by twentieth-century writers. However broad the poem's strokes, the speaker shares an important sense of guilt and shame with the author: "I live two lives and sometimes three. / The lives I live make life a death / For those who have to live with me" (*CP* 365). If the self-portrait here is not particularized, it is much more so in "Pershore Station" (1958), written not long after John and Elizabeth began their romance. "Pershore Station" sets the poet on a train platform on a lonely Sunday evening, his thoughts on the wife whom he has left behind and on the burden of guilt he now endures, "a deadweight in my heart," as "I dreamed of another wife / And lusted for freckled faces and lived a separate life." In the midst of this depressing reverie a blast of church bells rings out:

> When sudden the waiting stillness shook with the ancient spells
> Of an older world than all our worlds in the sound of the Pershore bells.
> They were ringing them down for Evensong in the lighted abbey near,
> Sounds which had poured through apple boughs for seven centuries here.

Instead of filling the poet's heart with comfort and joy, however, the bells convict him of his sin and fill the void in his heart with "Guilt, Remorse, Eternity" (*CP* 224). "Pershore Station" was not the first poem, nor would it be his last, to describe either church bells or eternity with anxiety and dread.

Betjeman's dread is really about death, for a natural connection exists between the measure of his spiritual doubt and his anxiety about dying. Worrying about what happens to the body and the soul preoccupied him to the point that at times he could barely function. Would his identity rot with his body into nothingness, or would he be doomed to an Eternity of pain and torment? In middle age, Betjeman publicly asserted that his fear of dying was "the one thing that motivates anything I write. Terrified of death. The loneliness of it. Anything rather than extinction."[22] Although at times he craved extinction, at other moments he seemed to fear extinction even if the alternative was damnation. Betjeman famously claimed in 1959, in conversation with Alan Neame, "Even so, I'd rather Hell than Nothing!"[23] Perhaps his preference for hell over oblivion was purely hyperbolic, but it sincerely and succinctly stated his desperation for eternity. As he confessed to Jonathan Stedall, "I remember hearing somebody say, 'Of course as a Christian I'm bound to believe in eternal life; but I prefer the idea of extinction.' That was a very good man, said that. And I thought it was really the most awful thing you could say. And now I find it's true."[24] Betjeman's statements on the subject of death and eternity are to be trusted only insofar as they are somewhat exaggerated expressions of what he is feeling at that moment. Consistency is not to be sought or found in his thinking on death and judgment. The one constant is fear: "Death frightens me. Desperately frightens me."[25] Yet even this fear might occasionally be mitigated; in "St Bartholomew's Hospital, EC1" (1978), Betjeman wrote that the "ghost of Rahere," the founder of the hospital, "looks on pain with a pitying eye / And teaches us never to fear to die."[26] Nevertheless, the fear of death was with him throughout his life: death poems frame his poetry, serving to inaugurate his first published volume of poetry and to conclude his final published volume.[27] Above all in his poetry there is, in the words of A. N. Wilson, "a foreboding that in all these changing scenes of life, the grinning skull of death catches his eye to torture and mock."[28] An elderly man, leaving an elegant Edwardian hospital with his wife and the dreadful news of his terminal diagnosis, seems in the marvelous and touching poem "Devonshire Street W.1" (1953) to speak for Betjeman's personal anxiety: "'Why was I made / For the long and painful deathbed coming to me?'" (*CP* 177). His wife's consolation is to create a distraction, but her attempt to figure out the schedule for their trip home cannot erase the horror of life. The old man's anguished cry embodies humanity's existential crisis: for what we were born but death?

Some of Betjeman's most powerful death poems are imaginative contemplations of living out one's days with the anxiety of a death sentence. In "Inevitable" (1957), inspired by his experiences in visiting terminal patients in St. Bartholomew's Hospital, Betjeman imagines losing a very dear friend, perhaps "too ill to know that he is dying," to a long and agonizing terminal disease. The first stanza is characterized by emotional distancing wherein the focus is not the patient but the disease; Betjeman creates further emotional distance in referring to the disease only as "it" instead of naming it. At the same time, he expresses his anxiety about death through the sound devices of the poem, the syllables a mouthful of purposeful inarticulation and the rhythms intentionally graceless and unsure:

> First there was putting hot-water bottles to it,
>   Then there was seeing what an osteopath could do,
> Then trying drugs to coax the thing and woo it,
>   Then came the time when he knew that he was through.

The poem grows more personal as Betjeman watches his friend become more remote as he accepts the inevitable end: "his large eyes seem to see beyond the day." The dying man's acceptance of the inevitable creates in Betjeman a deep appreciation for the profundity of the moment; in the final stanza the rhythms smooth into an iambic purity reflecting the calmness of the poet's emotional and spiritual state:

> Now from his remoteness in a stillness unaccountable
>   He drags himself to earth again to say good-bye to me—
> His final generosity when almost insurmountable
>   The barriers and mountains he has crossed again must be.

The poem concludes with the sense of spiritual possibility; anxiety gives way to wonder as Betjeman receives his friend's final good-bye as a benediction (*CP* 230).

In contrast is "Five o'Clock Shadow" (1966), in which Betjeman imagines himself a patient in the terminal ward of a hospital. The dominant impression is one of betrayal: the dying patients feel betrayed both by their own bodies and by the world of the living. Betjeman first creates an emotional bond by imagining himself as one among numerous dying souls, then induces an emotional distancing from his imagined terminal state by shifting pronouns from "we" to "he":

> This is the time of day when we in the Men's Ward
>   Think "One more surge of the pain and I give up the fight,"
> When he who struggles for breath can struggle less strongly:
>   This is the time of day which is worse than night.

While they endure physical and emotional agonies, anticipating their impending deaths, the dying suffer most, as Betjeman imagines it, from isolation. Life goes on about them, but the dying are excluded from normal activities. "This is the time of day when we feel betrayed," the poet writes, implying that the betrayal has been not by life but by the living. A "doctors' foursome" heads out for a round of golf, nurses take their late afternoon breaks, and worst of all loved ones anticipate a comfortable evening at home:

> Below the windows, loads of loving relations
>   Rev in the car park, changing gear at the bend,

> Making for home and a nice big tea and the telly:
> "Well, we've done what we can. It can't be long till the end."

The speaker imagines doctors and family members alike conspiring in an abandonment of the dying. Five o'clock shadows begin to fall, intensifying "the lonely terror I feel." Shadows at five p.m. suggest an image not only of impending nightfall but of an early death signified by darkness before night. The poem's title brilliantly captures the dual sense of the passing of one's own time and the lengthening of shadows to illustrate the anxiety and isolation that only the dying can know (*CP* 276).

"The Cottage Hospital" (1948) portrays the onset of death with equal insignificance though with a strikingly different perspective. Here the poet, trying to relax outdoors on a late summer Sunday, is suddenly forced to imagine his own death. The poem begins with imagery rich with summer abundance, but a closer look suggests something ominous:

> I lay under blackening branches
> where the mulberry leaves hung down
> Sheltering ruby fruit globes
> from a Sunday-tea-time heat.
> Apple and plum espaliers
> basked upon bricks of brown;
> The air was swimming with insects,
> and children played in the street.

Death imagery pervades it all: the blackness of the branches, the baking heat, the buzzing flies, and the tempting but forbidden fruit. Though innocence is implied in the play of children, Betjeman's suggestion is that the doom of experience is near; with it will come the knowledge of death. While the children are at play a fly is trapped in a web, "shrouded tight," and killed by a spider in a gruesome yet essentially innocuous display:

> Down came the hairy talons
> and horrible poison blade
> And none of the garden noticed
> that fizzing, hopeless fight.

The mundane events of the day fill the poet with an arresting sense of the banality of death. Insects buzz, children play, and death slips in. The concluding stanza of the poem reveals Betjeman imagining his own death rather like the fly's: unnoticed, insignificant, and void of meaning:

> Say in what Cottage Hospital
>   whose pale green walls resound
> With the tap upon polished parquet
>   of inflexible nurses' feet
> Shall I myself be lying
>   when they range the screens around?
> And say shall I groan in dying,
>   as I twist the sweaty sheet?
> Or gasp for breath uncrying,
>   as I feel my senses drown'd
> While the air is swimming with insects
>   and children play in the street?

The horror here is only the speaker's. His imagined groanings and writhings and gaspings go unheeded and perhaps entirely unseen. The dying suffer their physical and emotional agonies while the world continues in its unobservant or indifferent way (*CP* 178–79).

If Betjeman describes the process of dying in terrifying terms, when it comes to describing the aftermath of an actual death he has a strong tendency toward cold objectivity. With a sort of prying, journalistic nosiness Betjeman imagines what goes on around a life that has ceased to be. It is as if the dead still have some measure of being, a kind of emptiness or void around which the survivors must navigate carefully. The hole does not disappear right away, and it cannot be ignored. "Death in Leamington" (1930), for instance, combines the innocuousness of death with the ugly reality of life. An unnamed elderly woman with a "gray, decaying face" has died alone in a decrepit house; Betjeman apostrophizes her with a series of rhetorical questions:

> Do you know that the stucco is peeling?
>   Do you know that the heart will stop?
> From those yellow Italianate arches
>   Do you hear the plaster drop?

The old woman's nurse comes in with a tea tray, discovers she has died, and matter-of-factly tidies up the medicine bottles before turning down the heat and leaving the room in an appropriate chill and darkness, "As the calm of a Leamington ev'ning / Drifted into the place." There is little beauty here, and thus no dignity in the dying, other than that bestowed by fine starlight shining in the bedroom window:

> She died in the upstairs bedroom
>   By the light of the ev'ning star
> That shone through the plate glass window
>   From over Leamington Spa.

The light is unfathomably remote, and its intensity is diminished by the cheapness of plate glass. In this mise en scène of "chintzy cheeriness," the nurse, "alone with her own little soul," seems apathetic to the woman whether living or dead (*CP* 1–2).

"Variation on a Theme by T. W. Rolleston" (1948) explores what happens to the spaces once occupied by the formerly living.[29] A mother has died; she is clearly gone, yet most of the world is as oblivious of her absence as it had been insensible to her presence. All normal activities seem unaffected: "In the dying afternoon / Men from football, and women from Timothy White's and McIlroy's / Will be coming teawards soon." Betjeman describes her death in objectively realistic terms:

> Under the ground, on a Saturday afternoon in winter
>   Lies a mother of five,
> And frost has bitten the purple November rose flowers
>   Which budded when *she* was alive.

His exploration of the significance of her loss is curiously not from the perspective of her loved ones but that of shopkeepers and bureaucrats. Cobblers and grocers who hardly knew her wonder why she no longer comes round their shops:

> But her place is empty in the queue at the International,
>   The greengrocer's queue lacks one,
> So does the crowd at MacFisheries. There's no one to go to Freeman's
>   To ask if the shoes are done.

After "The tears, the prayers and the priest," civil servants obligingly organize her various documents and close her file with a frightening finality. What might the dead woman have thought, Betjeman wonders, if she knew that "Her clothing coupons and ration book were handed in at the Food Office / For the files marked 'deceased'?" Throughout the poem, Betjeman's asymmetrical rhythms and his images of working-class shops create a prosaic and conversational tone that not only masks the fact that this is poetry but also disguises the beauty of human life. The uniquely Betjemanesque qualities of this verse remind us of how little either our lives or our deaths matter, beyond a vague sense of emptiness created when the living depart for eternity (*CP* 204).

"Variation on a Theme by Newbolt" (1956) similarly describes the inescapable presence of the dead; our attention is drawn to City boardrooms and clubs, the golf course, and other public spaces where this man passed half his life.[30] The poem's speaker is a business associate preoccupied with the business of grief rather than by real sorrow:

> His death will be felt through the whole of the organization,
> In every branch of its vast managerial tree,
> His brother-in-law we suppose will attend the cremation,
> A service will later be held in St. Katherine Cree.

For the most part, the speaker utters sentiments appropriate to the occasion, though he is distracted by thoughts of golf and shooting and of how the deceased might have planned to dispose of his clubs and guns:

> But what of his guns?—he was always a generous giver.
> (Oh yes, of course, we will each of us send a wreath),
> His yacht? and his shoot? and his beautiful reach of river?
> And all the clubs in his locker at Walton Heath?

Is the speaker callous in thinking more of the disposal of the deceased's moveables than of expressing an appropriate grief? Probably, but Betjeman's point is not at all to satirize the speaker as cold and vicious. Instead he wishes to emphasize the normality of the speaker's thinking. What seems to frighten Betjeman is the thought that life does indeed go on for everyone but the deceased. The speaker's apparent apathy is furthermore converted to sympathy at the end:

> I do not know, for my mind sees one thing only,
> A luxurious bedroom looking on miles of fir

> From a Surrey height where his widow sits silent and lonely
> For the man whose love seemed wholly given to her.

Though the final stanza lifts us from the banality of death as the speaker contemplates the pain of the lonely and isolated widow, we are left with the reminder that the living cannot ever know what dying is (*CP* 229).

Understanding death in spiritual terms—dying as the departure of a sentient soul—was so difficult for Betjeman that such poems can only emphasize absence; the once living are now simply missing. Understanding death in physical terms—dying as the decaying of a body—was a simpler matter for a poet so connected to the material world. The fear of death was so strong that imagery of dying and decay pervades his poetry where one might not expect it: his youthful verse, his religious poetry, and even his love lyrics. One of his earliest poems, "For Nineteenth-Century Burials" (1927), touches gently on death's inevitability and passes lovingly over archaic death rituals in Victorian culture:

> These cold breezes
> Carry the bells away on the air,
> Stuttering tales of Gothic, and pass,
> Catching new grave flowers into their hair,
> Beating the chapel and red-coloured glass. (*CP* 9)

A poem in celebration of All Saints' Day, "Clay and Spirit" (1954), focuses more on the lingering permanence of clay than on that of spirit:

> Out of the clay the Saints were moulded,
> Out of the clay the Wine and Bread,
> But out of the Soul the heart that withers,
> As brains increase in the big white head.

The poem's imagery, finding decay around and in the church, excludes hope: "Elm trees rot in a still decay" as three lonely bells summon worshippers to "a cold stone chancel" with "a fungus odour."[31] "Late-Flowering Lust" (1950) finds death in an even more surprising place: in the caress and embrace of a lover:

> But I've a picture of my own
> On this reunion night,

Wherein two skeletons are shewn
　To hold each other tight;
Dark sockets look on emptiness
　Which once was loving-eyed,
The mouth that opens for a kiss
　Has got no tongue inside.

Though the imagery is gruesome, Betjeman is specifically reaching for a gothic effect: the speaker's inability to escape thoughts of death even in a moment of heightened sexual ecstasy is evidence of the poet's profound dread of dying and his unceasing torments of spiritual anxiety (*CP* 171–72).

Poetic representations of decay are not common among Betjeman's poems on death, but they are graphic and specific enough to grab any reader's attention. One of the most striking of these is "On a Portrait of a Deaf Man" (1940), a poem Betjeman wrote following the death of his father.[32] That his recollection of his dead father starts with a painting suggests perhaps that Betjeman is attempting to objectify his grief. However, his repressed sorrow is supplanted by emotions and images that are more painful yet, thoughts of his father's body rotting away in London's Highgate Cemetery. The portrait's "loosely fitting shooting clothes" are displaced in the poet's imagination with "A closely fitting shroud." The mouth of the man who once enjoyed eating "Potatoes in their skin" is now "wide to let / The London clay come in." He who would have liked to "Shake hands with many friends" might be surprised to find that "now his finger-bones / Stick through his finger-ends." And though the speaker claims "That now I do not like to think / Of maggots in his eyes," his obsessive contemplation of the decay of his father's body suggests otherwise. His inability to consider his father now in any condition but decay is merely a continuation of the antipathy and tension that characterized their relationship when his father was living. Betjeman's reaction to his father's passing sheds light, moreover, on his own state of unbelief at the point of the death:

You, God, who treat him thus and thus,
　Say "Save his soul and pray."
You ask me to believe You and
　I only see decay.

The loss of any filial bond underscores the poet's loss of faith, for the images of a rotting corpse, painful in themselves, are accompanied by the greater spiritual pain of disbelief in the promise of a reunion in eternity (*CP* 79–80).

The loss of faith is naturally expressed with symbols of decay. "Calvinistic Evensong" (1937) explores the effects of a punishing theology capable of producing the mind-set of the nanny whose cruelties Betjeman had endured as a child. In this poem Betjeman imagines eavesdropping on Evensong in an Anglican parish stricken and withered by a harsh and oppressive Calvinism with a congregation decayed into six elderly women who in "Cold silence wait the Calvinistic word" from a "Black gowned and sinister . . . / Curate-in-charge of aged parish fears." Death imagery pervades the poem: the parson preaches on death; the parish itself, shriveling in numbers, has the funk of decay; and the trees in the churchyard are hungry for their next feeding of parishioners' bodies:

> Pregnant with warning the globed elm trees wait
> Fresh coffin-wood beside the churchyard gate.
> And that mauve hat three cherries decorate
> Next week shall topple from its trembling perch
> While wet fields reek like some long empty church.

A life lived under the spirit of Calvinism Betjeman knew, embodied in that psalm "Which deals most harshly with the fruits of sin," is a miserable life spent fearing death, followed by the miserable fulfillment of that anxiety. If the poem contains a dark sense of graveyard humor, it is because Betjeman could find a temporary solace from this same anxiety by laughing grimly at it. In a nice bit of irony, the poem's only liveliness comes in Betjeman's comic description of the church music during this otherwise dead service: "Boy! pump the organ! let the anthem flow / With promise for the chosen saints below!" It is hard to imagine six elderly Anglican females singing with any gusto to match that of the organ. Likewise Betjeman's summary of the anthem itself suggests that these Calvinistic "chosen saints" are chosen not for "below" heaven but "below" ground (*CP* 32).

Betjeman's fear of dying not only describes his fear of being excluded from the world of the living but also reveals his greater fear of being excluded from eternity. His death poems are ultimately about the loss of faith; they are nothing if not expressions of his spiritual doubts. Nevertheless, those who could believe without any apparent doubt greatly intrigued Betjeman. Stephen Games has revealed Betjeman's attraction to "individuals for whom belief was either unproblematic or who had overcome difficulties in a way that he had not." In Games' view, it was a vicarious faith: if Betjeman "could not fully believe himself, he could at least worship God through the belief of others."[33] In his poetry he explored the phenomenon of being drawn to yet excluded from the estimable faith of others, and in a variety of poems he expresses this ironic compulsion in tones that range from admiration to frustration to comic amusement. One such poem is "The Sandemanian Meeting-House in Highbury Quadrant" (1931), inspired by a little-known Scottish sect, with tones moving between elegy and comedy.[34] From all over London come adherents to a meeting of this doomed faith:

> From Canonbury, Dalston and Mildmay Park
>   The old North London shoots in a train
> To the long black platform, gaslit and dark,
>   Oh Highbury Station once and again.

The elegiac quality of this journey is contrasted with the comedy of manners that Betjeman imagines going on in their services behind their locked doors:

> Away from the barks and the shouts and the greetings,
>   Psalm-singing over and love-lunch done,
> Listening to the Bible in their room for meetings,
>   Old Sandemanians are hidden from the sun.

The aspect of the Sandemanians that attracts Betjeman is their obscurity. Their meeting house is at a busy London junction; few people even notice it or the worshippers, and fewer still know what goes on behind the "fast-shut grained oak door." For Betjeman there is a mix of respect and amusement: respect for their quiet devotion and isolation from a sinful world, but amusement at what he imagines of their services, "the barks and the shouts and the greetings." While the poem condescends, it is refreshingly honest about human nature. This poem really tells us nothing of the Sandemanians; instead it reminds us of our natural instinct to find both amusement and inspiration in that which we do not understand (*CP* 15).[35]

As this poem indicates, Betjeman's passion for the Church of England did not preclude an interest in the larger church, and he was particularly fascinated, in almost an anthropological manner, by Protestant nonconformity. In a 1946 radio talk on the hymnodist Augustus Toplady, author of "Rock of Ages," Betjeman described him as "one of the most fascinating and attractive characters of the eighteenth century." What would have placed Toplady in ranks that ought to include Pope, Johnson, and Gibbon? To Betjeman, it was that Toplady "left behind him six large volumes of writing filled with love of God, vituperation of John Wesley and his followers and reflections on animals, history, philosophy, apparitions, devils, meteors, highwaymen and above all Calvinism, that great uncompromisingly logical system of theology of which Toplady was a violent upholder."[36] In the *Spectator* Betjeman wrote of his interest in the Muggletonians, a seventeenth-century sect that had survived until the nineteenth; Betjeman visited their meeting house in the City, recently converted into a carpet business, and came away with a prized acquisition: a gas bracket which had illuminated the "strange deliberations" of this sect.[37] The Agapemonites and their ornate 1892 church in Clapton preoccupied him as a poet as well as an architectural historian, both for the stunning Art Nouveau statues of the beasts of the Apocalypse carved below the steeple and for the scandalous stories of its leader, the Reverend J. H. Smyth-Piggott, who seduced wealthy female adherents into sexual and financial submission and who fancied himself Christ reincarnate.[38] Betjeman's interest in those branches of Protestant Christianity that dissented from the established church was due in part to a larger curiosity about aspects of English life obscured by and largely overlooked by the mainstream. It was also, however, because sacramental confession to a priest, which was encouraged by his Anglo-Catholicism, required him to empty his repressed conscience into a flood of guilt-ridden and self-condemnatory admissions. For a time in the 1930s he avoided this problem altogether by worshipping with the Society of Friends. (Perhaps there was a familial disposition toward nonconformity: his mother had dabbled in Christian Science, and his son Paul became for a period a Mormon following his emigration to the United States.) So strong was John Betjeman's interest in the various manifestations of Protestantism that he even decided that his Teddy bear Archie was a Strict Baptist.[39] In his poetry, these variants of low-church dissent, representing sects of Christian worship that the poet cannot quite understand or respect, serve as tests of his own faith. Though he is drawn to the seriousness and stability of the faith of their adherents, he stands outside their faith, sometimes quite literally as at the Sandemanian Meeting House, yet his sense of being excluded from the faith of others is ultimately a source of tremendous poetic inspiration, if not spiritual inspiration.

Such was the case with his response to the more evangelical sects. "Undenominational" (1937) describes an evangelical revival of emotional fervor. By placing himself near the action, Betjeman can reflect on this sort of religious experience more personally:

> I slipped about the chalky lane
>   That runs without the park,
> I saw the lone conventicle
>   A beacon in the dark.

Though drawn to the seriousness of the faith of these Christians, Betjeman is nevertheless amused by their manner of worship. Instead of describing the vigor and joy that generally characterizes the hymn singing of such congregations, Betjeman finds comedy and delight in a metrical arrangement of the titles of the hymn tunes the gathered worshippers are belting out:

> "Glory" "Gopsal" "Russell Place"
>   "Wrestling Jacob" "Rock"
> "Saffron Walden" "Safe at Home"
>   "Dorking" "Plymouth Dock."[40]

Despite his effort to distance himself emotionally from the revival, the speaker's proximity to the "conventicle" encourages a degree of involvement and even self-examination. Though at first he feels rather smug and superior to the congregation and its minister, he comes to sense that such a faith is "still the church of God" and that it can be "A beacon in the dark," a light of truth to guide one through the uncertain mists of a spiritual journey:

> Revival ran along the hedge
>   And made my spirit whole
> When steam was on the window panes
>   And glory in my soul.

Although this sensation of spiritual glory refreshes his spirit, the poet does not join the service, and he is left unconnected to the community of belief (*CP* 28).

"Matlock Bath" (1959) similarly finds the poet listening to hymn singing emanating from a Nonconformist congregation, this time in the eponymous Derbyshire town:

> From Matlock Bath's half-timbered station
>   I see the black dissenting spire—
> Thin witness of a congregation,
>   Stone emblem of a Handel choir;
> *In blest Bethesda's limpid pool*
> Comes treacling out of Sunday School.

Ultimately the Calvinistic hymns he hears outside the service, echoes of which comprise lines in the poem, burden him with anxiety of falling into damnation. Images of God's wrath in nature fill the poem as the poet imagines falling cliffs, giant crashing breakers, and "Whole woodlands snapp'd like cabbage stalks." He tries to mask his anxiety of falling spiritually behind the physical fear of slipping into the River Derwent below him, but his real dread—misinterpreting the message as he did with "World without end"—is that the Rock of Ages will swallow him into an eternal doom:

> Perhaps it's this that makes me shiver
>   As I ascend the slippery path
> High, high above the sliding river
>   And terraces of Matlock Bath:
> A sense of doom, a dread to see
> The *Rock of Ages cleft for me.*

The speaker's misinterpretation arises at least in part because he chooses to view the rock and the water with fear and because he equates these symbols with other childhood anxieties: "The shivering children wait their doom— / The father's whip, the mother's petting." The poem's numerous images of water seem to admit the possibility of baptismal regeneration, but his fear of the water and of submersion into God implies his inability to embrace this form and sign of spiritual union (*CP* 258–59).

A failed spiritual union signaled by subverted baptismal imagery undergirds two beautiful but frightening poems set on Betjeman's beloved Cornish coast. "Greenaway" (1954), a portrait of the beach Betjeman loved so much as a boy, begins with memorable images of familiarity and comfort: "clumps of sea-pink withered brown," "crackling layers of broken slate," and "squelching bladderwrack" adorn the shoreline, while "rounded smooth along the bay / The faithful rocks protecting stand." Just when the reader imagines that Betjeman will develop the shoreline imagery into a statement of faith in God's eternal love, however, he shifts suddenly to the memory of a nightmare. Dreaming he was back at Greenaway Beach, he "felt the breakers plunging white / Their weight of waters over me." He tries to recover the safety of the shore, but "With every stroke I struck the more / The backwash sucked me out of reach." The poem ends not just with the fear of death but with childish anxieties of monsters, a "water-world" of "waiting claws," "writhing tentacles" and "dreadful jaws" (*CP* 184–85). In a 1958 radio talk, Betjeman commented on what "a lonely place—especially out of season" Greenaway Beach was, and expressed some hope that the poem "gives some of the frightening quality of the North Cornish coast."[41] Betjeman was undoubtedly successful in rendering this fright. "Tregardock" (1966) describes another Cornish beach, though this one has none of the comforting childhood memories that characterize "Greenaway." Instead, "Gigantic slithering shelves of slate / In waiting awfulness" seem to do battle with "The long surf menacing and white / Hissing as far as it can reach." This is the end of Betjeman's world: literally, it is the edge of England, where Cornwall meets the sea; symbolically, it is where the poem's persona has come to end his life:

> And I on my volcano edge
> Exposed to ridicule and hate
> Still do not dare to leap the ledge
> And smash to pieces on the slate.

At Tregardock, this "final end of sea and land," the poet imagines cutting short his life (*CP* 239–40). In neither poem do the water images serve to revive the poet in a spiritual sense; drowning seems the more likely end. And yet in the midst of both of these spiritually empty poems there is an underlying desire for salvation. In "Greenaway" the poet struggles valiantly against the forces of death, and in "Tregardock" he refuses to capitulate to his depressive urge to take his own life, evidence indeed that Betjeman's Christian hope did guide him during periods of darkness and despair.

The failure of either church or nature to provide Betjeman with a sense of spiritual security and to comfort his soul is nonetheless a recurring theme. The poem "On Leaving Wantage 1972" (1972) begins with images of renewal in nature: "I like the mist of green about the elms / In earliest leaf-time. More intensely green / The duck-weed undulates." Images of spring naturally suggest a spiritual renewal, and Betjeman even specifically tells us that today is the "*Third Sunday after Easter.*" However, the passing of time since the celebration of Christ's resurrection suggests the waning of spiritual renewal, and the potential for baptismal symbolism in the imagery is countered with competing images: "Public ways / Reek faintly yet of last night's fish and chips. / The plumes of smoke from upright chimney-pots / Denote the death of last week's Sunday press." In the midst of these colliding images of natural beauty and human detritus comes yet a third image: "Suddenly on the unsuspecting air / The bells clash out. It seems a miracle. . . ." Indeed this is an apparently optimistic image of the struggle of the church to unite humanity in the symbolic act of bell ringing:

> From rumpled beds on far-off new estates,
> From houses over shops along the square,
> From red-brick villas somewhat further out,
> Ringers arrive, converging on the tower.

Despite this promise of renewal within a community of believers, however, Betjeman undercuts this potentiality for the restoration of faith. The bells "clash," implying not only their actual sound but also a conflict and a lack of harmony. The ringing of the bells might "seem a miracle," but the emphasis is on seeming rather than being. Moreover, the miracle is neither the convergence of ringers in the ancient art of campanology nor the renewal of faith implied in the summoning of believers by the ringing of bells; the miracle, perhaps used ironically, is the lack of effect: nature is untouched, nor is humanity, though the bells ring out. The "miracle" is "That leaf and flower should never even stir" or that the "great waves of medieval sound . . . / [that] ripple over roofs to fields and farms" rouse so few to church while so many more get up only to breakfast or return to sleep. Betjeman concludes with an image of the implacable force of time sweeping all things away:

> we now are whirled away
> Momently clinging to the things we knew—
> Friends, footpaths, hedges, house and animals—
> Till, borne along like twigs and bits of straw,
> We sink below the sliding stream of time. (*CP* 296–97)

Facing death and finding God absent from nature and church, particularly in his later poems, is something Betjeman is sometimes able to treat with a degree of acceptance. "Fruit" (1965), written several years before Betjeman was diagnosed with Parkinson's disease, anticipates the poet's inevitable decline and connects his physical and spiritual states with the natural world:

> Now with the threat growing still greater within me,
>   The Church dead that was hopelessly over-restored,
> The fruit picked from these yellowing Worcestershire orchards
>   What is left to me, Lord?

The question is rhetorical, for Betjeman makes clear that he has outstripped faith. His life's fruit is already plucked, his harvest has passed. There is nothing left for him but to bide his time until death washes all away:

> To wait until next year's bloom at the end of the garden
>   Foams to the Malvern Hills, like an inland sea,
> And to know that its fruit, dropping in autumn stillness,
>   May have outlived me.

The allusion to a "hopelessly over-restored" church is a curious one in this brief poem, recalling as it does the allusion in "Norfolk" to the damaging restorations of Fowler of Louth.[42] There, an over-restored church signifies a corruption of innocence, or more precisely a false and failed attempt to restore a lost innocence that can never be restored.

Thus here Betjeman implies that his innocence—that is to say, a pure and innocent faith uncorrupted by doubt—cannot be restored. Once doubts have crept in, it is too late to expunge them, just as when fruit is plucked it cannot be restored to the branch. Despite the grimness of the poem's theme, however, its tone is firm and balanced, accepting the inevitability of this truth without protest (*CP* 337).

"Loneliness" (1971) also joins images of church and nature to explore the absence of God and the loss of faith. In early drafts, the poem was variously titled "Edensor Bells" and "Easter in the Peak District,"[43] and indeed the poem is built upon powerful imagery of impending natural and spiritual regeneration:

> The last year's leaves are on the beech:
>   The twigs are black; the cold is dry;
> To deeps beyond the deepest reach
>   The Easter bells enlarge the sky.

Although it is spring, the trees, having not yet burst into bud, appear trapped in a wintry stasis. Subverting the usual associations of spring and rebirth with Easter, Betjeman in fact describes Easter bells ringing out amidst the bleakness of late winter and its icy air, blackened branches, and dried-out leaves. Even the bells have no warmth, only an "ordered metal clatter-clang." Apostrophizing the church bells, Betjeman describes the parabola of faith:

> You fill my heart with joy and grief—
> Belief! Belief! And unbelief . . .
>   And, though you tell me I shall die,
>   You say not how or when or why.

In the second stanza, the earliest signs of spring, echoing Eliot's "April is the cruelest month,"[44] mock the illusion of rebirth:

> What misery will this year bring
>   Now spring is in the air at last?
> For, sure as blackthorn bursts to snow,
> Cancer in some of us will grow.

The metaphor of spring growth as a tumor points to an analogy that comprises the poem's theme: the rituals we use to mask the ugly reality of death remind us that the rituals of religion mask man's isolation in creation:

> The tasteful crematorium door
> Shuts out for some the furnace roar;
>   But church-bells open on the blast
>   Our loneliness, so long and vast.

Here the church bells are more ominous and frightening than the crematorium; cremation may euphemize the ugliness and horror of dying, but church bells only increase humanity's isolation in the universe. In the end, "Loneliness" suggests that religion is little more than a tonic to fortify the mind against the fear of death (*CP* 322).

"Aldershot Crematorium" (1971) likewise describes the ways in which institutionalized religion offers cold comfort to the grieving. From the opening lines, it is clear that no matter how we order our lives, death is always right in the middle, indeed the central fact of life: "Between the swimming-pool and cricket-ground / How straight the crematorium driveway lies!" Though cremation makes a solemn, symbolic gesture heavenward, the poem denies meaning to any symbols of the resurrection of the dead: "And little puffs of smoke without a sound / Show what we loved dissolving in the skies." Instead of reminding the poet of Christ's ascension and the promise of eternal life, this image of the dead wafting skyward into nothingness mocks the poet's beliefs and reinforces the doubt he has acquired about Christianity's consolations: "And thus we try to dissipate our fears. / *'I am the Resurrection and the Life*': / Strong, deep and painful, doubt inserts the knife." Betjeman suggests that Christianity's promises are empty words which blow just as fruitlessly as smoke in the wind (*CP* 302). Around the same time that he was writing this poem, he was ironically expressing less agnostic thoughts in a letter to John Edward Bowle, an old school friend, concerning Bowle's aging mother: "I have recently had strange experiences which make it look as though Providence looks after us in an oblique and weird way. It will look after you and your mother, the difficulty is to trust it. If it doesn't sound too pi [i.e., pious], 'underneath are the everlasting arms.'"[45] When his dear friend Maurice Bowra, warden of Wadham College, Oxford, died the same year, Betjeman wrote to Kenneth Clark after the funeral of his conviction that Bowra was enjoying life eternal: "He is not dead," Betjeman insisted; "Maurice is quite all right." Still, an undercurrent of doubt remained: "Faith, Hope and Charity—for the faint-hearted such as yours truly, the greatest of these is Hope."[46]

If in his later life Betjeman seemed to accept the spiritual void caused by the absence of God with a measure of equanimity, when he was a younger man this sensation left him trembling in fear about the uncertainty of his fate. Would death bring oblivion or wrath? The only certainty he had was that either possibility was equally terrifying. One poem that beautifully illustrates his spiritual doubt and his terror of dying, his sense of God's absence and his anxiety concerning eternity, is "Before the Anaesthetic" (1945).[47] Here he imagines his terror at facing the unknown as he prepares for surgery, and he comes to realize that his faith may have been founded on nothingness. Throughout the poem, church bells are ringing, but their empty peals do not fill the poet with joy or hope, only unutterable horror at the absence of God: "Intolerably sad, profound / St. Giles's bells are ringing round."[48] Echoing the vast emptiness of the Easter bells in "Loneliness," the bells of St. Giles' replicate the parabola of belief and the dialectic of God's presence and absence: "Swing up! and give me hope of life, / Swing down! and plunge the surgeon's knife." "Is it extinction when I die?" fears the poet. "Oh better far those echoing hells / Half-threaten'd in the pealing bells / Than that this 'I' should cease to be— / Come quickly, Lord, come quick to me." Expressing a preference for hell over oblivion is surely poetic license; however, it aptly illustrates his anxiety about eternal life and underscores the frustration that his prayer for God's presence is unanswered. The great fear he then expresses is not hell but extinction; ironically, having given up hope of heavenly bliss, he finds himself wishing for the flames of hell as opposed to the alternative of an eternal nothingness promised by existential philosophers. When he read and discussed this poem in a 1949 radio broadcast, Betjeman insisted that these feelings were genuine and not merely clever poetic expressions: "I would rather there were an afterlife and that I should go to Hell than there should be extinction. That's how I feel about it. And I have an awful feeling too, and I expect a lot of other people do who believe in an afterlife, that they will go to Hell."[49] To Betjeman, at least hell is one kind of eternity—and thus perhaps an affirmation, however unfortunate, that all his efforts to worship and believe, however ineffectual, were not misguided and incorrect. To end up in hell would at least prove to him that he was right in trying to believe. The poem's speaker has certainly been a good Christian; he has observed all the necessary requirements of faith, and everything is in place, it seems, except faith itself:

> Illuminated missals—spires—
> Wide screens and decorated quires—
> All these I loved, and on my knees
> I thanked myself for knowing these
> And watched the morning sunlight pass
> Through richly stained Victorian glass
> And in the colour-shafted air
> I, kneeling, thought the Lord was there.

Perhaps the speaker's faith has failed because his focus was on the apparatus humanity has created with which to worship God, rather than on God himself, but whatever the cause, his faith has failed, and the bells of St. Giles' now mock his faith; they first tell him that he never truly sensed God's presence and then tell him that "that Lord did not exist." Despite the tremendous efforts he has taken to ensure for himself an eternity in heaven, despite every effort to believe and to worship, at this moment God is only an illusion. "Before the Anaesthetic" captures perfectly the sensation of the absence of God in the dialectic of Anglican faith. The concluding lines depressingly enunciate the pall of absence that covers the speaker facing death:

> Intolerably long and deep
> St. Giles's bells swing on in sleep:
> "But still you go from here alone"
> Say all the bells about the Throne.[50] (*CP* 106–8)

For Betjeman, doubt is not so much the absence of faith as its surrogate; paradoxically, the belief that God is absent supplants the belief that God is present. Betjeman's Anglicanism encourages him to see doubt as an integral part of faith, and this is the essence of the closing lines of "In Willesden Churchyard" (1957):

> I only know that as we see her grave
> My flesh, to dissolution nearer now

> Than yours, which is so milky white and soft,
> Frightens me, though the Blessed Sacrament
> Not ten yards off in Willesden parish church
> Glows with the present immanence of God.

The anxiety of eternity is reflected in Betjeman's fear of death coexisting with his avowal of God's presence. With echoes of both Raleigh and Gray, "In Willesden Churchyard" is predominantly an elegiac and dialectical meditation on England's past and present, on pastoralism and blight, on faith and doubt:

> Come walk with me, my love, to Neasden Lane,
> The chemicals from various factories
> Have bitten deep into the Portland stone
> And streaked the white Carrara of the graves.

Betjeman's persona and his beloved read the tombstones of the nobodies and the once-nearly-famous that fill the graves of Willesden churchyard.[51] Their speculation about the lives of those buried there points to a larger elegiac context than Gray's meditation on the ugly, looming inevitability of death: England's pastoral past is memorialized by tombstones now pitted by chemical pollution, and the speaker's romantic capacity gives way to fears of his own flesh decaying. But in the midst of this meditation the dialectic of presence and absence occurs: the poet moves from a fear of death in the absence of God to an awareness of God's "immanence" in the church nearby. What are we to make of this image and the speaker's possible epiphany? The word "Glows" suggests the vital intensity of God, yet the speaker's spatial separation from God seems to deny him full communion; God is in the church while the speaker remains in the churchyard. The diction and syntax of "Frightens me, though . . ." create the perfect measure of ambiguity necessary for identifying the dialectic of the presence and absence of God. Perhaps this construction means that the sacrament ameliorates the poet's fear; on the other hand, perhaps Betjeman means "even though," that is, he remains fearful of death despite the proximity of the sacrament: that God is present in the church, but absent for him. The ambiguity of faith could not be rendered more succinctly. Betjeman makes it quite clear that moments of profound uncertainty and disbelief define his Anglican faith. Rather than rendering his belief excessively tolerant or relativistic, however, the acceptance of the dialectic of the absence and presence of God is perhaps the only means to faith (*CP* 266–67).

The process by which doubt strengthens the convictions of the faithful is at the center of "The Conversion of St. Paul" (1955), a poem which describes the "Turning round" of Paul "From chaos to a love profound." The poem exemplifies Greek rationalism and stoicism as Betjeman ponders the faith of the church's founding apostle. The poem's very occasion—a public response to an agnostic's attacks on Christianity on BBC radio—demands that the poet deal with troubling questions of faith in a logical and rational manner.[52] It was Paul's extreme rejection of Christianity initially that led to his becoming such a committed and effective apostle and so devout in his faith; he was an extremist in both phases of his spiritual life. Paul's conversion, though so profoundly worthy of canonization, so vastly more significant than the typical Christian's conversion, and so idealized from pulpits as a model conversion for all believers, offers instead a hint of spiritual mockery to the doubting Betjeman:

> What is conversion? Not at all
> For me the experience of St. Paul,
> No blinding light, a fitful glow
> Is all the light of faith I know
> Which sometimes goes completely out
> And leaves me plunging round in doubt
> Until I will myself to go
> And worship in God's house below—
> My parish Church—and even there
> I find distractions everywhere.

Ever the tolerant Anglican, Betjeman knows that no conversion experience can provide a formula for all believers: some see Jesus and never lose his presence, while others see once and never see again. But most believers, Betjeman argues, only experience his "fitful glow," a symbol of the ebb and flow of faith in the heart of the struggling believer, the dialectic of absence and presence in one's faith:

> But most of us turn slow to see
> The figure hanging on a tree

And stumble on and blindly grope
Upheld by intermittent hope. (*CP* 382–84)

Certainly there was no "blinding light" for Betjeman. Less than a year before writing this poem he described a very different spiritual experience in the pages of the *Spectator*. "For me the growth of Faith is gradual and not a sudden revelation," he averred. "I have no memory of a blinding light striking me at the corner of a street, or of a fit of the shudders while people knelt around me in prayer. I cannot point to a date, time and place and say, 'That was when I was converted.'"53

A gradual faith was nonetheless set in motion. Despite the differences between their spiritual experiences, Betjeman did try to use the story of Paul's conversion to turn himself around from the absence of God to his presence. And despite his great preoccupation with death and his anxieties over his eternal destination, these uncertainties were indeed counterbalanced by periods of "intermittent hope" in which he enjoyed a settled belief and resolve in his Christian faith. This was not simply an emotional reaction but a clearly reasoned intellectual response. One of his unfinished poems captures the paradox of a rational acceptance of the impossibility of believing in something one knows is true:

I saw the light & I rejected it
I knew the Truth & I respected it
A glorious path was straight but I deflected it
Forgive me God made man if You exist.54

Betjeman's spiritual life was a constant negotiation of the razor's edge of belief and doubt. Generally, the most that he could hope for in the way of spiritual security was a slightly hopeful uncertainty. Such is the confession he utters near the end of *The Home Counties on Sunday*, a 1972 television film: "At half past six some villagers will go to Evensong. For evening is a time when some of us are thinking of the evening of our lives and of the vastness into which we go, or nothingness, or of eternal bliss." Betjeman then turns to the poignancy of poetry: "Whatever it is, for sure we've got to go / Alone, alone, and time will part us all / And somehow, somewhere, waits the love of God."55 How could an expression of spiritual ambivalence be any less ambiguous? Here Betjeman imagines the loneliness of death and the doubtfulness of eternity while simultaneously reassuring himself of God's love. As the subsequent chapters will reveal, his faith was complex and multifaceted, manifesting itself in various fashions. Belief simply could never be a simple matter for him, even in those moments when he felt a measure of security in his faith. Nevertheless, he always brought an intellectual honesty and a spiritual depth to his poetic reflections on Christian belief. As he admitted in an interview with Kenneth Allsop, "My only sustaining belief is that the Christian faith is probably true. Why, then, should I fear death? Well, if you don't have doubts what would faith be? Doubts are the test of one's faith."[56]

3

IN THE VAPORY INCENSE VEIL
Nature, Eros, and Spiritual Mystery

> So when we walk down a green lane like an ancient cart track towards
> the ringing church-bells, we can see the power of God in the blossom
> and trees, remember legends of the saints about birds and stones, and
> recall miracles that happened in the parish at this or that spot. . . .
> Chiefly in the figure of Our Lady do we see the tenderness and
> sweetness of this late religion.[1]

John Betjeman's short but exquisite poem "Uffington" (1966) is a tribute to the stunning medieval Church of St. Mary, Uffington, where
Betjeman was a member from 1934 to 1945. It begins with an ambiguous
couplet that describes the tension of village church bells: "Tonight we
feel the muffled peal / Hang on the village like a pall." The marvelous
consonance of "peal" and "pall" symbolizes the crux of the poem, the
fearful and majestic power of divine mystery. This eerie sound effect
creates an unsettled feeling that is reinforced by the image of a pealing
bell accompanied by death's pall. This spiritual ambiguity is heightened
furthermore by the metrical antithesis that initiates the first two lines,
as the regular iamb of "Tonight" is disrupted with an irregular trochee
in "Hang on." Paradox continues to characterize this poem. The bell
serves as a "death-reminding dying fall," yet it seems to summon the
presence of God: "The very sky no longer high / Comes down within
the reach of all." Of church bells Betjeman wrote, "Who has heard
a muffled peal and remained unmoved? . . . Some may hate them for

their melancholy, but they dislike them chiefly, I think, because they are reminders of Eternity. In an age of faith they were messengers of consolation."[2] The resonating church bells at Uffington paradoxically signify both death and life, a duality that captures the speaker's uncertainty about the nature of the divine and the necessity of embracing ambiguity. The poem's final line consciously eschews metaphor for prosaic simplicity: "Even the trivial seems profound." This ending suggests the power of God to endow with spiritual mystery even the mundane bits of human existence. Betjeman's belief is that we always live in the presence of this divine mystery; he cannot explain it, but he does not doubt that his feeling is based in genuine truth (*CP* 264).

Accepting the spiritual mystery of life, though an intellectual challenge, is essential to Anglican thinking and vital to an appreciation of the achievement of John Betjeman, whose thinking and writing is constructed with the stuff of Anglicanism in all its diverse nature. Characteristic of a large number of his poems is a deeply felt undercurrent of spirituality that embraces divine mystery. These range from celebrations of the birth of Christ to discoveries of God's presence in nature to the nearly divine delights of human sexuality. Betjeman's description of the Shrine of our Lady of Walsingham, "Here in this warm, mysterious, holy house," captures the complex and contradictory sense of spiritual mystery:

> Or do you think that forces are around,
> Strong, frightening, loving and just out of reach
> But waiting, waiting, somewhere to be asked?
> And is that somewhere here at Walsingham?[3]

Betjeman wonders whether the divine is a threatening power or a lover who must be coaxed and wooed, and in the end he allows the paradox to go unresolved. Living in the presence of mystery necessitates what Bishop Stephen Neill describes as a "conviction that truth is larger and more beautiful than our imperfect minds are able to apprehend or to conceive."[4] Betjeman was skeptical of absolutist theologies and resistant to rigid truth claims. He had, like many Anglicans, a "humility of awe before the divine mysteries of faith and a recognition of the incompetence of language to define the ultimate paradox of existence."[5] To accommodate himself to mystery meant accepting that truth could only be approached, that it could never be possessed or controlled.

The sense of mystery that typifies Anglican spirituality is partially explained by a deeply held incarnational faith. Certainly the key to Betjeman's own spiritual life was the mystery surrounding the doctrine of the incarnation. Among the clearest theological utterances Betjeman ever made is this straightforward assertion of an incarnational faith: "The one fundamental thing is that Christ was God . . . really I don't think it would be worth living if it weren't true."[6] Numerous Anglican apologists have argued that the incarnation is the most central doctrine of Christianity. For William Temple, archbishop of York from 1929 to 1942 and of Canterbury from 1942 to 1944, the incarnation was foundational to almost all of his theological and philosophical writings. In *Christus Veritas*, he argues convincingly that the incarnation was the opportunity not only for God to become human but for us to experience a glimpse of the divine. Taking on the human form, Temple asserts, becomes "the means whereby the Eternal Son, remaining always in the bosom of the Father, lays bare to us the very heart of Godhead." Therefore, he concludes, "Even had there been no evil in the world to be overcome, no sin to be abolished and forgiven, still the incarnation would be the natural inauguration of the final stage of evolution."[7] Thus for Anglicans the incarnation is not some consolation prize for the grave error of Adamic sin but is in fact the very reason that creation was formed out of inchoate matter; it was the very purpose of God's creative enterprise. Creation initiated the process of God's becoming incarnate and thereby experiencing human life and death, joy and grief.

A tone of restrained anticipation typifies Betjeman's contemplation of the mystery of the incarnation and the nativity. The season of Advent, the period of preparation for celebrating divine incarnation through the birth of Christ, is one that evokes from him an unambiguous appreciation for mystery and for the spiritual truth that we continue daily to live in the presence of this mystery. Several of Betjeman's poems speak to the intellectual dilemmas inherent in the doctrine of the incarnation. "Advent Bells" (broadcast in 1954, published in 2008) addresses the difficulty in believing in a mystery that some would consider "So highly primitive a myth." The response, characteristically

Betjeman, is that faith is an act, not a belief; that is to say, when the effort to believe intellectually fails, one can rely instead on acts of worship and ritual in order to receive God's grace: "We believe Him / When we in bread and wine receive Him."[8] In contrast, "Advent 1955" (1982) finds humor in the fact that most of humanity prepares for Christmas in ways that have nothing to do with belief in the incarnation: "Some ways indeed are very odd / By which we hail the birth of God." Betjeman enumerates these odd customs, namely the exchanging of cards and gifts with people we do not like or barely know, in order to remind us that Advent is the season for us to prepare for the gift of God to humanity, without which we would, quite simply, not be able to live in the presence of the divine: "Yet if God had not given so / He still would be a distant stranger / And not the Baby in the manger." A gently ironic poem that concludes with this direct statement, "Advent 1955" almost considers God's present of the incarnation as yet one more quotidian detail of modern existence (*CP* 369–70).[9] The poem "Christmas" (1947), however, which I examined in another context in chapter 1 (pp. 35–37), never lets us forget that the presence of God is an incredible (that is to say, both marvelous and implausible) mystery. Betjeman begins with the Advent bells reminding Christians to prepare, but as in "Advent 1955" most of the preparations are only vaguely religious, and not at all spiritual.

The central meaning of the poem "Christmas" develops from the contrast between the triviality of Christmas and the majesty and mystery of Christmas's true import: the nativity. Betjeman juxtaposes the banality of celebrations of Christmas against the mystery of the incarnation. In cities and villages, shops and houses, churches and pubs, people celebrate the best that they can:

> On lighted tenements I gaze
>   Where paper decorations hang,
> And bunting in the red Town Hall
> Says "Merry Christmas to you all."

In the midst of such mundanity, however, is the astonishing appearance of God. To Betjeman, the mystery is so profound, so inexplicable, that he can only describe the wonder with a question:

And is it true? And is it true,
  This most tremendous tale of all,
Seen in a stained-glass window's hue,
  A Baby in an ox's stall?
The Maker of the stars and sea
Become a Child on earth for me?

Betjeman uses ironically debased language to describe God's gift in order to express the way that all human efforts to celebrate this signal event of Christianity, the moment when the spirit assumed natural form, fail to offer appropriate glory. The gifts we exchange with each other—our symbolic reenactment of God's gift—are indeed trivial in comparison with Betjeman's "single Truth": "That God was Man in Palestine / And lives to-day in Bread and Wine."[10] What better illustration of the principle of mystery that characterizes Anglican spirituality could be found? In the midst of normal human triviality appeared God incarnate, and yet more mysterious is the fact that God remains incarnate today in the metaphysical reality of the Eucharist, where, as Betjeman wrote elsewhere, "the Greatest Mystery in the World happens Sunday after Sunday."[11] "And is it true?" Betjeman significantly asks in the poem three times. The poet approaches this truth, yet he will not express his belief in absolute or fundamental terms; he knows that this mystery can never be fully grasped or possessed. The best he can muster is an awareness of God's ultimate mystery; if this mystery cannot be understood it can at least be adored (*CP* 153–54).

For Betjeman a tenuous certainty allowed him to embrace the possibilities of an unpredictable grace from God and to trust that such surprising and undeserved gifts could happen anywhere and at any time. He used the opportunity of a 1953 radio address to talk about his Christian spirituality and his willingness to live with belief rather than proof.[12] First, he insists that he has to believe that "the force that created . . . the stars and the universe" loves him; otherwise "I would want to cut my throat or rush off and indulge myself in every physical excess of which my body is capable." His awareness of the Creator's love is what makes life worth living, but he makes sure to express this spirituality in specifically Anglican terms: "I know that my own Church is full of love—or charity as we call it—and I believe that it is the true Church. I know that Christ, who was Perfect Love, lives in it." If believing in the Creator's love is easy enough, accepting the doctrines of the faith is another matter. For Betjeman, nothing is more "difficult" to believe than that "God the Son, two thousand years ago, became Man in the womb of a Jewish virgin in Palestine." Initially Betjeman confesses doubt about this: "I *want* to believe that Christ was God become Man." But after expressing some anxiety about spiritual delusion, Betjeman affirms that "of course it is true." How can he know with such certainty? By embracing divine mystery and observing the incarnational faith of other believers:

> I have seen people die secure and believing that they are cared for and loved by God become Man, I have sat by deathbeds and I know that the Christian religion is true. I know that there is a world beyond this one that is all round us, that good and evil spirits are fighting here among us and that here we are born into this battle between good and evil—which is another way of saying that we were born in Original Sin. And I hope that when I die I shall understand more of the purpose of God. He hides much from me now because my finite brain would not be able to understand it.

Betjeman's faith is clearly steeped in spirituality rather than logical proofs, which is not to say his faith lacks rationality: it is rooted in personal feelings and the experience of others, couched in terms of living in mystery, and confirmed in the sense that God is all around him. This is the essence of an incarnational faith. As Michael Townsend puts it, Betjeman's "vision is primarily incarnational, fixed in a world of tangible things, perceptible to ordinary mortals, yet revelatory of the presence of the incarnate God."[13]

This public expression of Betjeman's creed expresses the spirituality that runs throughout his poetry, both religious and secular. Indeed his incarnational faith led him to create striking imagery mingling natural and divine, human and spiritual, and his expressions of belief are often poised in tense opposition to a robust and earthy sexuality. How better to understand the desire for God than through expressions of animal passion, and how better to describe the feelings of lust than through images of spirituality and divine mystery? If this seems contradictory, we should bear in mind that this is true not only of Anglican poetry (especially John Donne) but of Anglican spirituality broadly speaking. Spirituality within the Anglican tradition is characterized, writes A. M. Allchin, by "the link between grace and nature, faith and culture, divine and human."[14] Such linkages run throughout Betjeman's poetry because paradoxes like these speak to the very nature of Anglicanism. A. R. Vidler explains,

> Anglican theology is true to its genius when it is seeking to reconcile opposed systems, rejecting them as exclusive systems, but showing that the principle for which each stands has its place within the total orbit of Christian truth, and in the long run is secure only within that orbit or . . . when it is held in tension with other apparently opposed, but complementary principles.[15]

This same theological genius for reconciling contrarieties typifies Anglican poetry. Though Betjeman's expressions of the spiritual life often emphasize the natural and the erotic, underneath lies a sincere appreciation of divine mystery and a commitment to incarnational theology. It is through these theological positions concerning divine mystery and incarnational faith that he regularly expresses his spirituality with imagery that is natural and erotic. If the incarnation is about the divine putting on human form, he reverses the sequence and dresses the human with divinity. In both cases, the beloved divinity is objectified with the poet's desire. Descriptions of humans for whom he lusts are portrayed with trappings of divinity, and statements of faith are rendered with imagery dripping with sexuality and desire.

The erotics of Betjeman's incarnational spirituality should be considered first from a personal angle, underscoring which is a sense of mystery that conflates flesh and spirit into a mass of desire. It is as if the object of desire is divinity incarnate. As he wrote in the *Sunday Express* in 1973, "I like there to be a mystery between me and my beloved, and I don't think there was anything wrong with looking at her in church."[16] Indeed, the seemingly indiscriminate doubling of sexual and spiritual feelings is a significant motif in his poetry, perhaps most noticeably in the autobiographical *Summoned by Bells* (1960). As a child his first crush was on a memorably named little girl: "O Peggy Purey-Cust, how pure you were: / My first and purest love, Miss Purey-Cust!" Expressing his attraction for her in terms of moral decency, he connects this purity to the grandeur of her North London townhouse and its hilltop views that look "for miles across the chimney-pots / To spired St. Pancras and the dome of Paul's."[17] Betjeman here implies the remoteness and holiness of both cathedral and beloved, an intertwined duality of worship that is expressed over and over in his poetry. During adolescent summer vacations in Cornwall, Betjeman's affections were centered on a neighboring girl, Biddy Walsham, for whom he suffered "tender, humble, unrequited love," a "worshipping / That put me off my supper."[18] For Betjeman, this is perhaps an unusual instance of the spirit prevailing over the flesh; in general sexuality and faith enhance each other. At Oxford in the 1920s, which was undergoing a revival of Anglo-Catholicism, Betjeman may very well have found himself drawn to worship by the surprising path of lust:

> Those were the days when that divine baroque
> Transformed our English altars and our ways.
> Fiddle-back chasuble in mid-Lent pink
> Scandalized Rome and Protestants alike.[19]

It was not just the outward forms of spirituality that Betjeman could express in terms of desire; he could also describe a relationship with Christ as an "arduous love affair."[20]

Perhaps because his childhood was largely defined by single-sex educational institutions, many of Betjeman's sexual-spiritual allusions are homoerotic. Indeed the overwhelming allusion to homosexuality in many of his descriptions of spiritual matters is noteworthy, and it is therefore not surprising that some would find his attraction to the church to be rooted in homoerotic longing. Stephen Games, for instance, argues that Betjeman's love of the church and especially of its aesthetics contained "a strong erotic element in it, making his attendance at choral evensong and the sight of treble voices in surplices doubly compelling."[21] In many of Betjeman's verses, especially those that recall his childhood and youth, the idea of worship is united with that of ungovernable lust, expressed in the competing desires of the spirit and the flesh: "The muse inspired my pen: / The sunset tipped with gold St. Michael's church, / Shouts of boys bathing came from Highgate Ponds."[22] Ornate church interiors also mingle with desire that is at once spiritual and homoerotic:

> Jehovah Jireh! the arches ring,
> The Mintons glisten, and grand

Are the surpliced boys as they sweetly sing
  On the threshold of glory land.[23] (*CP* 37)

Betjeman expresses his earliest memories of being drawn into religious consciousness with the rhetoric of forbidden love. For him it was not "a conscious search for God" but "a longing" and "a slight sense of something unfulfilled" together with a "sense of guilt increasing with the years."[24] Though he would recall a playmate with whom he had engaged in exploratory touching of a nature his mother would call "unwholesome,"[25] he would also claim that his attraction to other boys was a "love / Too deep for words or touch."[26]

In public school at Marlborough College he would sit in the "glorious chapel," which was "the centre of my life," but, unable to heed the bishop's sermon, he found that all he "worshipped were the athletes, ranged / In the pews opposite."[27] As Betjeman's desire for other boys grew, he would continue to express his passion with Anglican imagery:

First tremulous desires in Autumn stillness—
  Grey eyes, lips laughing at another's joke,
A nose, a cowlick—a delightful illness
  That put me off my food and off my stroke.
Here, 'twixt the church tower and the chapel spire
Rang sad and deep the bells of my desire.[28]

Among his most favored symbols, the church bell is here appropriated to signal the painful yearning of unrequited passion. An earlier version of this passage suggests an even more intense desire. Here, however, resplendency is found neither in Anglican worship nor in the setting, but in the form of the boy who sat so intimately near to him in the service:

Ah, but that shabby chancel set us soaring
High to the skies above the Chapel bell,
The purring organ thundered to a roaring,
The stained glass windows rattled in the swell;
And I will never love again as when
I loved the boy with slick Anjora'd hair
Who smiled across the aisle . . .
So pure and so sexless that the spell
Still lingers in this moted evening air.[29]

The elements of Anglicanism—bells, organ, stained glass—all increase the poet's desire, a heightened passion indicated by his identification with the (other) organ's "swell" and by the fact that the desire itself, not just the memory, "Still lingers."

As for the nature of Betjeman's sexual orientation, from early childhood through boarding school and his undergraduate years at Oxford he felt deep attraction to members of both sexes, but as an adult he was strictly heterosexual.[30] Nevertheless, many of his closest friends being homosexual, Betjeman was sympathetic to homosexuality and remained intrigued by the possibilities of a homosexual aspect to his own personality, if not his active sex life. In 1949 he wrote several letters of advice to Anthony Barnes, who had recently left Eton and was now in the Royal Navy.[31] At Eton, Barnes had had an affair with another boy and was suffering some degree of religious guilt. Betjeman's response not only shows his sympathy for homosexuality but also suggests that displaying Christian charity is much more important than rigidly following the church's teaching on this matter. He himself—though he is clear not to speak for God on this matter—"will forgive the wildest sensual excesses for a spark of kindness, generosity and humour in the profligate. But those are my views and I doubt if God agrees with them."[32] Worried perhaps that he might have added anxiety to Barnes' burden, Betjeman wrote a week later to console him that his "splendid" affair would be the most memorable and emotionally "purest" incident of his life.[33] Betjeman's advice then turns to the relationship between faith and expressions of love, arguing that the important thing is to avoid being consumed by lust. He advises him not to be concerned about moral or theological questions, as long as it is love. If it should turn into lust, however, Betjeman writes, "then whether it is heter or homo makes little difference." He adds that among young men lust is common and that its uncontrollability makes it less sinful in youth. If Barnes continues to feel he is in mortal sin, Betjeman concludes, it is a simple matter to "confess it and receive absolution."[34] What seems significant in Betjeman's advice to the young Barnes is his suggestion that it little matters whether the love is expressed toward male or female, so long as it is not an obsessive lust; an expression of love is clearly a step toward the divine, while an expression of lust is a step away from God. This idea Betjeman worked into a sonnet; though the speaker is theoretically a woman, it is difficult to overlook the fact that it is a male writer who gives voice to this forbidden passion:

> Is He not good, God who such rapture gives?
>   Such overflowing ecstasy of joy.
> Touch, let me touch your warm enticing skin
> That I may know my lover breathes and lives.
>   My own, my darling sunkiss'd supple boy
> If this is sinful, what is wrong with sin?[35]

The speaker clearly associates the passionate delights of a young male lover with both grace and sin, suggesting the spiritual confusion caused by uncontrollable and unconscious desire.

If Betjeman's confessions of spirituality and sexuality tended toward homoeroticism in childhood, once he left the all-male confines of public school and university the same-sex attractions seemed to disappear and his latent heterosexuality began to blossom.[36] What remained consistent was the doubling of sexual and spiritual longings. Compelled by his childhood memories of the loveliness of Peggy Purey-Cust, Betjeman recreated other poetic women in her image:

> Your ice-blue eyes, your lashes long and light,
> Your sweetly freckled face and turned-up nose
> So haunted me that all my loves since then
> Have had a look of Peggy Purey-Cust.[37]

Unsurprisingly, the competition between flesh and spirit for the primacy of worship remained fierce. Betjeman's passion for athletic, gamine, golden-haired English goddesses manifested itself in numerous poetic muses whose natural and unselfconscious sexuality inspired the poet to rhapsodic delights of romantic self-confidence laden with imagery of Anglican worship. "Indoor Games near Newbury" (1947), written from the viewpoint of a child, recollects an intense moment of shared passion with a little girl while at a children's party; that night, while "the bells of all the churches" ring out, the boy's prayers constitute a lustful yearning for the girl:

> Wendy speeded my undressing,
> Wendy is the sheet's caressing

> Wendy bending gives a blessing,
> Holds me as I drift to dreamland, safe inside my slumber-wear. (*CP* 124–25)

Betjeman's adult persona continues this uncomfortable blend of worshipping in spirit and flesh. In "The Licorice Fields at Pontefract" (1950), the speaker meets his beloved in the eponymous fields for a sexual tryst, during which passionate encounter "From various black Victorian towers / The Sunday evening bells / Come pealing over dales and hills" (*CP* 155). Similarly, the Irish Unionist who laments his parting from his beloved Swedish beauty Greta Hellstrom remembers hearing the Angelus bell calling to him as they part forever.[38] In a slightly different vein the poet's passion for Pam, the "great big mountainous sports girl" in "Pot Pourri from a Surrey Garden" (1938), leads him to imagine not just a tennis match and a tryst but a good Anglican church wedding whose details occupy him as much as his passion for her "firm and hairy" arm, her muscular thighs, and her pouty lips:

> One fine Saturday, Windlesham bells shall call:
> Up the Butterfield aisle rich with Gothic enlacement,
>   Licensed now for embracement,
>   Pam and I, as the organ
> Thunders over you all. (*CP* 45–46)

"The Cockney Amorist" (1958) depicts a jilted lover recalling the places he and his beloved once frequented: cinemas, teashops, golf courses, and most notably churches:

> The vast suburban churches
>   Together we have found:
> The ones which smelt of gaslight
>   The ones in incense drown'd;
> I'll use them now for praying in
>   And not for looking round. (*CP* 282–83)

That lover may echo the experience of the female persona in one of Betjeman's earliest poems, "Blisland, Bodmin" (1927), who recalls discovering "First love and life" while exploring the "moorland shrine" of Blisland parish church.[39] The speaker's discovery of a spiritual side of himself in the middle of a sexual reverie is a surprising pattern in a number of Betjeman's poems, for ecclesial imagery is not merely decoration but indeed serves a larger purpose. In "Ireland with Emily" (1944), the devotion of Roman Catholic peasants arouses the speaker to poetic flights of devotion to his beloved, where five of the six stanzas describe churches and churchyards. As the poem opens, "Bells are booming down the bohreens" while lovely Irish lasses "Move between the fields to Mass." Here Betjeman is drawing connections among the scenic natural landscape of Ireland, the devoted faith of its people, and the sexual allure of the young women. The "decent whitewashed chapel" and its "Gilded gates" suggest the purity of the girls for whom the poet lusts at a distance; if only he could redirect their devotion for the Mass toward himself. Again the poet connects nature, sexuality, and spirituality in one seething image:

> See the black-shawled congregations
>   On the broidered vestment gaze
> Murmur past the painted stations
>   As Thy Sacred Heart displays
> Lush Kildare of scented meadows.

The poet remains outside this Roman Catholic Mass, however, and his thoughts turn to the churchyard where the remains of the faithful departed unite in luxuriant splendor with the natural landscape, and to his friendship with Emily, with whom he has explored on bicycle the ruins of Ireland. Significantly, it is a ruined church that captivates the speaker and provides him with an important connection to his beloved:

> Till there arose, abrupt and lonely,
> A ruined abbey, chancel only,
> Lichen-crusted, time befriended,
> Soared the arches, splayed and splendid,
>   Romanesque against the sky.

Here it is the image of the church rather than the beloved that dominates the poem and the poet's thoughts; although Emily drifts into the background, the speaker's romantic feelings for her help to stimulate his passion for the faith of the Irish people (*CP* 98–99).

An empty church serves a more explicitly erotic purpose in "An Archaeological Picnic" (1940), a poem that describes a sexually charged outdoor luncheon shared by a young man and woman in a churchyard during a day of rambling through old churches. The opening stanza unites riotous and erotic imagery of nature with an alluring country church:

> In this high pasturage, this Blunden time,
>   With Lady's Finger, Smokewort, Lover's Loss,
> And lin-lan-lone a Tennysonian chime
>   Stirring the sorrel and gold-starred moss,
>   Cool is the chancel, bright the altar cross.

In the second stanza the speaker urges his beloved to drink her "fizzy lemonade" and hasten to the important activity of the afternoon, to find the key that "lies underneath the mat." Here the sexual underscores the spiritual as Betjeman transposes the speaker's desire for one sort of forbidden ingress into another. Inside the church, the speaker describes what he sees with the breathless intensity of transmogrified desire:

> Sweet smell of cerements and of cold wet stones,
>   Hassock and cassock, paraffin and pew;
> Green in a light which that sublime Burne-Jones
>   White-hot and wondering from the glass-kiln drew,
>   Gleams and re-gleams this Trans arcade anew.

The stained-glass window by the pre-Raphaelite artist Edward Burne-Jones is especially charged with sexuality, a "sublime" experience fraught with natural wildness and danger. In the midst of the poet's ecstasy, in the final stanza, stands the beloved in "freckled innocence." Perhaps she does not find arousal in the wonders of the church's interior, but there is plenty to arouse her outdoors, where the "flattened pattern" in the "meadow grass" implies that a sexual encounter has indeed occurred, a digging and unearthing of hidden layers not normally implied by the title's adjective, "archaeological." This is not to suggest that the speaker is so rapt in his ecclesial reverie that he is oblivious to her willing desire; in fact it is fair to suggest that the speaker's arousal inside the church heightens his sexual enjoyment of the beloved (*CP* 95).[40]

Such poems reveal that Betjeman fetishizes the normal stuff of churches with a latent sexuality. In "Myfanwy at Oxford" (1938), Betjeman effuses over the sensual delights of an undergraduate whose bicycling about the city arouses many of the young scholars:

Sancta Hilda, Myfanwyatia
   Evansensis—I hold your heart,
Willowy banks of a willowy Cherwell a
   Willowy figure with lips apart,
Strong and willowy, strong to pillow me,
   Gold Myfanwy, kisses and art.

Betjeman imagines her an essential part of nature—a flower, a tree—
and yet paradoxically a statue to be worshipped and adored. Transfixed
by this deity, Betjeman imagines himself an acolyte bound in devotion
to her divinity. Though outward signs of Anglo-Catholicism abound in
Oxford, his worship is directed entirely toward Myfanwy, whose name
evokes spiritual mystery. Here Betjeman describes, though with a touch
of mock-innocence, the symbiosis of sexual and spiritual desire:

Tubular bells of tall St. Barnabas,
   Single clatter above St. Paul,
Chasuble, acolyte, incense-offering,
   Spectacled faces held in thrall.
There in the nimbus and Comper tracery
   Gold Myfanwy blesses us all.

"Myfanwy at Oxford" embodies perfectly the tendency in Betjeman's
poetry to find a spiritual vision in the midst of a sexual reverie (*CP*
71–72).[41] His attitude toward the church is much too complex, however,
to dismiss such lines as evidence of a sacrilegious nature. His friend
Lord David Cecil emphasized that the "very idea of believing in the
Church but at the same time making fun of it," though it would have
been "distasteful" and "bewildering" to Betjeman's Oxford tutor C. S.
Lewis, was central to Betjeman's character. And yet Betjeman had no
problem dropping a girlfriend after witnessing her sacrilegious behavior during a church crawl on which she accompanied him. In Bevis
Hillier's recounting, he "gave her up when she performed dance steps
in the aisle of Gloucester Cathedral."[42] Perhaps sacrilege is easier to
spot in others than in oneself, but the fact remains that Betjeman had
little difficulty in reconciling his own sexuality to Anglican spirituality.

   The double helix of spirituality and sexuality is imbedded in
"Lenten Thoughts of a High Anglican" (1971), a poem in which Betjeman describes watching a mysterious and alluring woman receiving

Communion each Sunday.[43] The minister of the church, perhaps in an
effort to increase parishioners' attentiveness, has told his congregation
that one should not stare around and become distracted during the
church service, "Or the Unknown God we are seeking / May forever
elude our search." But Betjeman's point is that as long as we are hunting for God, he will elude us. We cannot possess, control, or grasp him;
we cannot make him come to us; we must in fact wait for his manifestation. And just where, in this poem, does God become incarnate?
Just what causes Betjeman to become conscious of God's presence? It
is, strangely, the mysterious and alluring woman, whom Betjeman has
decided looks too well kept to be anyone's "legal wife":

> But I hope that the preacher will not think
>   It unorthodox and odd
> If I add that I glimpse in "the Mistress"
>   A hint of the Unknown God.

What better illustration could one find of the principle that God's
manifestations are surprising and extraordinary? In the midst of fan-
tasizing about this woman's sexual life, Betjeman suddenly becomes
aware of the presence of God. As Geoffrey Harvey puts it, "Betjeman
suggests that we learn the world's spiritual frame by knowing its Creator in another and in oneself."[44] The woman may or may not be some-
one's mistress, but her aura of mystery creates more than intrigue and
arousal. Her mystery reminds the speaker that God is mysterious; she
is a visible symbol of spiritual mystery:

> How elegantly she swings along
>   In the vapory incense veil;
> The angel choir must pause in song
>   When she kneels at the altar rail.

Though clearly we are meant to laugh at Betjeman's mock-blasphemy,
we are still reminded of the idea that the incarnation of God is mysterious and inexplicable (*CP* 310–11).

   If spiritual metaphors inform his sexual poetry, it is also true that
sexuality informs his spiritual poetry and can be put to serious and
religious purpose. The mystery surrounding the presence of God is
at the heart of the baroque solemnity of "Holy Trinity, Sloane Street"

(1939).[45] This is among the most mysterious and elusive of Betjeman's poems. Sensuous imagery of candles and incense, ornate decor, and penitential liturgy fill the poem. The poem is passionate; the religious experience borders on the sexual, or at least is expressed in poundingly physical terms:

> Light six white tapers with the Flame of Art,
> Send incense wreathing to the lily flowers,
> And, with your cool hands white,
> Swing the warm censer round my bruised heart,
> Drop, dove-grey eyes, your penitential showers
> On this pale acolyte.

The speaker's faith, his sense of the truth of Christianity, is found not in the physical features of high Anglican worship but in the mystery symbolized by these features, such as the maternal power of the Virgin Mary. The worship described in this poem may occur on Mothering Sunday; the second stanza alludes to Whistler's mother, and the third to the red roses carried on that day.[46] Here, filial piety is yoked metaphysically with sexual arousal to symbolize the emotional pitch of devout religiosity commanded by Anglo-Catholicism:

> Bronze triptych doors unswing!
> Wait, restive heart, wait, rounded lips, to pray,
> Mid beaten copper interset with gems
> Behold! Behold! your King!

Religious expressions of fervor and intensity are relatively rare in Betjeman's verse; typically, his poetry is rational and cool. Anglicans after all are generally suspicious of emotional expressions of faith and understand that such effusions may in fact impede a spiritual encounter. As Stephen Neill puts it, Anglicanism is marked by "a certain restrained and sober quality of devotion . . . based more on the direction of the will than on the stirring of the emotions."[47] "Holy Trinity, Sloane Street" is thus highly unusual in its passionate depiction of the pulsating heart of the Christian awaiting God's mysterious penetration of his soul (*CP* 47).

Underscoring the erotic and the spiritual in Betjeman's poetry is indeed a sense of mystery; for Betjeman a beautiful woman and a beautiful church were equally alluring, elusive, and mysterious. As a school child exploring the many churches around Oxford, Betjeman found St. Aloysius, the Roman Catholic church, "very sacred and alarming." The whole aura was one of feminized mystery with its "candles, polished brass and jewels" and its "apse of coloured saints and its smell of incense and many *dévoués* crossing themselves and looking back at us while on their knees."[48] Consider as well the following passage describing St. Chad's Cathedral (the Roman Catholic cathedral of the Archdiocese of Birmingham), from his radio talk on the architect A. W. N. Pugin: "The stained glass glows like jewels; the great rood screen in front of the altar adds mystery to what would otherwise be a rather obvious place; the altars blaze with gilding and colour."[49] Indeed what creates the beauty in St. Chad's is its mysterious femininity. Likewise Betjeman adored cathedral screens and baldachins for the way they create a sense of privacy and mystery within the vast spaces. Sir Ninian Comper was a contemporary architect who understood this principle; his churches were not only "an expression of his own Faith" but were moreover "designed to bring you to your knees when you see the altar through the mystery of screens or under the golden canopy of a vast ciborium."[50] In contrast, Betjeman expressed doubts about Basil Spence's design for a new cathedral in Coventry because it had all the mystery of an exhibition hall or auditorium: "It lacks mystery and the endlessness of vista upon vista characteristic of our faith itself."[51] Mystery is central to Betjeman's concept of ecclesial beauty. The interior of Holy Trinity Church, Kensington Gore, "is pale green many vista'd twilight hung with mighty chandeliers."[52] The inherent mystery within a place of worship was what gave it its beauty and what inspired Betjeman's faith, and this mystery could be enhanced or destroyed depending on the lighting in the church. Noting the increasing rarity of a candle-lit church, Betjeman offers the "supreme example" of the beauty and mystery created by the lighting in the chapel of King's College, Cambridge: "I know no more wonderful sight than to enter that chapel on an autumn evening when the time of Evensong synchronises with the end of day. The colours of the great stained-glass windows that line the walls fade away, the huge stone-vaulted roof disappears in misty darkness and warm and golden around us glow the candles, burnishing the white surplices of the choir."[53] The setting is both eroticized and naturalized by the lighting, which is responsible for the spiritual mystery of the chapel at King's.[54]

Even moving beyond his overtly erotic writing one can sense a genuine and profound appreciation in his work for divine mystery, but if Betjeman's poetry commonly joins together flesh and spirit, it is only because this union is central to his theological thinking. The poetic union of flesh and spirit neatly symbolizes for him the mystery of the incarnation. Of all Christian creeds, the incarnation, whereby divine spirit is made human flesh, is of singular importance, and yet belief in this doctrine requires a leap of faith that necessitates accepting a mystery as truth. That leap essentially involves the ability to live an incarnational faith. Because he believed God is incarnate in the world, not merely in the church, Betjeman finds evidence of the incarnation in the everyday world, even in the banal details. This belief leads to a rejection of a dualistic view of the church and the world, of the spiritual and material, because the spiritual life happens largely in the secular world. Likewise, grace is unpredictable, a surprising and undeserved gift that can never be obtained through any human effort or found in any consistent place. As L. William Countryman writes, "the Holy will meet us when it chooses, not just when we choose. And when it does so, the moment of meeting may well be neither in the church nor in the mountain, but in the midst of life's dailiness."[55] Indeed, foundational to an incarnational faith is the idea that God did not merely become incarnate on Christmas Eve two thousand years ago but that God remains incarnate in the world. The concept of "immanence," meaning both *appearing in* and *remaining in*, helps to explain how God abides in this world. According to this belief, as God made himself incarnate in the most mundane way, by being born to unwed parents in a stinking barn, so God is just as likely to be found today in the mundane world, whether of man's or God's creation, as in the church or on the altar. The idea of a surprise meeting with the holy underscores much of Betjeman's writing, and he was especially fond of celebrating those discoveries of God in nature, sentiments that surface with particular frequency in his prose. In his 1947 radio talk, "Christmas Nostalgia," Betjeman finds God even where life is rotting away: "I can turn over a piece of decaying wood in our garden and see myriapods, insects and bugs, startled out of sluggish winter torpor by my motion. Each is perfectly formed and adapted to its life. From the immensity of the stars to the perfection of an insect—I cannot believe that I am surrounded by a purposeless accident."[56] In a letter to his publisher John Murray written that same Christmas Day, Betjeman justified the religious emphasis of his natural descriptions: "When I am describing Nature, it is *always* with a view to the social background or the sense of Man's impotence before the vastness of the Creator."[57]

This is especially true in his descriptions of the ocean, for it seemed that he was most likely to encounter the holy along the wild Atlantic coast. "Polzeath," a 1950 radio broadcast celebrating one of his favorite bits of Cornish shoreline, presents evidence of the divine in nature. Nestling among forests of seaweed, starfish, and rosy cowries, magnified by a heterogeneity of color, he finds God in a rock pool: "Never was such colour, never is the wonder of God's creation more brought home to me than when I see the strange, merciless bright-coloured world of these Cornish rock pools."[58] The seaside and faith became inextricably linked in Betjeman's mind, and to consider one was inevitably to stimulate imagery of the other. The conclusion of his semiautobiographical poem "North Coast Recollections" (1947) makes the link explicit:

> Then pealing out across the estuary
> The Padstow bells rang up for practice-night
> An undersong to birds and dripping shrubs.
> The full Atlantic at September spring
> Flooded a final tide-mark up the sand,
> And ocean sank to silence under bells,
> And the next breaker was a lesser one
> Then lesser still. Atlantic, bells and birds
> Were layer on interchanging layers of sound. (*CP* 139–40)

In "Trebetherick," a 1975 essay, Betjeman recalled a carefree Cornish childhood. Memories of coastal explorations are embellished with echoes of church bells:

> The finding of extra-big cowries in Cowry Cave. The seaweeds to collect, wild flowers and blue butterflies. The tiny tinkle on a hot Sunday afternoon from the crooked steeple of St Enodoc. The magic mournful call of Padstow

bells across the Sunday estuary, and far inland the lovely ring from St Minver. Blackberry picking in the woods at Grogley. Collecting green seaweed that fringed the pools at the very lowest tides. . . .[59]

Betjeman indeed finds God in unlikely places. The surprising discovery of God is the essence of looking at the world from the perspective of incarnational Christianity.

Indeed his perception of nature is a reliable gauge of his spiritual state. As Philip Payton writes, "Betjeman's imagination . . . mirrored in the landscape his innermost struggles, not least those of religious faith."[60] Evidence of Betjeman's seriousness about spirituality is his perception that God remains incarnate in the world, if in neither a strictly literal nor a strictly metaphorical sense. A recurring pattern in his poetry is his simple delight in suddenly becoming aware of God's creation and his continuing presence in it. In "Wantage Bells" (1954) the speaker encounters God quite plainly in a garden, on a spring Sunday morning, with church bells sounding. Composed in three stanzas of seven lines each, to reinforce the idea of God's immanence in his creation, the poem begins with the bells gradually rising into the consciousness of the speaker, but the speaker is moved not by this sound but by the prolific beauty of his garden: the bright and various hues, the intense fragrances, the cycle of blooming and fading, and the astonishing invasion of color. The bells remain in the background of his mind, but they subconsciously remind the speaker that this garden is no accident of nature but is in fact the intentional and exceedingly generous gift of a Creator who remains present in the world He created:

> Where are the words to express
> > Such a reckless bestowing?
> The voices of birds utter less
> > Than the thanks we are owing,
> > Bell notes alone
> > Ring praise of their own
> As clear as the weed-waving brook and as evenly flowing. (*CP* 208)

In his 1950 radio broadcast "Highworth," Betjeman describes a similar scene in which an after-storm "rainbow glowed brighter against the black sky" on a late Sunday afternoon in an unspoiled West Country village of unutterable perfection: "And suddenly with a burst the

bells of Highworth church rang out for Evening Service. As though
called by the bells, the late sun burst out and bathed the varied roofs
with gold and scooped itself into the uneven panes of old windows.
Sun and stone and old brick and garden flowers and church bells. That
was Sunday evening in Highworth. That was England."[61] It was not
in church where the speaker found God, although church did subtly
remind the speaker of God's bounty and love. In fact, Betjeman may be
suggesting that God is as likely to be found in nature as in the church.
The point is more fully developed in "St. Barnabas, Oxford" (1945).[62]
Here he describes the displacement of God's splendor with an edifice
of Byzantine grandeur and haughtiness:

> Where once the fritillaries hung in the grass
> A baldachin pillar is guarding the Mass.
> Farewell to blue meadows we loved not enough,
> And elms in whose shadows were Glanville and Clough.

Ironically, this monument to the worship of God and to the praise of
God's creation has cut humanity off from the very source of creativity.
In a vein of Romantic effusion, Betjeman writes that the best place to
find God—as to find poetic inspiration—is in a temple of God's making, not man's; in a meadow, not in a church (*CP* 94).

The notion that the church cuts off man from nature is not at
all a consistent position taken by Betjeman. In fact he just as frequently indicates that both the beauty and the spirituality inherent in
old churches are owing to their being rooted in the natural landscape.
"It is impossible to think of English scenery," he wrote in 1954, "without seeing the towers and spires of churches as an essential part of
it." Though villages are altered beyond recognition, and cottages and
country houses are condemned and fallen, "churches remain to remind
us of how beautiful England once was."[63] His 1945 poem "South London Sketch, 1944," suggesting both resurrection and ascension, pays
tribute to the London skyline so inexorably altered by Hitler's bombs
and the "dust of dead explosions":

> And calmly rise on smoky skies
>   Of intersected wires
> The Nonconformist spirelets
>   And the Church of England spires. (*CP* 122)

Indeed the church itself seems to be a vital and living element of the English sky and soil, as Betjeman remarks in his 1974 BBC film *A Passion for Churches*:

> What would you be, you wide East Anglian sky,
> Without church towers to recognise you by?
> What centuries of faith, in flint and stone,
> Wait in this watery landscape, all alone?[64]

His 1953 poem "Essex" noted that "out of elm and sycamore / Rise flinty fifteenth-century towers" (*CP* 159). In 1948 he wrote of the effect of a Wiltshire parish church, which "stands in the Kennet water meadows," as entering "a forest of the most magnificent oak joinery, an ocean of box-pews stretching shoulder high all over the chancel."[65] In 1950 he described Inglesham parish church as a "lichen-crusted country church among the whispering grasses."[66] And in 1956 he admired Maidstone's parish church of All Saints, which hung, "tree-embowered and picturesque, above the Medway."[67] Even as early as 1937, Betjeman was noting the inherent mystery in the rootedness of English churches in their local landscape. Imagining an idealized setting, he describes the ruins of "Godley Abbey" (likely inspired by Chertsey Abbey in Surrey, whose land grants included the Hundred of Godley) rising "among the willows and elms of the valley. The pile is a monument to superstition but, at the same time, it has much of the sublime, seeming to draw towards it the surrounding hills."[68]

The mysterious sublimity of English churches derives from their inherent connection to the natural landscape. All across England, churches seem to spring organically from the native soil and rock:

> Down what lanes, across how many farmyards, resting in how many valleys, topping what hills and suddenly appearing round the corners of what ancient city streets are the churches of England? The many pinnacles in Somerset, of rough granite from the moors in Devon and Cornwall, of slate by the sea coasts, brushed with lichen, spotted with saffron, their rings of five and six bells pouring music among the windy elm trees as they have poured their sound for centuries, still they stand, the towers and spires of the West.[69]

In this 1948 radio talk, "St Protus and St Hyacinth, Blisland, Cornwall," the first in a three-part series on West Country churches, Betjeman describes a rare old unrestored church in a remote corner of England. This church is not just connected with the landscape but seems to sustain life: "The church . . . looks over the tree tops of a deep and elmy valley. . . . An opening in the churchyard circle shows a fuchsia hedge. . . . When I first saw it, the tower was stuffed with moss and with plants that had rooted here and there between the great stones." Yet the church structure seems more living organism than building: "The church itself which seems to lean this way and that, throws out chapels and aisles in all directions. It hangs on the hillside, spotted with lichens which have even softened the slates of its roof."[70] Betjeman concludes the talk with a brief reminiscence about his first visit to the Church of St. Protus and St. Hyacinth as a child during a Cornish summer holiday. The dominant image is one of God incarnate not in the church per se but in nature, of which the church is a vital but not singular part: "Valerian sprouted on the Vicarage wall. A fig tree traced its leaves against a western window. Grasshoppers and birds chirruped. St. Protus and St. Hyacinth, patron saints of Blisland church, pray for me!"[71] Betjeman's "memory" is of course carefully and imaginatively constructed; that one of the saints bears a floral name adds to the natural context of this church. Perhaps cleverest of all is Betjeman's choice of the healing herb valerian to grow on the wall of the vicarage; Protus and Hyacinth were martyred in a massacre instigated in 258 by the Roman emperor Valerian. Altogether, this scene is one of healing and renewal made possible by the unity of nature and spirit.[72]

A sense of spiritual mystery, harmonized between faith and nature, is at the heart of Betjeman's 1949 broadcast, "St. Endellion." St. Endellion is a coastal Cornish village with strong happy childhood associations for Betjeman.[73] Its church was one of several Betjeman identified with Celtic mysticism, where "Caverns of light revealed the Holy Grail / Exhaling gold upon the mountain-tops; / . . . / And past and present were enwrapped in one."[74] In his broadcast, Betjeman put it more prosaically and modestly: "There is something strange and exalting about this windy Cornish hill top looking over miles of distant cliffs, that cannot be put into words."[75] The church itself sits atop this "exalting" hill, and it seems a living element of the landscape: "It looked, and still looks, just like a hare. The ears are the pinnacles of the tower and the rest of the hare, the church, crouches among wind-slashed firs." In his memory the approach to St. Endellion was also hastened by the ringing of its six bells, the sound of which is an integral part of nature: "[T]heir music was scattered from the rough lichened openings over foxgloves, over grey slate roofs, lonely farms and feather tamarisks, down to that cluster of whitewashed houses known as Trelights."[76] After recounting the life of Endelienta, the church's sixth-century patron saint, Betjeman describes the rather generic physical properties of the church itself, concluding indeed that "though at first glance it is unmysterious, its mystery grows."[77] Our final image of the church is also his, a last longing look from a cliff top above the sea. His incarnational faith embraces the spiritual mystery adumbrated in time and nature:

> Man's life on earth will last for seventy years perhaps. But this sea will go on swirling against these green and purple rocks for centuries. Long after we are dead it will rush up in waterfalls of whiteness that seem to hang half-way up the cliff face and then come pouring down with tons of ginger-beery foam. Yet compared with the age of these rocks, the sea's life is nothing. And even the age of rocks is nothing compared with the eternal life of man. And up there on the hill in St Endellion church, eternal man comes week by week in the Eucharist. This is the supreme mystery of all the mysteries of St Endellion.[78]

Like these two radio broadcasts, the poem "Autumn 1964" (1966) presents an image of incarnational Christianity that emphasizes a balanced and reciprocal relationship between God's creation and man's institutional efforts to celebrate and preserve for eternity the fact of God's incarnation. During a glowing autumn Sunday sunrise, apples ripe but poised to fall, the sky clean and slowly burning off a morning fog, the poet anticipates the approaching bells of worship, which will peal out in praise not of God himself but of the beauty of God's creation as evidence of the incarnation: "In half-an-hour a day of days / Will climb into its golden height / And Sunday bells will ring its praise." In response, all of creation joins in praising God's gift of eternal life, an image Betjeman depicts in the language of baptism and salvation: stones, trees, vines, berries, and "The watery sky washed clean and new, / Are all rejoicing with the dead." The astonishing beauty of creation is for Betjeman less a reminder of God's grace than material evidence of his reckless generosity. No element of Christian worship can adequately honor or thank God for his bounty, let alone reciprocate him;

all Christian worship can do is to remind us of the utter profundity of his gift:

> Never have light and colour been
> So prodigally thrown around;
> And in the bells the promise tells
> Of greater light where Love is found.[79] (*CP* 270)

Betjeman's perception of God's incarnation in the natural order and of the relationship between nature and the divine is fundamental to Anglican spirituality. What William J. Wolf writes of Thomas Traherne applies equally to Betjeman: "Concrete elements of nature fairly shine for him with divine translucence, giving an ecological orientation to his meditation."[80]

This idea characterizes the brief but emotionally powerful "Olney Hymns" (1940). This poem is inspired by the evangelical faith of the eighteenth-century writers John Newton and William Cowper, whose poems and hymns (including "Amazing Grace" and "O for a Closer Walk with God") have rooted themselves into the Protestant consciousness.[81] Their collaboration continues to provide poetic and spiritual inspiration as Betjeman finds himself motivated to grow in faith by their hymns and by the village where they lived and wrote:

> Oh God the Olney Hymns abound
> With words of Grace which Thou didst choose,
> And wet the elm above the hedge
> Reflected in the winding Ouse.
>
> Pour in my soul unemptied floods
> That stand between the slopes of clay,
> Till deep beyond a deeper depth
> This Olney day is any day. (*CP* 78)

Rooting evangelical spirituality in the naturally scenic Buckinghamshire soil, Betjeman finds points of connection between the words of faith contained in the poems and Olney's landscape features, its hills and trees and river. Echoing both the language and rhythms of evangelical hymns, his poem suggests an enduring faith to be found through the pastoral countryside, ultimately elevating Olney as a destination on the map of English spiritual pilgrimages, worthy perhaps to be compared with the more prominent Lindisfarne, Little Gidding, or Iona.

"Saint Cadoc" (1940), a tribute to the Celtic mysticism of a sixth-century Cornish saint who "sheltered God," distinctively evokes a gentle religiosity in a setting of natural intensity.[82] The poet imagines Cadoc still "in his cell beside the sea," with its "holy walls and holy well," and "to the west the thundering bay / With soaking seaweed, sand and spray." As he walks the ocean paths along the rugged Cornish coastline once known to Cadoc, Betjeman transforms this place, so familiar from his childhood summers in Trebetherick, into a destination worthy of a pilgrimage for religious renewal. He invokes the saint to pray for him and begins to celebrate the natural unity of all things in God—sea, earth, saint, and poet:

> Somewhere the tree, the yellowing oak,
> Is waiting for the woodman's stroke,
> Waits for the chisel saw and plane
> To prime it for the earth again
>   And in the earth, for me inside,
>   The generous oak tree will have died.

The unity Betjeman imagines within nature is not, however, a result of death; in fact, this conjunction of living and dead, divine and natural, time and eternity seems altogether a spiritual unity: "He had no cowering fear of death / For breath of God was Cadoc's breath." The idea of Cadoc's unity with God and the sense of Cadoc's eternal presence in the landscape offer comfort and hope to the poet, whose anxieties about death are diminished by the realization of God's immanence in the natural world. Even nature joins Cadoc in celebrating the spiritual blessings that emanate from God: "As ocean rollers curled and poured / Their loud Hosannas to the Lord." In the end, the poet finds his solace from the fear of death in the comforts of spiritual unity suggested by the mystical union of nature and spirit central to his incarnational faith (*CP* 81–82).

This mystical union also characterizes "Old Friends" (1962), an elegiac lament for lost acquaintances. This poem is infused with an intense and personal sense of loss as the poet's spirits sink at the memory of dead friends with whom he once summered on the Cornish coast. However, his mood is lightened by an arrestingly beautiful Cornish sunset, the coastal tidepools, and the distant chiming of the bells of St. Minver's Church, followed by the sudden beauty of the night sky:

> What a host of stars in a wideness still and deep:
>   What a host of souls, as a motor-bike whines away
> And the silver snake of the estuary curls to sleep
>   In Daymer Bay.

The emergence of the stars and the stillness of the bay remind the poet of the wideness in God's mercy; however, the poet finds consolation not in the Christian hope of eternity but in the dawning awareness that he, the deceased, and the Celtic saints of the distant past may all be united in an eternity of stars and sea:

> Are they one with the Celtic saints and the years between?
>   Can they see the moonlit pools where ribbonweed drifts?
> As I reach our hill, I am part of a sea unseen—
>   And oppression lifts.

"Old Friends" concludes with a sense of the unity across time and space of all of God's creation. Church bells along the Cornish coast, the gently rippling waves below, and the stars above all serve to comfort the poet in the loss of his childhood companions and to reassure him of God's love and the promise of life eternal. This spiritual awakening in a setting of idyllic nature is at the heart of Celtic Christianity, at least as he understood and appreciated it (*CP* 245–46).

Since his adolescent summers in Cornwall, Betjeman had been intrigued by Celtic Christianity. This posed no dilemma for the devout Anglo-Catholic, and to him the two forms of Christianity were forever linked. As Philip Payton has argued, Betjeman saw the Anglo-Catholic church in Cornwall as the "direct inheritor" of the ancient Celtic church. A Celtic manifestation of Anglo-Catholicism thus appealed to Betjeman's "religious sense of reverence, ritual, mystery and beauty, . . . an intimacy reflected in his poetry."[83] This is clearly evident in *Summoned by Bells*, where he describes having searched "In quest of mystical experience," the mutual dangers of nature and a life of faith wrapped together in one spiritual encounter:

> Somewhere among the cairns or in the caves
> The Celtic saints would come to me, the ledge

> Of time we walk on, like a thin cliff-path
> High in the mist, would show the precipice.[84]

The wildness of the natural landscape is what attracts the poet to the precarious life of spiritual commitment. The unpredictable Cornish landscape not only made it physically attractive to Betjeman; it kept his faith vibrant. In 1939 he gave a radio talk called "The Parson Hawker of Morwenstow," part of a series called "Western Worthies." Though much of the broadcast was given over to describing the life and accomplishments of this eccentric nineteenth-century vicar and poet, Betjeman connects the man's faith to the natural world. Hawker's spirituality is rooted in the Cornish landscape, which Betjeman reiterates is nothing at all like England. In England, the landscape suggests that "Christianity here is a matter of indifference. Its roots are shallow." Not so in Cornwall, this "kingdom of contrasts": "But you can stand in some parts of Cornwall—little valleys where there are old churches and the wells of Celtic saints who lived 1,400 years ago—and feel the land is soaked in Christianity. Other parts feel intensely evil." Thus Betjeman finds religious inspiration as Parson Hawker did, through an intimate connection between nature and spirit: "Hawker held that each man lived in a spiritual element that clouded over him like a pool over one's head. And in this element angels and devils slid up and down," though this state could only be perceived by "souls of people spiritually alive." That experience of spiritual vitality came from Hawker's close connection with the natural world. As Betjeman poetically puts it, "above the noise of wind and waves which roars through his life and through most of his poetry, there is an upper stillness in which he really lived."[85]

"Felixstowe" (1958) likewise employs an oceanside setting to comment on the incarnational faith that unites nature and spirit in an "upper stillness." The poem commences with mournful seaside echoes of Matthew Arnold's "Dover Beach":

> With one consuming roar along the shingle
> The long wave claws and rakes the pebbles down
> To where its backwash and the next wave mingle,
> A mounting arch of water weedy-brown
> Against the tide the off-shore breezes blow.
> Oh wind and water, this is Felixstowe.

In contrast with Matthew Arnold's exploration of the loss of faith, Betjeman's speaker—a nun who is the last surviving member of her order—continues to find faith in God's love, despite her isolation and loneliness. The nun observes people going about their daily business, oblivious to her and to the work of God, and in spite of worldly temptation her devotion and faith never waver; while "all the world goes home to tea and toast / I hurry past a cakeshop's tempting scones / Bound for the redbrick twilight of St. John's." Unlike "Saint Cadoc," however, where faith was enlarged by the experience of nature, the faith of this speaker is increased by escaping the winter "sea winds chill and shriller" for the warmth and security of St. John's Church: "Here where the white light burns with steady glow / . . . / Safe from the surging of the lonely sea / My heart finds rest, my heart finds rest in Thee." Though the nun rejects nature in favor of a constructed space in which she feels that human and divine can more easily commune, the poem nonetheless emphasizes the genuine potential for a relationship between nature and spirit (*CP* 222–23).

Betjeman's poetry insists that God is incarnate in the world and that we will encounter God if we will be still long enough. But the poet's discovery of God is not the result of his diligent search for God at long last rewarded with this personal triumph. Betjeman instead suggests that God finds us, rather than vice versa, and that his appearance will always surprise and delight. That this might happen most fortuitously with a blend of formal worship and natural unity is a key element in "Sunday Afternoon Service in St. Enodoc Church, Cornwall" (1944).[86] The poem begins with descriptions of coastal Cornwall, as the speaker hikes alongside tidal pools and traverses sand dunes across the St. Enodoc golf course, and the vibrant imagery of Cornish scenery is rhetorically punctuated with the anaphoric phrase, "Come on! come on!" In his *Collins Guide to English Parish Churches*, Betjeman described the spiritual effect of walking through this sort of natural landscape: "So when we walk down a green lane like an ancient cart track towards the ringing church-bells, we can see the power of God in the blossom and trees, remember legends of the saints about birds and stones, and recall miracles that happened in the parish at this or that spot."[87] When the speaker in "Sunday Afternoon Service" at last reaches the church, however, his attention is not on preparing for worship; he is not kneeling in prayer but instead contemplating the sticky pews, a map of France, the bells, the organ stops, and the church's anachronistic architectural elements (which he chooses not to criticize, as he is here to worship, he reminds himself, rather than for ruin-bibbing). The minister enters the church and begins the service, and immediately Betjeman's mind is released from its attention to the actual service:

> He [the priest] runs his hands once, twice, across his face
> "Dearly beloved . . ." and a bumble-bee
> Zooms itself free into the churchyard sun
> And so my thoughts this happy Sabbathtide.[88]

His thoughts free, Betjeman roams his imagination across the gorgeous Cornish coast with romantic lines of natural description that echo Edgar's lines to Gloucester as they approach the cliffs of Dover where Gloucester intends to end his life. Betjeman describes the Cornish cliffs in Shakespearean blank verse:

> Where deep cliffs loom enormous, where cascade
> Mesembryanthemum and stone-crop down,
> Where the gull looks no larger than a lark
> Hung midway twixt the cliff-top and the sand,
> Sun-shadowed valleys roll along the sea.
> . . . .
> And tufts of sea-pink, high and dry for years,
> Are flooded out of ledges, boulders seem
> No bigger than a pebble washed about
> In this tremendous tide. . . .

The Shakespearean allusion is not incidental, for Betjeman has in mind the scene in *King Lear* wherein Gloucester is taught by his son, "Thy life's a miracle."[89] But where is God in Betjeman's poem? Does God appear to him in the church service, or in nature? It seems God's incarnation lies in the combination of the two, as "this House of God" and the institution of *The Book of Common Prayer* and its liturgical orders are juxtaposed upon the natural wildness of the Cornish landscape. Here in the service of Evening Prayer, Betjeman is reminded that God is alive in this world, and that he himself is an integral part of the long history of God's creation. Humanity is helpless like the crashing wave Betjeman imagines:

> Now she breaks
> And in an arch of thunder plunges down
> To burst and tumble, foam on top of foam,
> Criss-crossing, baffled, sucked and shot again.

Despite this vulnerability, humanity has relied on the incarnate God for hope, security, and the promise of eternity:

> Oh kindly slate of these unaltered cliffs,
> Firm, barren substrate of our windy fields!
> Oh lichened slate in walls, they knew your worth
> Who raised you up to make this House of God
> What faith was his, that dim, that Cornish saint,
> Small rushlight of a long-forgotten church,
> Who lived with God on this unfriendly shore,
> Who knew He made the Atlantic and the stones
> And destined seamen here to end their lives
> Dashed on a rock, rolled over in the surf,
> And not one hair forgotten. Now they lie
> In centuries of sand beside the church.[90]

Simple elements of Christian faith are rendered by Betjeman's poem in stark profundity: what could be more amazing than the fact that even in this most hostile of environments men and women have rediscovered throughout the ages that God is incarnate in his own creation, and that he dwells among us and never abandons us even in death? Ultimately, the poem suggests, God's incarnation is remarkable not so much for where he reveals himself to us, but for the very fact that he never disappears from us and his creation even when we stop looking (*CP* 113–17).[91]

That significant Anglican quality that embraces mystery and ambiguity and refuses to simplify truth into a finality is at the heart of "A Lincolnshire Church" (1958). Unusual among Betjeman's poems, where churches are typically named with a surprising specificity, this church is unnamed; it is historically and architecturally insignificant, and Betjeman uses only generic identifiers to describe the building. "Lincolnshire middle-pointed" is the Pevsner-style classifier, but apparently the church stands out in no unique way at all:

"Cathedral Glass" in the windows,
A roof of unsuitable slate—
Restored with a vengeance, for certain,
About eighteen-eighty-eight.

Instead of rendering the church insignificant, however, the poor restoration and the general homeliness of the place seem to add meaning to the structure by suggesting that it is just a typical English country parish church. Indeed, the church, whose tower looms on "a gentle eminence," shares in the natural spirit of Lincolnshire's wolds and marshes. This church, however, must somehow service a modern Britain with its "usual sprinkle of villas," a Britain "Seemingly so indifferent / And with so little soul to win" and exemplified by "The usual woman in slacks, / Cigarette in her mouth." As Betjeman synecdochizes it, this Lincolnshire church seems to embody the larger spirit of "Dear old, bloody old England, / Of telegraph poles and tin."[92] Sensing the church's rootedness in the natural English landscape, the speaker opens the door, stands on the threshold, and instantly perceives a spirit of presence much larger than the parish of people who live nearby. Aroused by the ineffable, the speaker comes into contact with the mysterious presence of the divine:

And there on the South aisle altar
Is the tabernacle of God.
There where the white light flickers
By the white and silver veil,
A wafer dipped in a wine-drop
Is the Presence the angels hail,
Is God who created the Heavens
And the wide green marsh as well
Who sings in the sky with the skylark
Who calls in the evening bell,
Is God who prepared His coming
With fruit of the earth for his food
With stone for building His churches
And trees for making His rood.

The mystery of the divine cannot be explained or defined, but it is, as it was for George Herbert, "something understood."[93] It is something that creates beauty, grants life, and even joins people into inexplicable common bonds:

> There where the white light flickers,
> Our Creator is with us yet,
> To be worshipped by you and the woman
> Of the slacks and the cigarette.

As the church door shuts behind him, the speaker is overwhelmed by the spiritual mystery of the place, and he falls to his knees, aware that he is in "the Presence of God Incarnate." The speaker realizes that God is both spirit and flesh; being in the presence of this mystery spiritually excites him, but it is not something he can explain or define. This is the urgency of a personal meeting with God. Adding to the spiritual mystery is the Trinitarian nature of the "mysterious Godhead," which Betjeman underscores by repeating the phrase "There where the white light flickers" three times. Where the light flickers is the place where the poet can only see darkly. It is the place where truth cannot be determined absolutely, yet it is the place where the known and unknown come face to face. It is where humans approach God (or he approaches us), where God becomes incarnate in the elements of Communion. In the mystery of the Eucharist, Betjeman experiences a peace against the onslaught of doubt (*CP* 141–43).

Betjeman's deep appreciation of the power of spiritual mystery, his willingness to embrace ambiguity, is a triumph over the anxiety of eternity. In his film *A Passion for Churches*, standing in a graveyard that surrounds a derelict church, he finds not despair for the end of England or of his own faith, but hope in the salvation that comes through God's grace and love. This is a hope born in paradox and raised in mystery:

> Christ, son of God, come down to me and save:
> How fearful and how final seems the grave.
> Only through death can resurrection come;
> Only from shadows can we see the light;
> Only at our lowest comes the gleam:
> Help us, we're all alone and full of fear.
> Drowning, we stretch our hands to you for aid
> And wholly unexpectedly you come.[94]

4

Dear Old, Bloody Old England
Sacramental Politics and Anglican Pastoralism

Here lies the England we are all beginning to wish we knew, as
the roar of the machine gets louder and the suburbs creep from
London to Land's End.[1]

On a cold and dark day in May 1984, with a raking wind and rain
soaking the mourners, John Betjeman was laid to rest in the
graveyard of St. Enodoc Church, near Trebetherick, Cornwall, the setting that had inspired his 1944 poem, "Sunday Afternoon Service in
St. Enodoc Church, Cornwall." The church, which was within walking
distance of Betjeman's home in Treen, was one he had known since
childhood. It was fifteenth-century, nondescript beyond its memorably crooked spire and the romanticized local legends of the saint above
whose cell the church was constructed. More importantly, it exhibited
the very ethos of Betjeman's world. According to Simon Jenkins,

> St. Enodoc's embodied all that Betjeman valued in English life and landscape.
> Landward are the secure Edwardian villas of Trebetherick, hidden among the
> Scots pines and cedars. Holidaying children play adventures in large gardens
> and along sandy footpaths. Between the beach and the site of the church is a
> golf course that barely harms the scenery.[2]

Though unremarkable in the usual aspects of architectural merit, it
has about it nonetheless a "dark and ancient" air of mystery that continues to fascinate visitors and a remoteness from the "telegraph poles

and tin" of the rest of "Dear old, bloody old England."[3] The church's presence here is moreover miraculous. Drifts of sand from the surrounding dunes began to settle and rise in the nave of the church in the nineteenth century, and before its restoration in 1864 it remained consecrated by the vigilance of a vicar who annually entered the church by a hole in the ceiling in order to utter the words of a divine office, though this appearance of devotion is diminished by the rather prosaic fact that at least one service per year was required for the parson to collect his yearly stipend.[4] It was just the sort of story—and just the sort of place—to inspire Betjeman to poetic flights. The efforts of the parishioners in the nineteenth century to empty the church of sand, to restore the damaged interior, and to resuscitate the parish must have been of particular inspiration to Betjeman, who dedicated a nearly unimaginable measure of his life to the preservation of England's threatened ecclesial heritage.

Indeed the preservation of English churches was probably as important to Betjeman as his poetry. In "The Fabric of our Faith," an essay in *Punch* written in 1953 as an appeal for readers to contribute to the Historic Churches Trust Fund, Betjeman asked, "Yet what would England be without her old churches? Not the England we know and love." Indeed England's churches, which Betjeman believed existed in a richer variety of styles than in any other country in the world, "are the living record, not the museum, of English craftsmanship." But more importantly they "are the history of the people of the parish." Betjeman reminds readers that parsons have more important tasks than fundraising for repairs and should not be "diverted from their work of ministering to the sick and feeding the souls of the faithful and converting indifference to belief, by having always to bother about money for the fabric of their churches." He explains why the faith of the parishioners and their parsons is no longer enough to sustain the buildings threatened by disrepair or by apathy: "Too many bishops to-day, worried by finance and the need for new churches in the growing suburbs and new towns, show a lack of faith by shutting some of them and selling the sites—often important ones in the heart of a city—in order to find money to build other churches and halls in the new suburbs." Betjeman's desire to preserve endangered churches is rooted in his desire for a spiritual conservation of the England he knows and loves. Such bishops driven by the bottom line "forget that a church as a building is a more lasting witness to our Christian faith than any bishop, vicar, churchwarden or congregation. A civilization is remembered and judged by her build-ings. That is why every church, however remote and, maybe only tem-porarily, unsuccessful, must be kept in repair and open and alive." Thus Betjeman concludes in confidence that his readers, no matter to what "version of the Christian faith" they adhere, will contribute to the His-toric Churches Trust, "If we have any faith left, any love of what makes England beautiful and England for us."[5]

As "The Fabric of our Faith" shows, Betjeman was more anxious about the future of churches from the example set by its leaders than from the apathy of its parishioners. How could the church survive the deadening reduction of faith to economics? "Not Necessarily Leeds" (1954) is a poem occasioned by the efforts of the Church of England in the 1950s to sell off churches deemed redundant.[6] The poem's humor, reinforced by the inherently comic rhythms of a rollicking metrical pattern of anapestic tetrameter, masks the poet's rage at the callous economy of Anglican bishops toward their own churches and their soulless schemes to enhance their coffers. After the bishop of London sold St. Peter's, Great Windmill Street, Betjeman was determined to prevent further disaster, and in this poem he caustically attacks the bishop of Ripon and the archdeacon of Leeds for their plan to demol-ish Holy Trinity, Leeds, and sell the land.[7] Here the bishop praises the archdeacon for his financial wizardry and administrative dexterity:

> Yes, he is a man with his feet on the ground,
> His financial arrangements are clever and sound.
> I find as his bishop I'm daily delighted
> To think of the livings his skill has united.

Though perhaps tempted to defend the church on grounds of historic and architectural merit, Betjeman relies on a more powerful appeal, satirizing the bishop for following demographic trends instead of evangelizing:

> Its strange congregation was culled from afar,
> And you know how eclectic such worshippers are.
> The stipend was small but the site was worth more
> Than any old church I have sold here before.

The bishop, motivated not so much by greed as by an obsession with financial stability, is all too happy to close an urban parish with declining attendance and create a united benefice if it will boost his budget. Betjeman also attacks the bishop for his intolerance of the aesthetic extremes within the Church of England and for targeting any church whose services are "impossibly High" or "needlessly Low." Betjeman's attack on the bishop's apparent apathy to the spiritual needs of an urban, postwar people worked, and Holy Trinity was not closed, yet the struggle to save vulnerable churches from the craft and scheming of the church itself was unrelenting.[8]

Preserving church buildings was of course central to his nature, but there was always a primary element of spiritual conservation. The endurance of the church was, as Peter J. Lowe has noted, "its own eloquent testimony to the strength of the creed to which they [Christians] adhered."[9] His commitment to the preservation of churches began in the 1930s and continued to the end of his life but was particularly significant following the successful campaign for Holy Trinity, Leeds. In addition to joining the Council for the Care of Churches and the Historic Churches Preservation Trust, Betjeman was involved in numerous campaigns to save individually threatened churches, often initiating as well as joining others in these efforts.[10] In his remarks there is always the sense that buildings are to be preserved as sites of worship, not merely as architectural examples. The 1961 campaign for St. Mary Redcliffe in Bristol, one of the largest and grandest of English parish churches, was about much more than its aesthetic merit: "For close on 800 years its beauty has witnessed to the eternal truth and goodness of God and helped men to worship Him."[11] In 1977 Betjeman joined with Trevor Huddleston, the bishop of Stepney (and British leader of the movement to end apartheid in South Africa), in campaigning to preserve Nicholas Hawksmoor's London churches. Betjeman and the bishop put this pointed question to England: "Yet what in fact is the nation prepared to do to ensure that they are preserved and used for the glory of God and the benefit of the community?" Churches, they insisted, are embodiments of the nation's cultural ethos. Saving those threatened buildings "would demonstrate our concern as a nation for the preservation and the revitalization of those values upon which our civilization is built."[12] Betjeman's last important campaign to save a threatened church was for

St. Barnabas, Pimlico. His letter to the *Times* in 1982 is a brilliant summation of his belief in the communal value of the church and merits quoting in full:

> Sir, I am appalled by the news that St Barnabas, Pimlico, is to become redundant.
>
> Architecturally it is a jewel of a church, not least the Comper Lady Chapel. And historically it is central to the history of the Church of England in the nineteenth century: riots, Bennet, the Vicar in a *Punch* cartoon, Lord Shaftesbury attacking it in pious evangelical horror and, during the Second World War, Winston Churchill attending the church for the baptism of his Sandys grandchild. It was from its vicarage that the *English Hymnal* was produced and it was always a place of devout prayer.
>
> The church needs to continue as a living focus of love—God's love and ours for him. And it is in the centre of literally hundreds of working-class flats whose inhabitants are the congregation.
>
> Yours faithfully,
> JOHN BETJEMAN,
> 29 Radnor Walk, SW3.[13]

Though Betjeman was too old to participate fully in the campaign to save St. Barnabas, his letter was a significant contribution, and the triumph of St. Barnabas is due in part to Betjeman's vision of this church as a repository of living history as well as the spiritual home of a still vibrant parish community. Despite the individual instances of success, he knew that the church would remain under constant threat from enemies as varied as land values, apathy, and neglect.

The need to preserve England's churches was no doubt stimulated by Betjeman's deeply held religious impulses, but it is part and parcel of his larger drive for the conservation of England's built heritage. No matter what one's religious beliefs, Betjeman insisted, churches "are the most lasting memorial of our civilisation," which itself "is remembered by its buildings, when its art and literature and music are forgotten."[14] Thus Betjeman wanted to save threatened buildings because they were innately humanized by those who built them and lived, worked, and worshipped in them. As Bevis Hillier succinctly puts it, "Buildings were the spoors of human beings."[15] Hillier has recounted at length many of Betjeman's campaigns (some successful, some not), among the most celebrated of which were to save Waterloo Bridge, Euston Arch, the Coal Exchange, Bedford Park, St. Pancras Station, and the London sky-line.[16] In 1974 he was galvanized by a proposal to demolish the Royal Agricultural Hall. To Betjeman, this building was worth saving not just for its architectural value, though that was high; it was because the hall embodied the nation's living history: "It was a vital focus of national life: the rumbustious surge of a nation at the height of its powers and confidence passed through its doors and was caught vividly in a thousand pictures of that period. It would be a very great tragedy, tantamount to an historical amnesia, if the Royal Agricultural Hall were to be razed from the London townscape."[17] After lengthy debate, the "Aggie" was saved, though other sites remained under regular threat from developers who coveted the real estate. Proposed new buildings could generate resistance from Betjeman almost as frequently as the threatened destruction of old ones. Plans in 1980 to construct the so-called "Green Giant" building on the South Bank across from the Tate Gallery mobilized Betjeman and numerous others to protest. Betjeman wrote that the artist's rendering of the design was unreliable: "It does not show how the cruel tusks of the building will look in the London sky from such familiar places as the Royal Parks, Hampstead Heath or Putney Common. It does not give the scale of this inhuman thing which is going to turn London into Chicago."[18] Even more offensive to Betjeman than their obtuseness about beauty and history was the insensitivity of developers to the human spirit. In 1971 he joined a campaign to protest a proposed motorway that would cut across the cathedral city of Winchester. The damage to the historic and pastoral surroundings from aural and olfactory pollution was of great concern, but the focus remained on the people and spirit of Winchester:

> This route would be a disaster, not only for the many citizens of Winchester who walk through the meadows every day, but also for the thousands of visitors who come every year. Winchester and its immediate neighbourhood provide a record of English culture stretching from Roman times to the present day. It would be a tragedy if the twentieth century were to destroy what has existed in peace for hundreds of years.[19]

Betjeman's Anglicanism was always sequestered behind these campaigns. The human element of English buildings and spaces, with a suggestion of a spiritual connection to history, underpinned his commitment to preservation. There was something sacred about endangered places, and his commitment to their preservation was sacramental, as if he were saying, This do in remembrance of England. He affirmed that in the conclusion of his essay "Topographical Verse":

> I love suburbs and gas-lights and Pont Street and Gothic Revival churches and mineral railways, provincial towns and Garden cities. They are, many of them, part of my background. From them I try to create an atmosphere which will be remembered by those who have had a similar background, when England is all council houses and trunk roads and steel and glass factory blocks in the New Europe of after the War.[20]

These things are not merely loved by Betjeman; they are sacred. What Auden says of the impulse to creativity in his 1956 Oxford lecture, *Making, Knowing and Judging*, seems especially apt of Betjeman: such an impulse constitutes a desire to express a "passive awe provoked by sacred beings or events . . . in a rite of worship or homage. . . . This rite has no magical or idolatrous intention; nothing is expected in return."[21] Betjeman's rites of worship of the spaces sacred to him are equally visible in his poems and his acts of cultural preservation. Because the things he wishes to preserve are indeed sacred to him, it is fair to say that his commitment to preservation has about it a holy, sacramental quality. Perhaps nowhere is this quality of his faith clearer than in a letter he wrote in 1943 explaining his return to England from wartime service in Ireland. In addition to his and his family's homesickness, he was motivated by "the need to be in England during all the post-war reconstruction schemes and to put in a word, everywhere possible, for Christian bases. Living in Ireland has been a wonderful experience, because it is a wholly Christian country. I am sure it is my duty to go back and help to remake England one so far as I can."[22] (One assumes this vision excludes the internecine warfare between Catholics and Protestants that Betjeman seems to ignore in Ireland.)

Behind each of Betjeman's campaigns to preserve or rebuild England lay his hopes for the reconstruction of a national faith. This duty to England's Christian history and heritage underscored his commitment to England's natural as well as built environment, and his protests against natural despoliation could instigate from him responses that varied from the elegiac to the denunciatory. In 1947 a proposal to construct a television relay station atop Berkshire's White Horse Hill elicited this pastoral effusion: "The strange chalk dragon, the great bowl of the manger, the green rampart of Uffington Castle, comprise one of the fairest downland scenes in England. The beauty of this hill, with its wide views from that rippling sea of wind-blown grass, was in its remoteness from the present age, when one stood on it. And from the vast vale below, its beauty was in the bareness of the noble outline of down."[23] When the hill was saved, it was then threatened by tourists. Nearly thirty years later he wrote of the need to protect the White Horse from those who loved it too much: "There is not another of its age or character throughout the world. It has been part of our national heritage for at least two thousand years and should be cherished with far greater care than is now being shown."[24] Beauty, remoteness, purity, and uniqueness were under constant threat in the twentieth century. Among his many causes, Betjeman led or contributed significantly to protests over the erection of wireless masts across Dorset hills and electrical pylons through the Berkshire Vale, the building of nuclear plants along the Essex shoreline, the decapitation of Dulcote Hill for quarrying, the construction of a motorway through the Berkshire Downs, the development of Stansted Airport in the Hertfordshire countryside of thatched-roof cottages, the appropriation of Cornish moorland for military training, and the disposal of china clay mining waste just off the Cornish coast.

An interesting pattern emerges in his connections between the built and natural environments; at times it is difficult to distinguish between them. Southend Pier should be saved because, though man-made, it allows one the rare chance to escape other human constructions: "One can walk on the pier, one's nose unafflicted by fumes of oil, one's ears unassaulted by the internal combustion engine, one's fears unaroused by road traffic, one's eyes delighted by the far flat coasts of Kent and Essex and the long straight line of the sea."[25] The town center of Bury St. Edmunds should be saved from new housing estates because of the aesthetic illusion it presents that it is a part of nature: "Of course the town has the usual fringe of harsh industrial estates, but what makes it so appealing is that real Suffolk country, where the Lark and Linnet rivers flow through Gainsborough-like landscape, comes up to its very doors on the eastern side of the place. Thus the country is felt in the very heart of the place."²⁶ Likewise the proposed "Green Giant" tower to be built beside the Thames is to be rejected because London is not New York but a pastoral village: "The Thames is not the Hudson. The Thames is slow-flowing in a wide gravel and clay basin in a small and old country. It was never meant to be a canal between tall tower blocks. At its best, it is flanked by bushes and marshes under wide skies. This quality has been made world famous by poets and painters."²⁷

Betjeman's desire to protect buildings and nature from destruction was based in his simple belief in the soul. What makes us human is the soul, he believed, and what makes human spaces worth saving is the soul that is imparted to them through centuries of care. It is important to bear in mind his notion of beauty and to understand that for him beauty was not determined by the simplistic determiners of ancient heritage and unpolluted vistas. He loathed the clean and open green spaces of England's new towns because of their artifice, satirizing in "Inexpensive Progress" (1955) the inevitable "rockeried roundabout" and "patch of shaven green" to be found in such places (*CP* 286). Age obviously added to the beauty of an English scene, but the lack of age or aesthetic merit did not inherently diminish the worth of a building or street to Betjeman. For him beauty emanated from within, that is to say, when the subject's spiritual or human worth was apparent. This explains his deep appreciation for a place as unlovely as Swindon. In his 1948 radio broadcast, "St Mark's, Swindon, Wiltshire," he asserted his preference for "a red-brick rash like Swindon enlivened with Victorian towers and steeples sticking out of it" over "a gleaming glass city of architect-designed flats with never a church but instead only the humped backs of super-cinemas, the grandstands of the greyhound tracks and the other shrines of the modern barbarism."²⁸ For all its clean lines, modern architecture was stripped of spirit and humanity. "Where can be the heart that sends a family / To the twentieth floor in such a slab as this?" he asked poetically in a 1969 television program, *The Englishman's Home*. Despite the attention to landscaping and to stunning views, the result of all this newness could only be "New loneliness, new restlessness, new pressure," and people reduced to living in such a world would not find a life of the spirit. Instead of finding God, they would "find / A God who fits in."²⁹ No wonder the deities worshipped by most Londoners care so little for humanity. As Betjeman succinctly expressed it in the *Times*, "As Londoners, we must not allow our home to be dehumanized."[30]

Though the destruction of England's urban heritage occupied much of his preservation energies, Betjeman had his eye equally on the forces threatening the end of its rural heritage, and in particular the virtues of the village.[31] "The Dear Old Village" (1947) is Betjeman's ironic celebration of the English village transformed, updated, and improved in this "age of progress." The poem archly employs archaic language more appropriate to Goldsmith or Crabbe, to whose famous village poems Betjeman undoubtedly alludes. The church is an "embattled, lichen-crusted fane," and if one listens closely one can hear "the water lapsing down the rills"; though "lapsing" is an archaic term for the flow of a stream, its more common meanings imply neglect and apostasy, and though a "fane" is a temple, a more common meaning is a weathercock. Betjeman seems to imply that the village is unfixed, turning indiscriminately with the wind and suffering a moral fall: "Nature is out of date and GOD is too; / Think what atomic energy can do!" Much of the poem lashes a greedy and hypocritical local farmer who sells his "undrainable and useless" land for the construction of council houses. Residents suffer in ugly and unsafe houses while village children are sent by bus to a distant, modern school whose imagined curricula of "Civics, eurhythmics, economics, Marx" teaches them "to scorn / The old thatch'd cottages where they were born." On Sundays the church has little reason to open its doors to its three feckless parishioners, while the village youth ride off to the cinema on motorbikes that drown the echoing church bells (*CP* 187–91). Betjeman would echo these sentiments in a variety of prose pieces. In 1948 he campaigned to save Letcombe Bassett from utter destruction and the depopulation of its village, arguing that the spiritual qualities of a home included all aspects of village life: family, house, friends, and social institutions but especially the visual shape of the place. "Then, and more lastingly as we grow older," he urged, "it means loved outlines of hills, shapes of fields, turns of lane, trees and houses of the landscape."[32] Though this battle was won and Letcombe Bassett was saved, the war against village life would continue. In 1954 he predicted that rural England would soon "be wholly transformed into a series of soulless council estates with a few dead museum pieces preserved here and there for educational and 'art-historical' purposes."[33] (Betjeman undoubtedly privileged aesthetics over social welfare, preferring not to consider the unfortunate necessity that these ugly estates were housing people bombed out of London during the war.)

Betjeman's satirical essay "High Frecklesby Has a Plan" (1953) is a further development of the range of his thinking on the subject of rural destruction. The essay, presented in the language and tone of a developer's proposal for the transformation of the imagined parish of Frecklesby into an exemplum of modern life, devastatingly parodies the civil servant as a soulless madman. Betjeman writes in the persona of such a planster:

> The parish of Frecklesby . . . has been chosen for this survey and plan because it represents a particularly wasteful rural unit which, by economic development and the co-operation of local authorities with enlightened surveyors, sanitary inspectors and planners, might be transformed into a model community of national significance, thus contributing to the progressive crusade towards a world target of planned production, without which, etc., etc.

In the planster's mind, the problem with High Frecklesby is both natural and social. The village is "infested" with abundant verdancy and riddled with "needlessly tortuous lanes" and "unhygienic hedges," two features of the English landscape of which Betjeman was especially fond. The haphazard arrangement of traditional cottages around the central "antiquated" church offends the geometric symmetry of the planster's brain, and all will have to be demolished. Although the planster expresses regret at losing "an historic relic" which might have served some educational purpose, he celebrates "the compensatory saving of space and the provision of an inter-denominational meeting room" of which the village atheists might also avail themselves for civic enhancement. The planster then lays out neat solutions to problems with agriculture, housing, education, and transport. Hedges are to be uprooted "to ensure maximum land utilisation," flats in a high-rise building of glass and plastic will accommodate the villagers, whose children will attend a new school "under expert Government control," while newly straightened roads will be illuminated by concrete standards.[34] Wishing that the rest of English villages could "be rehabilitated on these lines," Betjeman's planster concludes his proposal with the brilliant irony of a frightening and apocalyptic New Jerusalem: "We have built Jerusalem / In England's green and pleasant land."[35]

Though an entire nation was to blame for these execrations against the traditional English landscape, the locus of Betjeman's rage was the civil servant with a passion for expunging the past and a loathing for the preservationist's instinct. His poem "The Planster's Vision" (1945) captures remarkably the sort of voice never before heard in a sonnet. This is the voice of bureaucracy, a town planner anxious to erase the symbols of English history and replant the landscape with a Maoist vision of collective banality. Betjeman fulminates against a dystopic future in which church bells are silenced by loudspeakers indoctrinating the masses until they have become brainwashed drones.

> Cut down that timber! Bells, too many and strong,
>   Pouring their music through the branches bare,
>   From moon-white church-towers down the windy air
> Have pealed the centuries out with Evensong.
> Remove those cottages, a huddled throng!
>   Too many babies have been born in there,
>   Too many coffins, bumping down the stair,
> Carried the old their garden paths along.
>
> I have a Vision of The Future, chum,
>   The workers' flats in fields of soya beans
>   Tower up like silver pencils, score on score:
> And Surging Millions hear the Challenge come
>   From microphones in communal canteens
>   "No Right! No Wrong! All's perfect, evermore." (*CP* 104)

In the words of Peter J. Lowe, this poem "offered a bleak view of a post-war Britain in which architectural redevelopment went hand in hand with the loss of the communal way of life and, more worryingly, the spiritual foundation of that way of life."[36] In short, a system of faith that underscored the cycle of life for centuries of Britons was threatened by a nightmarish alternative. "The Town Clerk's Views" (1949) is a lengthier elaboration of this same nightmare, leisurely unfolding in a plan "to turn our country into hell." The vision begins with pulling down traditional cottages in favor of massive flats of concrete, glass, and steel. It then encompasses the restructuring of county borders wherein a disregard for history means that some counties no longer have any justification for an independent existence; their names too are out of date and ought to be reconfigured with terminology redolent of London's postal codes. Blandness and uniformity are the operative principles in the town clerk's vision of England. In its academic centers, Oxford, having carelessly thrown up concrete blocks everywhere, is on the right path, but poor Cambridge, clinging still to its useless chapels, halls, and Backs, is out of touch with the march of progress:

> As for remote East Anglia, he who searches
> Finds only thatch and vast, redundant churches.
> But that's the dark side. I can safely say
> A beauteous England's really on the way.

As religion has no place in this utopia, cathedrals can now be transformed into cultural centers, and sermons on the effects of sin will be supplanted with lectures of a civil or sociological nature. The crowning glory of the town planners' vision for a modern England is the expunging of religion. God has no place in this hellish future, and the horror for Betjeman is that England will have arrived at its holocaust (*CP* 144–47).[37]

He simply had no patience with developers and planners, and at times he erupted in rage at the inhumanity and soullessness of modern planning.[38] His 1965 poem "Mortality" envisioned the death by car crash of "a senior civil servant" whose "first-class brains . . . / Are sweetbread on the road today" (*CP* 288).[39] This is the sort of man responsible for (in his mind) the ruination of the town of Bath, a planner who spends his days, as Betjeman puts it in his satirical poem "The Newest Bath Guide" (1973), "In working out methods of cutting down cost— / So that mouldings, proportion and texture are lost / In a uniform nothingness." To such a man, "houses are 'units' and people are 'digits,'" resulting in a blind and desexed world: "Official designs are aggressively neuter, / The Puritan work of an eyeless computer" (*CP* 303–4).[40] As early as 1937, however, Betjeman still had faith in the concept of national planning if not in the actual planners. "Strategically, economically, and aesthetically, England needs a national plan," he wrote in the *Criterion* in response to a controversial highway development survey for

London. His faith in planning is couched in typically religious language tinged with doubt: "There is no hope for national salvation until a central planning authority is established with dictatorial powers overriding property owners and local authorities and vested interests."[41] His early belief in the potential success of a central government planning agency may come as a surprise; his faith in it, however, was short lived. Like the rest of the world, he was soon to see just what "dictatorial powers" meant. In 1943 he delivered a BBC broadcast, "'Oh, to be in England . . .,'" that perfectly encapsulated what there was to love and to loathe in England. Among its many memorable passages was this attack on the insidious fascism of England's town planners:

> Planning is very much in the English air now. And that is a good thing if by planning we also mean preserving. But let the planners be careful. It would not be worth our being away from England, those of us who live in the country, if we had to come back to find our villages transformed into single blocks of flats towering out of unfenced fields, with an interdenominational religious room at the top of each tower for services conducted by wireless (voluntary attendance). And those of us who live in old towns do not want to see everything swept away to open vistas where vistas were never intended. Hitler has opened up a few good ones. Let us leave it at that.[42]

This was a theme to which he would return throughout the rest of his life, with increasing anger. In the *Daily Telegraph* in 1952, he fulminated against the "soulless theorists" who "look at places from the height of an aeroplane and think in terms of maps and figures." Such planners, he raged, would "turn us from a nation of house dwellers into a nation of flat dwellers living in huge hygienic Karl Marx Hofs, ants in an insect world of the future."[43] Ten years later he rampaged in the *Daily Express* against the economic self-interest of developers and the even "More sinister . . . grey men—the pseudo-progressive professors, the exploded functionalists, and the permanent civil servants anxious to retain their power." He then launched into a jeremiad against the junta of soulless "grey men" responsible for the desecration of England:

> We are ruled by the most vandalistic Government departments and local authorities Britain has ever known. We must rescue the country from developers and the motor-car. Young and old are joined in a

battle against grey men without eyes or heart, whose only literature is a cheque book and to whom beauty is an indecent word.[44]

Such battles gave purpose and meaning to his life. "The most important thing I do," he wrote in 1961, "is to try to stop the planners and businessmen, the bureaucrats and mass manipulators, from destroying England."[45]

In such writing, Betjeman may come across as a Luddite, but his full-frontal assault on modern "progress," symbolized by his seemingly pointless attack on the automobile, is in fact a broad-minded and progressive commitment to a cultural and natural ecology. Betjeman's attitude toward the motor car was complex and paradoxical. In 1955 he wrote that the natural and ancient beauty of Oxford had been destroyed by the internal combustion engine: "Parked cars make the streets hideous by the garish and untidy contrast they make against old buildings. The roar of moving cars destroys the peace. Those adjuncts of the motor-car, a tarmac surface replacing cobbles and a smell of petrol drowning that of burning leaves or damp earth, take away from Oxford's beauty too."[46] Betjeman's preference for "fritillaries in the Cherwell water meadows" is cast, however, with a sensitive awareness of the laborers in Oxford's automobile factories, who are "chained to the conveyor belt for most of their lives."[47] It was underscored as well with the knowledge that the car was here to stay and had thus to be accommodated.[48] As Leena K. Schröder has shown, through his "Shell Guides" to English counties Betjeman was actively and shrewdly involved in marketing his notions of traditional Englishness with a modern automobile-based economy specifically in mind.[49] He had, moreover, a deep admiration for the accomplishments of modern technology and its feats of engineering, including the Clifton suspension bridge and Bristol's Temple Meads railway station, both by I. K. Brunel.[50] As Stephen Games' anthology *Tennis Whites and Teacakes* reveals, Betjeman was (at least early in his life) a proponent of modernism and the machine age and believed that the changes wrought by industrialism needed to be accepted.[51] In "The Passing of the Village" (1932), Betjeman deplored the "escapist who has not the courage to face the creations of the machine age in which he lives," and concluded his essay with this surprising manifesto: "We have created a machine age and we should not be afraid of it but rather become accustomed to it and control it. The machine age may be a roaring lion in the land but the lamb of agriculture can lie down beside it. It is a shorn and shivering lamb that it is hardly worth the eating."[52] Though some of his writings are tinged with a wistful or nostalgic yearning for a lost past, to think of him simply as one who wanted fondly and foolishly to sustain a simpler pre-war Britain is entirely to misinterpret this "firebrand moved . . . by anxiety and alienation."[53]

With this understanding of Betjeman in mind, the charge of nostalgia is applicable only within a narrow context. Betjeman himself claimed, "I don't like that word 'nostalgia': it sounds like 'neuralgia' and gives me a headache."[54] A few years later he would appropriate and redefine nostalgia to suit himself: "I regard 'nostalgic' as a term of praise, myself, for it implies reverence and a sense of the past and an awareness of, though not necessarily a slavery to, tradition."[55] Geoffrey Harvey astutely noted that such nostalgia looks forward as well as backward: "Betjeman's concern for the preservation not merely of fine buildings but of the human frame of things which they represent, is not reactionary but, ironically in modern society with its commitment to size, growth and change for their own sakes, economically and politically subversive."[56] Indeed his opposition to the new was only partly rooted in his love of the old and his commitment to preserving the buildings of the past. He also believed that what was new now was too cheap and ugly to have any chance of some day becoming old and meaningful. In a 1960 film he surveyed the buildings of the 1951 National Festival of Britain and remembered "how tremendously modern it seemed and contemporary," but now only nine years later the buildings were already showing signs of dereliction, and thus he mused, "there's something sad now, looking at it, how quickly contemporary rusts and decays."[57] Betjeman's conservatism was in short neither retrograde nor insensitive but at once spiritually minded and forward-thinking. Indeed, in the words of Timothy Mowl, if the Church of England "ever had the nerve to canonize, what a patron saint of the Environment John would have made."[58]

His campaigns to preserve the built and natural environment were informed by his religious beliefs, even though this faith was often opaque in the public forum of newspapers. In his poems, essays, and radio broadcasts concerning the environment, however, his beliefs were much more transparent and reveal the manifestations of a political framework that was distinctly religious, for his opinions about conservation and preservation were intrinsic to his faith. To his mind, England was a sacred land suffering systematic desecration by both apathy and bureaucracy. Betjeman's commitments were thus outward and visible signs of his belief in the eternal verities of Christianity, and his rejection of the aesthetic horrors of contemporary culture stemmed from his awareness that such a culture depresses and corrodes the spirit. Much of his poetry and prose is characterized by a sacramental politics, a politics that is informed and guided by his adherence to Anglicanism and in particular to the church's historic teaching on and definition of a sacrament as an outward and visible sign of an inward and spiritual grace.[59] A good illustration of his sacramental politics can be found in his early essay, "1837–1937: A Spiritual Change Is the One Hope for Art" (1937). Here Betjeman explores what he perceives as a "drift toward ugliness" in English taste during the preceding one hundred years, a drift he attributes to "the increase in population, mass production, [and] absence of any uniting faith."[60] Betjeman traces the history of an imaginary English town through its architecture, in typical fashion focusing largely though not entirely on its ecclesial structures. His thesis, argued consistently through this essay, is molded by his sacramental view of the world: "And there is no doubt that architecture is the outward and visible form of inward and spiritual grace or disgrace."[61] Disgrace is, perhaps not surprisingly, the spiritual state of English life and architecture, though a taste of innocence and purity "is still traceable underneath the hoardings, neon signs and wires with which progress has strung every feature of urban and even rural landscape."[62] Much of the essay describes architectural evolution in "Boggleton," though its features represent almost all of England. The essay's strength rests in its condemnation of modern culture's appropriation and transformation of the spiritual and unique qualities of the architecture for secular and collectivist aims. On the site of the ruined abbey, for instance, lectures are now given on "socialism, eugenics, eurythmics, hygiene, economics and other important problems."[63] These ideas, force-fed to the masses, have supplanted the power of religion and have led to the despoliation of the landscape. Many people once had faith in God, and many others once had faith in the Machine; now "no one knows what to believe." Thus he dispiritedly concludes, "The Machine is discredited, God is discredited, human nature is discredited. We are turning ourselves into the material of which slaves are made—time slaves, machine slaves and money slaves."[64]

Many of Betjeman's poems evolve out of ideas from this essay, comprising harsh attacks on what he perceived to be a desecration of both city and country, from litter to pylons to concrete office blocks. His anger and bitterness, though sometimes disguised by an ironic serenity, are always meant to reflect the increasing ugliness in his beloved nation. If his poetry laments the enervation of English culture while expressing outrage and anger at the ruination of the English landscape, it also yearns for a lost pastoral England of the imagination. Thus "Middlesex" (1954) is a place "Where a few surviving hedges / Keep alive our lost Elysium" (*CP* 163). Elysium is imaginary, however, for the pastoral, as a poetic subject, is something just beyond our grasp. And "Essex" (1953) was once "Sweet uneventful countryside," but "Now yarrow chokes the railway track, / Brambles obliterate the stile, / No motor coach can take me back / To that Edwardian 'erstwhile'" (*CP* 158–59). The dream of restoring a pastoral Edwardian England is a strong one, and in "Dilton Marsh Halt" (1968), Betjeman imagines a return to an age in which steam trains brought one in touch with a natural and unpolluted England:

> And when all the horrible roads are finally done for,
>   And there's no more petrol left in the world to burn,
> Here to the Halt from Salisbury and from Bristol
>   Steam trains will return. (*CP* 321)

Similarly, a ride in a horse-drawn gig brought Betjeman into "a paradise of rain-washed scents and sights."[65] The latent pastoralism in his work is rooted in a long tradition of semimythological English landscape poetry that blends pastoral yearning for an imagined past with a sense that such cultural loss has a moral or spiritual dimension. This diverse context includes John of Gaunt's paean to England in Shakespeare's *Richard II* ("This other Eden, demi-paradise") and William Blake's "Jerusalem" ("And was the holy Lamb of God / On England's pleasant pastures seen?") as well as popular songs such as Ivor Novello's "The Land of Might-Have-Been" ("Somewhere there's another land, / Different from this world below"), all of which evoke an imaginary but spiritual England just beyond our reach. If Betjeman's poems on a lost or declining England are set within this poetic context, it becomes quite clear that his views on progress and preservation are rooted in his religious beliefs. To him England was once Edenic but has been recklessly ruined by modern progress, and his protests against the depredation of the English landscape, both natural and human, are riddled with spiritual and religious language. In updating the image of dark Satanic mills with one of power stations, Betjeman sustains Blake's notion that progress is a euphemism for social action that masks the sinful nature of humanity. The result is a fallen world; England is only a memory, a land that might have been. As he wrote in 1944, "Neither despairers nor Christians believe in the progress myth that was all the rage in the last century."[66] Reading Betjeman in this light allows us to see that he has infused with spirituality his opinions of architectural and landscape preservation, of urban and pastoral blight, and of the forsaken symbols and customs of England.

His love of England is not merely a case of topophilia, though that is how it has been addressed by many, including W. H. Auden and Betjeman himself.[67] Betjeman's friend and editor John Sparrow deepened the discussion of Betjeman's topophilia, noting that it was rooted in an appreciation of the human properties of place: "For the landscape that most appeals to him is the inhabited landscape: he cannot see a place without seeing also the life that is lived in it, without becoming conscious of its human associations."[68] This was clearly a critical step forward, though Betjeman himself pointed out that his topophilia was rooted as much in a love of God as of humanity. Having read a draft of Sparrow's essay, he responded that he believed he shared a poetic bond with William Cowper but not with John Clare, a mere poet of place; the difference, he insisted, concerned their worldviews. Like Cowper, Betjeman believed "that man is born to fulfil the purposes of his Creator i.e. to Praise his Creator."[69] Revealing the symbiosis of nature and faith was Betjeman's means to praise his Creator, and many of his descriptions of nature embody a sort of Anglican pastoralism. His essay "Winter at Home" (1948) synthesizes the natural beauty of England in winter with the eternal verities of Anglican worship:

> Ploughed fields take on a look like a farming scene in the initial letter of a
> medieval manuscript. Bricks are an intenser red and Cotswold stone is more
> golden, the limestone and granite of the north is more silver, bare branches
> are like pressed seaweed against the pale blue sky. Whatever remains green is
> more deeply, richly green than it was before.

Like the colors of winter, especially the enhanced greenness, this wintry period of "waiting, intense stillness" suggests to Betjeman the everlasting faith, and thus "even across three miles of still, misty fields,
it is possible to distinguish all six of the church bells as men practise
method ringing in the oil-lit evening tower."[70]

Coastal regions of Britain seemed especially effective at preserving this pastoral sense of England. For example, when he describes
the cell of St. Petroc, situated between the Cornish peaks of Rough
Tor and Brown Willy, time disappears, the ancient Celtic church survives, and nature is untouched: "Not a motor car, nor aeroplane, nor
modern sound was heard, only sheep bleating and larks singing and the
startled thud of a nearby moorland pony. A silence so deep and so long
that the chirps and scurryings of nature only made it greater. Here,
as to St Petroc, because nature was near, so was the Creator."[71] Cornwall seemed to sustain that quality of Anglican pastoralism better than
other parts of England. To Betjeman, Blisland was especially vibrant
with an ancient faith:

> I was on the edge of Bodmin Moor, that sweet brown home of Celtic saints,
> that haunted, thrilling land so full of ghosts of ancient peoples whose hut
> circles, beehive dwellings and burial mounds jut out above the ling and
> heather. Great wooded valleys, white below the tree trunks with wood anem-
> ones or blue with bluebells, form a border fence on this, the western side of
> Bodmin Moor.[72]

The Essex coast, being closer to London, was more susceptible to
technological encroachments. In a piece for the *Spectator*, Betjeman
described attending an inquiry in Maldon concerning plans to construct an atomic power station on Essex's Dengie Peninsula: "It is a
place of narrow lanes which take sudden right-angle bends revealing
rows of weather-boarded cottages, small hills with elms on them, and
finally the great salt marshes, with their birds and sea lavender. . . . It
is the remotest possible country, and the only sea coast near London

which has not been exploited." Betjeman concludes his pastoral reverie with a personal memory of his first journey there, by bicycle to
attend services in "the chapels of the Peculiar People, that Essex sect
which goes in for healing, whose women wear black bonnets."[73] And in
his film *Beside the Seaside*, broadcast on Christmas Day 1969, he com-
pares the undeveloped remainder of the shoreline to the "holy hush"
of Christmas morning: "We must keep the rest of it for the good of
our souls."[74] The motif in each of these passages is the harmonizing
of landscape and faith.

Whether he is describing a natural landscape, a country house, the
seaside, or suburbia, Betjeman endows his vision of a primal England
with purity and spirituality, often with an implication or foreshadowing
of loss. The ringing of church bells by the seaside fills his early poem
"Westgate-on-Sea" (1930), reawakening memories of playful childhood
innocence and stirring him with vivid images of a blissful suburban
pastoralism:

> Happy bells of eighteen-ninety,
> > Bursting from your freestone tower!
> Recalling laurel, shrubs and privet,
> > Red geraniums in flower. (*CP* 12)

Here English pastoralism is also associated with prelapsarian innocence
and depicted with images of a carefree childhood, a theme developed
further in "May-Day Song for North Oxford" (1945): "And open-necked
and freckled, where once there grazed the cows, / Emancipated children swing on old apple boughs." This freedom is threatened, however,
with an ironic movement from emancipation back into slavery, for the
apple tree that now functions both as a means of play and as a connection with the earth is laden with heavy symbolism of original sin
(*CP* 96). "Trebetherick" (1940), based on memories of childhood summers on the Cornish coast, mourns the loss of innocence associated
with childhood, when "Waves full of treasure then were roaring up the
beach." All was not carefree, however, as Betjeman recalls:

> And we were in a water-world
> > Of rain and blizzard, sea and spray,
> And one against the other hurled
> > We struggled round to Greenaway.

The physical danger of the seaside is reinforced with images of sin and evil lurking in the coastal woods:

> The lichened branches of a wood
>   In summer silver-cool and still;
> And there the Shade of Evil could
>   Stretch out at us from Shilla Mill.
> Thick with sloe and blackberry, uneven in the light,
> Lonely ran the hedge, the heavy meadow was remote,
> The oldest part of Cornwall was the wood as black as night,
> And the pheasant and the rabbit lay torn open at the throat.

Despite the unpolluted appearance of this ancient, pastoral landscape, dangers physical and moral lurk everywhere, signaled by the inexplicable violence against animals in their natural environment and as well by the darkness and isolation of the setting. Refusing to sentimentalize childhood or romanticize nature, Betjeman concludes with a prayer addressed jointly to Trebetherick's patron saint and to the landscape: "Blessèd be St. Enodoc, blessèd be the wave, / Blessèd be the springy turf, we pray, pray to thee" (*CP* 52–53).

Probably no setting could elicit the pastoralism from Betjeman's pen quite so eloquently as the coast of Cornwall. "Cornish Cliffs" (1966) demonstrates a beauty in nature emanating from its awe-inspiring force: "A far-off blow-hole booming like a gun," "The veined sea-campion buds burst into white," "And gorse turns tawny orange, seen beside / Pale drifts of primroses cascading wide / To where the slate falls sheer into the tide." Throughout the poem Betjeman emphasizes nature's power, but more distinctive is the poem's evocative portrayal of the persistent beauty of Cornwall despite the recurrent intrusions of humanity:

> From today's calm, the lane's enclosing green
> Leads inland to a usual Cornish scene—
> Slate cottages with sycamore between.
>
> Small fields and tellymasts and wires and poles
> With, as the everlasting ocean rolls,
> Two chapels built for half a hundred souls.

What is significant here is the image of eternity, associated with the ocean. No effort of man can compare with this, neither his intentional efforts to worship, which are here rendered relatively inconsequential, nor his careless defilement of the cliffs. Such inconsiderate additions to the environment will be subsumed by the bountiful generosity of Cornwall: "nature spills / A wealth of heather, kidney-vetch and squills / Over these long-defended Cornish hills." Time and nature will efface the scars humanity leaves behind, for this Cornwall, Betjeman here asserts, will always triumph: "A gun-emplacement of the latest war / Looks older than the hill fort built before / Saxon or Norman headed for the shore." Cornwall's natural force is such that its age and beauty are lent even to the symbols of humanity's propensity for evil and destruction (*CP* 237–38).

Betjeman's abiding love of England's coastal landscape manifests itself in poetic ocean motifs that recur almost as frequently as church bells. "Beside the Seaside" (1947), an extended blank-verse, autobiographical poem that foreshadows much of *Summoned by Bells*, concludes with a meditation on the end of England and the one constant and unchanging force—the ocean's waves crashing and caressing England's shoreline:

> And all the time the waves, the waves, the waves
> Chase, intersect and flatten on the sand
> As they have done for centuries, as they will
> For centuries to come, when not a soul
> Is left to picnic on the blazing rocks,
> When England is not England, when mankind
> Has blown himself to pieces. Still the sea,
> Consolingly disastrous, will return
> While the strange starfish, hugely magnified,
> Waits in the jewelled basin of a pool. (*CP* 134)

This passage contains key motifs and themes: the comforts of life at the seaside, the priceless beauty of a tidepool, the ocean's paradoxical power to soothe and to destroy, and the imminent demise of England. Perhaps most significant is that Betjeman's pastoral elegy is coupled with his recurring anxiety of eternity. That the ocean is eternal is small comfort for him, for this is an eternity in which humanity has wiped itself out, an echo perhaps of his fear that any eternity for him would mean hell. However, the final two lines, containing the symbols of a star and a jewel, plausibly suggest the birth of Christ and the public acknowledgment by the Magi of this promise of redemption. Betjeman thus ends this pastoral reverie on a note that indicates the possibility of a spiritual renewal in the landscape.[75]

Elsewhere in England, away from the shore, nature might not be so successful at appropriating the detritus of humanity in re-forming a pastoral landscape. "Great Central Railway" (1962) depicts the view of an uncorrupted countryside as seen from a train window on a journey, according to the poem's subtitle, from "Sheffield Victoria to Banbury." Here Betjeman glimpses a pastoral landscape infused with his Anglican imagination:

> And silver shone the steeples out
> > Above the barren boughs;
> Colts in a paddock ran from us
> > But not the solid cows.

By recasting classical pastoralism within a Christian setting, Betjeman suggests that the violation of the landscape is evidence of humanity's moral fall. As the train passes "A village street—a manor house— / A church," all is well in the landscape of Betjeman's England, for these are essential elements of a pristine landscape. But this setting is disrupted by visual clutter as

> We pounded through a housing scheme
> > With tellymasts a-row,
> Where cars of parked executives
> > Did regimented wait
> Beside administrative blocks
> > Within the factory gate.

Though this train still pursues "A trail of glory," Betjeman makes clear it is to the West—perhaps Cornwall?—where "'Unmitigated England'" may still be found.[76] Though he does not specifically condemn the housing scheme and television aerials in this poem, he does suggest that an unspoiled landscape is associated with the age of rail travel rather than motor cars (*CP* 256–57). "Meditation on a Constable Picture" (1970) takes the reader back one generation further in time, when travel was not yet by steam train but by "hay barges sailing, the watermen rowing / On a Thames unembanked which was wide and slow-flowing." Again the pastoral setting is infused with Anglicanism, for in Betjeman's interpretation of Constable's depiction of the Thames, the London skyline remains dominated at one end by the "towers of the Abbey" and at the other by, "steeple-surrounded, the dome of St. Paul's." This London of faith was a "cluster of villages" ensconced in a "wide-spreading valley, half-hidden in haze." Betjeman does not allow the reader to enjoy the reverie of early nineteenth-century pastoral London, however. He concludes with a plea that launches us back into the present age, the post-Edenic fallen world of aesthetic horrors: "Let us keep what is left of the London we knew" (*CP* 314). At other occasions he would despair that nothing was left: "Where is the old London now? . . . It is gone, with the smell of straw and horse-dung from every mews beyond the high Palladian terraces of South Kensington. It is gone, with the fish-tail gas-jets which flared, a long unsteady row, around the black clerestory inside St. Bartholomew-the-Great."[77]

Perhaps the most literary of Betjeman's pastorals is "The Old Liberals" (1949), an elegy for a lost world of Edwardian drawing rooms. The poem begins with a scene of a father and daughter playing hymns from the high church hymnal on woodwind instruments; typifying the ethos of the country house, windows and doors seem to be open to allow a natural flow of the landscape inside: "Daylight swims / On sectional bookcase, delicate cup and plate." The light itself is infused with a mysterious religiosity: "And many the silver birches the pearly light shines through." And the elegant musicians are seemingly transformed into shepherds: "Such painstaking piping high on a Berkshire hill." The middle stanza enacts the classic *ubi sunt* motif of the pastoral in deliberately archaic language reminiscent of the English literary renaissance, which popularized the pastoral:

> For deep in the hearts of the man and the woman playing
>   The rose of a world that was not has withered away.
> Where are the wains with garlanded swathes a-swaying?
> Where are the swains to wend through the lanes a-maying?
>   Where are the blithe and jocund to ted the hay?
>   Where are the free folk of England? Where are they?

Pastorals often contain political subtexts, and "The Old Liberals" is no exception. The question about the "free folk of England" points not to the liberated shepherds and shepherdesses that populate the poetry of the sixteenth century but instead to the denizens of modern Britain who having survived Hitler's intentions must now grapple with the onslaught of planners and councils and agencies. "In a single week of our planning, centuries of texture can be brushed away," he raged. "Is all to be replanned. . . ?"[78] The poem ends with death imagery and the loss of hope. While packed buses transport workers into congested suburbs, birch trees drop their leaves, the "wet woods [are] weeping," and the woodwinds up in the country house "only moan at a mouldering sky" (*CP* 183).

True to the pastoral tradition, Betjeman indulges in fantasies of escape from the ugliness and misery of the present for a fantasy of the past. The fantasy varies widely from the Cornwall of his childhood to the London of Constable; it even includes the country house, as in "An Edwardian Sunday, Broomhill, Sheffield" (1966): "High Dormers are rising / So sharp and surprising, / And ponticum edges / The driveways of gravel." Such a house is rendered distinctly pastoral: "A sylvan expansion / So varied and jolly / Where laurel and holly / Commingle their greens." But however "Serene" this setting, it is painfully close to "back street and alley / And chemical valley" (*CP* 260–61). Betjeman's urge to escape was essential to his faith. As he wrote in his 1951 radio broadcast "The Victorian Sunday," Sundays were about evading the brutalities of the workaday world: "Sunday is, thank goodness, *different* and we must have one day in seven different or our nerves collapse, our way of living goes too fast and there is no escape from the machines that all but control us."[79] Thus the poem "Lines Written to Martyn Skinner" (1964), which praises the poet's friend for his flight from the urban wasteland of modern Oxford into a bucolic England of boyhood dreams:

> Return, return to Ealing,
>   Worn poet of the farm!
> Regain your boyhood feeling
>   Of uninvaded calm!

Here Betjeman connects an unspoiled landscape with the purity and innocence of childhood, but he infuses it as well with a religious sensibility: "In Ealing on a Sunday / Bell-haunted quiet falls." If an uncorrupted landscape is rooted in the historic and communal faith, in Ealing Skinner will find a euphonic paradise of church bells and birds and milkmen, though the anxieties of urban England and the grating cacophony of modern life are never far behind:

No early morning tractors
  The thrush and blackbird drown,
No nuclear reactors
  Bulge huge below the down,
. . . .
No lorries grind in bottom gear
  Up steep and narrow lanes,
Nor constant here offend the ear
  Low-flying aeroplanes.

On the contrary, here in Ealing the pastoral moment is sustained by soothing images of "leafy avenues / Of lime and chestnut" and by euphonious language that harmonizes man and nature: the bicycle that "smoothly glides," the River Brent that "softly flows," the "gentle gale" that "Sends up the hayfield scent" (*CP* 262–63).

In contrast with both the Ealing of Martyn Skinner and the Cornish cliffs of Betjeman's memory, "Delectable Duchy" (1967) observes the horrifying transformation of pastoral England into a site of ugliness, waste, and apathy. The natural emptiness of the scenic Cornish coastline has been corrupted by humanity and its detritus: cellophane wrappers, abandoned toys, portable toilets, caravans, and, perhaps the most offensive litter of all, villas that "hog" an ocean view once open to all.[80] Where once "The mint and meadowsweet would scent / The brambly lane," today "A smell of deep-fry haunts the shore." The contrast with the remnants of unpolluted nature is poignant:

And on the sand the surf-line lisps
With wrappings of potato crisps.
The breakers bring with merry noise
Tribute of broken plastic toys
And lichened spears of blackthorn glitter
With harvest of the August litter.

Betjeman equates a pristine landscape with the carefree days of childhood, "the years when she [Cornwall] was young and fair":

The white unpopulated surf,
The thyme- and mushroom-scented turf,
The slate-hung farms, the oil-lit chapels,
Thin elms and lemon-coloured apples.

Though these images are beautiful, they are ominous with overtones of sin and damnation. Imbuing his poem with a spiritual dimension, Betjeman suggests a link between an unmolested countryside and prelapsarian innocence, which further implies that the ongoing despoliation of the English landscape has resulted from a moral fall. Though he imagines a time when Cornwall's "golden" shores were "unpeopled," now the duchy is "gone beyond recall." And thus he concludes with a vision of divine destruction, in which the duchy will be once again "unpeopled":

> One day a tidal wave will break
> Before the breakfasters awake
> And sweep the cara's out to sea,
> The oil, the tar, and you and me,
> And leave in windy criss-cross motion
> A waste of undulating ocean.

Although this flood cleanses, it does not renew. Betjeman concludes the poem without rainbow or dove, without symbols of baptism or the promise of rebirth (*CP* 306–7).[81]

If the beauty of the English landscape symbolizes the innocence of childhood, then the desecration of that landscape points to a loss of innocence. "Hertfordshire" (1956) connects a childhood mortification with the devastation of natural beauty. Though the poem is predominantly a meditation on a memory of a humiliating hunting trip with a humorless, impatient, and authoritarian father, "Hertfordshire" concludes with a disaster much greater than the poet's shame at mishandling his gun and disappointing his "knickerbockered sire": the raping of the pastoral countryside by the emblems of progress—electric wires, concrete light poles, and suburban sprawl. Though "Colour-washed cottages reed thatched" remain alongside "weather-boarded water mills" and "Flint churches, brick and plaster patched," London is encroaching, and "the shire / Suffers a devastating change":

> Its gentle landscape strung with wire,
>   Old places looking ill and strange.
>   . . . .
> Tall concrete standards line the lane,
>   Brick boxes glitter in the sun.

Perhaps surprisingly, considering his usual hostility to his father (and to his father's memory), Betjeman accepts the burden of his father's anguish at having "such a milksop for a son." More significantly, however, he transfers his own anguish over the destruction of the countryside to his father: "Far more would these have caused him pain / Than my mishandling of a gun." His transference of emotion serves the purpose of mediating the hostility between father and son through a shared bond of outrage at what has happened to Hertfordshire (*CP* 225–26).

Betjeman makes brilliant use of irony to expose the cheapness of modern progress and the vast expense of its devastation nationwide. "Inexpensive Progress" (1955) includes offenses major and minor: power stations and nylon stockings are among his targets, along with electrical pylons, motorways, landing strips, and plate-glass windows. In addition to green spaces, other traditional features of the English landscape lost to progress include country lanes, hedgerows, inn signs, and unique village high streets. Because they are ancient, even these man-made features become integral to the natural landscape. What is lost, however, is less horrifying than what is gained:

> When all our roads are lighted
> By concrete monsters sited
>   Like gallows overhead,
> Bathed in the yellow vomit
> Each monster belches from it,
>   We'll know that we are dead.

Throughout the poem the denunciation of modernity is rendered in moral and religious terms: to Betjeman this is an "age without a soul"; the effect of progress is a "raw obscenity," and the result of this moral fall is death. The degree of his wrath can be measured in his suggestion that progress is a kind of monstrous intestinal effluvium, yet the religious fervor of the poem turns his anger from bitterness into righteousness (*CP* 286–87). This tone also characterizes the poem "Harvest Hymn" (1964), which, as its title suggests, appropriates an ecclesial probity in its assault on agrarian England. Parodying the familiar harvest hymn, "We Plough the Fields and Scatter," Betjeman reveals himself as an ardent ecological preservationist. Here he asks us to recall a traditional farming life, now essentially gone forever. Small, bucolic farms having been swallowed up by monstrous cooperatives, the new farm is a nightmare of pesticides, over-production, and materialism. Except when spraying poisons and burning ancient hedgerows, farmers are entirely cut off from their land and their history. Without thought for the future, their mantra is "The earth is ours today" (*CP* 284).

Betjeman castigates this new England of destruction, pollution, and blight, a nation either apathetic to or oblivious of the horrors besetting not only farms and villages but also cities and counties. Illustrating the crisis with the example of the growing problem of litter, he laid the blame on a national trend toward self-absorption. "Let us remind ourselves that this is a free country," he wrote in satirical vein in 1954, "and we can throw what we like where we like and feel proud of it." Though his target in this piece for *Punch* was ostensibly litter, Betjeman enlarges the problem to a moral and political dilemma: "Finally let us remember that everything belongs to everyone and we can do exactly what we like with anything we see."[82] Such collectivist thinking is a product of mental confusion, a pattern he satirizes in two ruthless poems. "Cheshire" (1982) describes an entire county corrupted by transgression of aesthetic principles. Everywhere is an architectural impropriety plastered onto nature, from rooflines in the Dutch style to faux medieval golfing clubs, an aesthetic jumble worsened by a mishmash of transportation routes and a horizon criss-crossed by wires: "And metalled roads bisect canals, / And both are crossed by railway lines." Betjeman's point is to create a mental hodgepodge that not only confuses but also offends against both taste and morals (*CP* 352). If the countryside is denied even an illusory purity and piety, the city is worse yet. Such is the brazen horror and doom of "Chelsea 1977" (1977), in which "the dying embers of the day" come not from a lovely sunset but from the conflagratory ruins of the city. Here Betjeman describes the beauty of a city sunset despoiled by piles of excrement, building materials, sewage pipes, and so forth. He transforms this urban wasteland into a literal hell as Satan lurks just beneath the streets, fanning his flames to heighten the eternal torment for those who have blighted England (*CP* 392). In mock-pastoral vein, he described "The Romance of the Thames" in 1955. Stagnant water, a nauseating stench, and a "sliding train of filthy intimate objects" have polluted this sacramental emblem of England: "So it goes backwards and forwards through the middle of London until time and tide dissolve it."[83]

If pollution was an obvious landscape or cityscape horror, an artificially hygienic environment could prove even more unsettling. In Betjeman's nightmare vision of the future of England, the state's displacement and appropriation of the church has not only debilitated the village but also hastened the rise of an alien and fatuous modern city. "Huxley Hall" (1953) suggests a brave new world indeed, a dystopian vision of an England where every town has become Letchworth or Hatfield, new and overplanned garden cities intentionally built as social experiments but so aesthetically hygienic that uniqueness was eradicated. Despite the efforts of modern planners to undermine the influence of religion, the persona instinctively dwells on the evidence that humans are by nature sinful and have fallen as a result: having come to hear a lecture in this garden city, he finds instead his thoughts are drawn naturally to "the Fall." The behavior of innocent children at play as well as of hypocritical bureaucrats bolsters his belief "that we may be born in sin." The state, having supplanted the church, tries futilely to perfect human existence, maintaining the pleasant fiction of evolutionary progress for humanity in "the folk-museum's charting of man's Progress out of slime." As Betjeman asked rhetorically in a 1953 radio broadcast, "Has evil been charmed or psychoanalysed out of all children?"[84] The state not only lies about having cured humanity of sin and evil; it even denies him pleasure by regulating his diet, feeding him a "vegetarian dinner" and a "lime-juice minus gin." He has sunk into a "Deep depression" caused by the state's every effort to improve society. The state, having presumed to usurp God as redeemer of humanity, has failed and fallen, creating instead a "bright, hygienic hell." This life, as he wrote elsewhere, is "a fool's paradise of imagined culture, a sort of Welwyn Garden City of the mind."[85] Having lost the Garden of Eden, we are now banished to the garden city, which in Betjeman's mind embodies not only the fallen nature of humanity but also the state's emphasis on physical and mental health to the exclusion of spiritual health.[86] Hope of life accrues only to those rare souls still residing in traditional pockets of rural England, metonymized by the woman eating "greasy crumpets" and "dropping butter on her book" while she curls up reading "snugly in the inglenook / Of some birch-enshrouded homestead," the enshrouded inglenook and porous crumpet suggesting that pockets of life survive where salvation might still be found (*CP* 160).

While "Huxley Hall" accords the modern city the comfortable fiction of hygiene, Betjeman's early and notorious poetic jeremiad "Slough" (1937) puts such fantasies to the lie. With its infamous refrain, "Come, friendly bombs, and fall on Slough," the poem reduces the town of Slough not merely to an excrescence of arresting ugliness and mundanity but also to a moral morass of modernism that has rendered it unfit for human occupation. So powerful was his assault that the town of Slough continues to suffer the slings and arrows of the reputation it gained simply from Betjeman's poem.[87] Yet Betjeman would come to regret his poem, and he emphasized in subsequent writings and interviews that the poem actually alluded to Slough's Trading Estate, a horrible conglomeration of factories and light industry built on valuable agricultural land.[88] Moreover, "Slough" was to stand for a new trend developing across England, "the menace of things to come," the defacing of open countryside with the effrontery of cheap commerce.[89] "Slough" is perhaps Betjeman's harshest indictment of humanity: he rebukes our materialism, our insensitivity to the environment, our moral and sexual corruption, and our indolent preference for the benefits of modern technology at the expense of traditional culture. The desecration of culture and landscape being complete and irreversible, "Slough" suggests that annihilation is to be desired. Only a decimation of blitzkrieg proportions can purge and purify the England synecdochized by Slough and prepare it for a reawakening. Despite the apparent viciousness of Betjeman's apostrophic petition, "Come, friendly bombs," the poet is motivated by righteous indignation. The poem feels like a jeremiad yet ends with a hopeful image in its depiction of the postapocalyptic aftermath:

> Come, friendly bombs, and fall on Slough
> To get it ready for the plough.
> The cabbages are coming now;
>   The earth exhales.

The bombs will make the place more attractive and fit for habitation; they will expunge the evils of Slough in order to restore to it a traditional, agrarian England. The bombs may be coming, but after them will come the plough and the cabbages. As the earth renews it "exhales," as if it has been holding its breath all this while against the stench of modern Slough. The renewal of a bucolic vision for England is undoubtedly a restoration of religious proportions (*CP* 20–21).[90]

Despite the contumely of "Slough," the landscape of England, comprising both natural and human features, was sacred to Betjeman, and in all his writings he imbued it simultaneously with Anglican and pastoral features. Perhaps no poem more perfectly embodies this duality than "Before Invasion, 1940" (1942):

> Still heavy with may, and the sky ready to fall,
> Meadows buttercup high, shed and chicken and wire?
> And here where the wind leans on a sycamore silver wall,
> Are you still taller than sycamores, gallant Victorian spire?
>
> Still, fairly intact, and demolishing squads about,
> Bracketed station lamp with your oil-light taken away?
> Weep flowering currant, while your bitter cascades are out,
> Born in an age of railways, for flowering into to-day! (*CP* 97)

Betjeman's rhetorical questions add poignancy to the impending losses. Blending seamlessly with pastoral images of springtime flowering are a Victorian church and a Victorian railway station, threatened by German bombs and "the sky ready to fall." He was firm in his belief that this England was worth defending, was worth the effort to preserve, not only from German invasion but also from depredations at home. Though England would win the war against German fascism, Betjeman despaired that the values of fascism were already taking root in England; these included "the group mind, the state instead of the individual, theory instead of man himself, theories instead of human beings, the annihilation of man as an individual, the setting up of the ants' nest." To him, whose political views were always informed by faith, the only "revolutionary force likely to contend with fascism" was Christianity.[91] Only rarely did he express complete and utter hopelessness in the future of "Dear old, bloody old England," but these rare exceptions could bring shock to readers unprepared for pessimism. Such was the effect in 1952 when Britons picked up his new anthology of prose pieces and read the introductory essay, "Love Is Dead." Here Betjeman launched into an uncharacteristic jeremiad harsher and more polemical than anything he had written before, of which the following is characteristic: "We have ceased to use our eyes because we are so worried about money and illness. Beauty is invisible to us. We live in a right little, tight little clinic." The growing interest of Britons in culture is only evidence of the loss of faith: "It is a desire for the unworldly. It is a search for religion and it is far smarter than Christianity."[92]

Such pessimism was the exception rather than the rule. Even here, though, there is the slightest evidence of optimism, the slightest suggestion that Betjeman might still think Britain worth fighting for, for he concludes with a prayer for the Holy Spirit to send a renewing breath of charity into the hearts of the British people.[93] For what value had life if nothing was worth fighting for? As late as October 1939, Betjeman had described himself as a Christian pacifist; in a letter to Ninian Comper he wondered "if I can persuade myself it is right to fight at all. At present fighting in a war seems to me to be committing a new sin in defence of an old one."[94] It took little time for Betjeman to clear his conscience, volunteering in the Observer Corps and then taking employment in the Ministry of Information and as press attaché in the British Embassy in Dublin.[95] Returning to England in 1943, he delivered his memorable BBC radio broadcast, "'Oh, to be in England . . . ,'" extolling the nation's beauty, praising its recent social improvements, and attacking the town planners who, sweeping all away, would accomplish what the Nazis had not yet done. England could remain pastoral, "where roads wind like streams among the elms; the bulging barrows of the chalk downs, where thatched houses cluster among elm trees in hollows and white roads wind up from them to the sheep-folds." Always hanging over Betjeman's pastoral vision is his Anglican sensibility: "hundreds and hundreds of unspoiled places with stone churches, heavily ticking church clocks, modest post offices, creeper-clad wardens' cottages, rusty croquet hoops on rectory lawns, swinging inn signs, and well-stocked gardens where brick paths lead through thyme and vegetables." This immense and varied beauty of England "is so easily destroyed, not by bombs but by witless councillors, people on the lookout for building land, electric-light companies, county councils with new road schemes, the wrong sort of 'planner.'"[96] Philip Larkin astutely noted that Betjeman, perhaps more robustly and realistically than any other twentieth-century poet, captures what it means to be English and to live in England: "Betjeman's poems would be something I should want to take with me if I were a soldier leaving England: I can't think of any other poet who has preserved so much of what I should want to remember, nor one who, to use his own words, would so easily suggest 'It is those we are fighting for, foremost of all.'"[97]

5

THE CHAIN-SMOKING MILLIONS AND ME
Anglican Culture and the Community of Faith

And should we let the poor old churches die?[1]

In his poem "A Lincolnshire Church" (1958), Betjeman visits an obscure church situated in an uninspiring and unsightly setting. Though he is only on a church crawl, the poet's thoughts turn from the aesthetic to the conjunction of social and spiritual, and he begins to wonder how the Anglican community could survive or thrive amid such apathy and ugliness:

> And around it, turning their backs,
> The usual sprinkle of villas;
> The usual woman in slacks,
> Cigarette in her mouth,
> Regretting Americans, stands
> As a wireless croons in the kitchen
> Manicuring her hands.
> Dear old, bloody old England
> Of telegraph poles and tin,
> Seemingly so indifferent
> And with so little soul to win.

The church's setting in a "green marsh" beneath "a huge cloud cavern of gold" is spoiled by the sacrilege of the English landscape and the detachment of its people. The spatial arrangement of England's modern housing schemes further suggests a nation that has turned its back on God. Despite apparently having so little soul left, the England synecdochized in this poem may yet be won, a salvation made possible by the renewal of a communal spirit. Betjeman's hope is that if renewal begins at the community level it will spread gradually across the nation, one parish at a time. When the poet enters the church, aiming to explore its architectural possibilities, he is immediately transported by its spiritual mystery:

> There where the white light flickers,
> Our Creator is with us yet,
> To be worshipped by you and the woman
> Of the slacks and the cigarette.

The spiritual mystery is the very source of the church's communal spirit. Despite the poet's instinct to distinguish himself socially and spiritually from other English sinners, it begins to dawn on him that all believers are united into a spiritual community whose worth overpowers the walls of social distinction that the speaker's innate snobbery urges him to construct. Becoming aware of God's immanence in the place, the poem's speaker confesses his sins, only to become aware of the priest: "An Indian Christian priest" borne by "heaving waters / . . . from sun glare harsh / Of some Indian Anglican Mission / To this green enormous marsh." The poet naturally wonders how this priest came to this corner of England, yet as spiritual mystery overwhelms his curiosity a deeper and more profound sense of community is created. The poet asks no questions, resting assured in the sense that "The same mysterious Godhead" that unites him with the woman with the cigarette is also "welcoming His friend" from India. This is a spiritual union more vital than any social union; differences of class and ethnicity are erased by the spiritual community created by the Church of England— and this was something Betjeman imagined well before the onset of the civil rights movement. This is a community that is Anglican, not English; it is an identity that is Anglican, embracing Englishness while encompassing so much more (*CP* 141–43).

Irrespective of his faith, John Betjeman had a deep and abiding commitment to the history, buildings, and institution of the Church of England. To him being English meant being Anglican, his faith and

identity thus inextricably woven. Patrick Taylor-Martin has argued
that the "Englishness" of Betjeman's religion was its fundamental quality; his church was "a social and spiritual entity rooted in the English soil. . . . It was the national religion and, as such, demanded his
allegiance and loyalty."[2] To Betjeman, the church was undoubtedly
the most significant institution in England, in fact the nation's central
defining characteristic. In addition to its architectural and liturgical
beauty, he embraced the Church of England's role as the storehouse
of English history and tradition, its symbolic locus as the center of the
community, and its function as the primary source of cultural identity for the English people. When he wrote about the church, he was
recounting the great narrative of English history. One of his favored
ideas, a refrain that recurs in many places in his writing, is that the
story of England could be found in its churches. When he went church
crawling, that "richest of pleasures," he learned "the history of England
in stone and wood and glass, which is always truer than what you read
in books."[3] When he went to church to worship, it was "to hear the old
story told anew," and this was as much England's story as the gospel. In
his marvelous 1974 BBC film, *A Passion for Churches*, Betjeman turns the
restoration of church paintings into an elaborate analogy for recover-
ing the forgotten past:

> Each generation makes itself heard. The past cries out to us even when we
> try to smother the cries. Medieval saints peer at us through godly warnings
> put over them by pious Elizabethans who had more use for the written word
> than the painted picture. We can help the past come through a hundredth of
> an inch at a time.[4]

Betjeman's reflection on the restoration of medieval ecclesial art serves
to metonymize the act of remembering. The church may preserve the
faith in beautiful spaces, but more importantly it creates and sustains
community as it nurtures the endurance of living tradition.

In short, the rituals of the church may have encouraged and main-
tained Betjeman's faith during times of doubt, but he never lost faith
in its social role; indeed as an Anglican and as a religious poet, he was
shaped by the Church of England perhaps even more by its cultural
authority than by its spiritual authority. To Betjeman Anglicanism was
vital as much for its culture as for its faith, and a simple correlative in

his thinking was that a healthy culture demanded a healthy faith. What a fearsome thing it was, therefore, for him to consider the decline of the church. It sorrowed him to witness not only this national loss of faith but also what he perceived to be an inevitable decline in English culture and society broadly speaking, of "Dear old, bloody old England." This anxiety undergirds *A Passion for Churches*. In a remarkable scene near the end, the vicar of a small Norfolk church rings the bell for a weekday service while Betjeman comments on this vital communal ritual: "The Vicar of Flordon has rung the bell for matins each day for the past eleven years." The camera focuses on the vicar reading the office of Morning Prayer, then pans back to reveal that the church is empty. While surely the village's spiritual apathy is cause for concern for Betjeman, he insists that "It doesn't matter that there's no one there. It doesn't matter when they do not come. The villagers know the parson is praying for them in their church." Betjeman well knows that this is better than nothing: "In some churches all prayer has ceased." He shows a church reduced to its tower, another reconstituted as a warehouse, a further converted to artists' studio space. "Better that than let the building fall," he laments.[5] At least these churches have survived, in whatever altered form, maintaining still some semblance or echo of a communal spirit. Betjeman decried the growing phenomenon of locked churches, for how was a community of faith to be sustained when access to the altar for private prayer was denied? In 1941, following the devastations to the City by German incendiary bombs, he described the condition of London's churches: "There was something grimly ironic about St. Vedast's, Foster Lane, when I visited it; the doors were, as usual, locked and the gate in front of them padlocked. But there was no church behind the doors, just an arcade and a heap of rubble to the sky and a smashed font and a brown smoke-streak across the stone steeple."[6] Locked churches were doomed churches in any sense of the word. Betjeman's faith, though certainly spiritual, was clearly cultural as well. This cultural faith manifests itself in an exploration of Englishness that is defined by the privileged status of its established church and by the importance that Anglicanism places on the idea of a community of believers.

Among the many things he liked about the Church of England was its official establishment as a national church. The union of church

and state, an alien concept in other democratic societies, was fundamental to Betjeman's appreciation of the church. He was, in short, the
embodiment of antidisestablishmentarianism. In a 1948 series of radio
talks sharing his delight in church crawling with the public, Betjeman
described a group of churches that had given him particular pleasure.
One theme that recurs in this series is that an established church is a
natural idea, not a political one; that is to say, he makes an undemo-
cratic political concept seem to be natural. He specifically celebrates
St. John the Baptist, a Georgian church in Mildenhall, Wiltshire, as "a
patriarchal church. It is the embodiment of the Church of England by
law established, the still heart of England, as haunting to my memory
as the tinkle of sheep bells on the Wiltshire Downs."[7] Indeed the concept of a union of church and state is made natural in two senses: the
idea evokes pastoral images of the natural English landscape, and at
the same time it exists according to natural law, fundamental to English identity. This idea is thus embodied in the decorated interior of
Mildenhall church: "Over the chancel arch, where once hung Our
Lord and Our Lady and St John, is a huge Royal Arms symbolizing
the alliance of Church and State."[8] Coming from a believer who so
often professed his catholicity, it may seem a surprise that Betjeman
does not find fault with the loss of the medieval figures; however, this
talk was written and delivered in the summer of 1948, following his
wife's conversion to Roman Catholicism and his epistolary theological exchanges with Evelyn Waugh, a context that may well explain and
justify this adamant endorsement of establishment. (One shudders to
imagine Waugh's outrage had he been listening to the wireless that evening.) Not surprisingly, Betjeman was equally committed to the monarchy, finding within its patriarchal traditions an order that explains by
analogy the supernal mysteries of the divine. Of the investiture of the
Prince of Wales in 1969, he wrote: "Suddenly all Creation's near / And
complicated things are clear, / Eternity in reach!" (*CP* 334).[9] These con-
cepts of monarchy and established church, so inseparable in his mind,
served to simplify complex spiritual matters for him, and though some
might find his political thinking to be rather fuzzy, his adherence to
these ideas helped him to stave off doubt.

Because it is a national church, the Church of England has about
it the notion that it is the spiritual embodiment of the English people.

The aim of the Church of England has always been, as Bishop Stephen Neill has argued, "to gather into one all those whom God had united as members of a single nation."[10] Betjeman himself poetically expressed it thus in *A Passion for Churches*: "The Anglican Church has got a bit of everything. It's very tolerant—and that is part of its strength. . . . Most tolerant and all-embracing Church. Wide is the compass of the Church of England."[11] The idealized universality of Anglicanism helps to explain how religion and culture are so intrinsically interwoven in Betjeman's poetry. It also helps to explain why his poetry is so much more concerned about the social aspects of religion than it is with the niceties of Christian theology.[12] This gives the Anglican Church a social significance beyond its spiritual function in assisting believers in communing with God. Anglicanism, in its perception of itself, defines and unites a people into communing with each other and with generations across time.[13] In Anglicanism, a communal tradition of worship is in fact more important than the sharp distinctions in doctrine or faith that define and divide other traditions. If that made the Anglican church excessively tolerant in the eyes of Evelyn Waugh and of legions of other English Catholics, it should at least have made the Church of England broad, inclusive, and welcoming. It was inexplicable then to Betjeman why his church was in such straits, why Anglican cathedrals were "crumbling to decay / Half empty" while Roman ones, "though brash and cheap, / Are always, always, crowded to the doors" (*CP* 381).[14] The answer to that question he could barely fathom, but he tentatively implied the possibility that spiritual apathy might be at the root of the declining English church: "They are not backwaters—or they shouldn't be, if the clergy and people love them—but strongholds."[15] Betjeman nonetheless embraced and adhered rigidly to the Anglican theory that its church was the body of the English people.[16] This idea of an Anglican community expresses itself in distinct ways in Betjeman's poetry and prose: by turns he celebrates the communal function of the church and mourns the loss of this communal spirit.

In a 1938 broadcast, "How to Look at a Church," one of his earliest radio talks about his love of church crawling, Betjeman makes specific reference to the concept of how the church embodies living history and sustains a sense of community. He begins this talk with an extended metaphor of the church as home—not merely the House of God but in fact as domestic abode: "There's something much kinder about a house which has been lived in for generations than a brand-new one," he writes, and here the word "kinder" suggests not only the obvious connotations of gentler and more caring but the older meaning of "natural." Why is this? Betjeman asks. It's "better built," he argues; it "reflects the generations that have lived in it"; and most importantly "it's part of England, not a bright red pimple freshly arisen on its surface." Betjeman here distinguishes what is organic and beautiful (and old) from what is bacterial and hideous (and new), all with a delightful rhetorical figure about the architectural carbuncle of modernism—a metaphor that Prince Charles would echo as an offense to the British architectural community at the end of the century. But how does this analogy point to the church? Betjeman begins to draw the points together at the end of the first paragraph, where the traits of an old house are greatly reminiscent of the Church of England at mid-century: "It may be a bit inconvenient and muddled, but it is human." Just in case his listeners do not catch his drift, Betjeman spells out the analogy: "But of all the old houses of England, the oldest and the most interesting are the Houses of God—the Churches." Because each generation is reflected in the architecture and decoration of an English church, it is "a living thing." Medieval stained-glass windows, Elizabethan sacramental silver, and Georgian marble monuments: these are vital to sustaining a community of people across time. Perhaps not surprisingly, it is the church bell that in Betjeman's imagination most effectively achieves this communal spirit: "And from the tower a bell, cast soon after the Wars of the Roses, lends its note to the peal that ripples over the meadows and threads its way under the drone of aeroplanes."[17] To Betjeman then, a church endures across time by drawing people together in a bond of living history that resists the degradation of modern life.

As in his radio talks, one of the most distinctive aspects of his verse is his praise for the capability of the church, with its symbols and traditions, to summon its parishioners to unite heart and mind. The imaginary idea of the English nation as a little community united in the act of common worship by the peal of church bells is a central theme of many of his poems. In "Verses Turned" (1952),[18] the peal of a single church bell draws an entire parish into both social and spiritual communion:

> It calls the choirboys from their tea
> And villagers, the two or three,
>   Damp down the kitchen fire,
> Let out the cat, and up the lane
> Go paddling through the gentle rain
>   Of misty Oxfordshire.

Together, these villagers will not only take communion but raise the funds necessary to preserve St. Katherine's, Chiselhampton. Betjeman's poem was occasioned by a plea to the nation to contribute to the restoration of this obscure church built in 1762, but it was not because St. Katherine's has historical or aesthetic significance:

> And must that plaintive bell in vain
> Plead loud along the dripping lane?
>   And must the building fall?
> Not while we love the Church and live
> And of our charity will give
>   Our much, our more, our all.

The poem emphasizes that even obscure, remote, or forgotten churches are significant; as a village is a microcosm of the nation, so a parish history recounts the history of England.[19] "Verses Turned" emphasizes that even this church is socially important; its history is both the history of its innocuous village and the history of the Church of England. The "plaintive bell" of St. Katherine's, Chiselhampton, is a plea to save both this little parish church and the national church as well. St. Katherine's is worth saving because the Church of England is worth saving; thus the "plaintive bell" in "Verses Turned" appeals to the Anglican's cultural love for the Church (*CP* 149–51). Betjeman's plea was not merely poetic, for he was among those who signed a letter to the *Times* in 1952 appealing "to all who admire Georgian architecture and love our country churches" to contribute toward the preservation of St. Katherine's, "both a perfect example of all that is best in eighteenth-century Anglicanism and a living parish church."[20]

One of the many features of Anglicanism that he admired was the diversity of liturgical style within it. "Church of England Thoughts" (1952)[21] describes how a ring of bells, emanating from Magdalen Tower in Oxford, reminds the poet of the variety of worship experience the

Church of England tolerates: high church, broad church, and low. This is a church sufficiently capacious to allow for either "Morning Prayer or Holy Mass," for "churches blue with incense mist" or "Chapels-of-ease by railway lines." These Anglican divisions and distinctions are rendered insignificant, however, as worshippers are united into a single community of Englishmen:

> A multiplicity of bells,
>> A changing cadence, rich and deep
> Swung from those pinnacles on high
> To fill the trees and flood the sky
>> And rock the sailing clouds to sleep.

Ultimately the bells call one to be English as much as they call one to be Christian. Betjeman hears "the plaintive ting-tangs call" from settings as various as urban "humble streets" with their "smells of gas" and country gardens with their "resin-scented chines / And purple rhododendrons." What creates the unity is the bells: "A Church of England sound, it tells / Of 'moderate' worship, God and State." The poem ends with a degree of ambiguity, however. These are collegiate bells, not church bells, and as the sound dissipates, the poet is dragged out of an illusory stupor and back into the harsh reality of a modern society oblivious to the capacity for communal regeneration that the Church of England offers:

> Before the spell begin to fail,
>> Before the bells have lost their power,
> Before the grassy kingdom fade
> And Oxford traffic roar invade,
>> I thank the bells of Magdalen Tower.

The poem's final lines, with their anaphoric potency, serve as a prayer for the sense of community to endure, masking the anxiety that such communal spirit is in fact threatened (*CP* 156–57).

In a number of poems, the magnificent aural image of church bells serves symbolically to unite a disparate community, a disconnect created by social class, by modern technology, by personal angst, or by death. In "On Leaving Wantage 1972" (1972), Betjeman describes the cohesion created among bell ringers despite their socially and economically distinct backgrounds:

> From rumpled beds on far-off new estates,
> From houses over shops along the square,
> From red-brick villas somewhat further out,
> Ringers arrive, converging on the tower. (*CP* 296)

A community is created across time by the activity of bell ringing in "On Hearing the Full Peal of Ten Bells from Christ Church, Swindon, Wilts" (1945). Here, bell ringing unites past, present, and future generations, the living, the dead, and the yet-to-be-born, despite the disruptive effects of modern technology, which tempts us into social disharmony:

> Oh still white headstones on these fields of sound
> Hear you the wedding joybells wheeling round?
> Oh brick-built breeding boxes of new souls,
> Hear how the pealing through the louvres rolls!
> Now birth and death-reminding bells ring clear,
> Loud under 'planes and over changing gear. (*CP* 109)

"Bristol" (1945), which makes a tribute to a "mathematic pattern of a plain course on the bells," finds comfort against existential despair through the musical beauty and orderly rationality of campanology, expressed through perfect tercets of trochaic octameter. The poem associates the peal of church bells with all that is beautiful in English towns and landscapes, its setting in the aftermath of a gentle rain suggesting the sensation of purity and restoration that accompanies the lovely flood of music as the listener is roused out of melancholy and into joy:

> Green upon the flooded Avon shone the after-storm-wet-sky
> Quick the struggling withy branches let the leaves of autumn fly
> And a star shone over Bristol, wonderfully far and high.
>
> Ringers in an oil-lit belfry—Bitton? Kelston?[22] who shall say?—
> Smoothly practicing a plain course, caverned out the dying day
> As their melancholy music flooded up and ebbed away. (*CP* 89)

The church and its bells also give physical form to the abstractions of eternity that Betjeman so craved. "Village Wedding" (1959) blends imagery of natural beauty, a rain-purified atmosphere, and church bells with a festive occasion that spans the generations. Time is eclipsed by eternity in this moment and in this place:

> And all the souls of Uffington,
> The dead among the living,
> Seem witnessing the rite begun
> Of taking and of giving.

Here Betjeman creates the perfect sensation of a community existing across time. The entire parish is brought together by pealing bells into the ancient church to witness a sacrament that binds together not just a young couple but all the living and dead with the timeless communal rituals of Christian faith.[23]

Perhaps it was only his deep love for the idea of Anglican community that could grant him relief from his anxious dread of death. In a very few poems, he expresses hope in the face of death simply because death—like marriage—can both symbolize and create unity as the living believer is joined with the countless generations of the past. "House of Rest" (1953) suggests that in the Eucharist we experience the communion of the living and the dead. In this poem, an elderly woman contemplates the recent death of her husband, a vicar, and the long-ago death of her sons. She invites the poet, who appears to be visiting her in a nursing home, to share their living presence in photographs, memories, and in such seemingly mundane objects as her husband's tobacco jar. The woman embraces Christian consolation, knowing that she will soon be reunited with them and that for now Anglican worship and common prayer symbolize this promise:

> Now when the bells for Eucharist
> Sound in the Market Square,
> With sunshine struggling through the mist
> And Sunday in the air,
>
> The veil between her and her dead
> Dissolves and shows them clear,
> The Consecration Prayer is said
> And all of them are near.

For the old woman, the Eucharist lifts the veil dividing her from her loved ones and draws them to her, but the poet is not quite certain. For Betjeman, the sun struggles to penetrate the mist, and he may still be wondering what becomes of the dead. The vicar is gone yet not gone, a paradox symbolized by the tobacco jar now filled with lavender (*CP* 161–62).

"The Commander" (1966) is another poem that uses the inevitability of death to celebrate the vital importance of a communal faith. In this tribute to George Barnes, a senior BBC official who died in 1960, Betjeman honors his friend by attributing to his example the necessity of accepting the onset of death with fortitude and embracing a simple trust in God's promise of eternal life:

> "Lord, I am not high-minded . . ." The final lesson you taught me,
>   When you bade the world good-bye,
> Was humbly and calmly to trust in the soul's survival
>   When my own hour comes to die.

Barnes' humility in the face of death, implied in the quoted Psalm,[24] is of some comfort to Betjeman, yet it is ultimately the communal spirit of shared Anglican values that restores his soul:

> I remembered our shared delight in architecture and nature
>   As bicycling we went
> By saffron-spotted palings to crumbling box-pewed churches
>   Down hazel lanes in Kent.
>
> I remembered on winter evenings, with wine and the family round you,
>   Your reading Dickens aloud
> And the laughs we used to have at your gift for administration,
>   For you were never proud.
>
> Sky and sun and the sea! the greatness of things was in you
>   And thus you refrained your soul.
> Let others fuss over academical detail,
>   *You* saw people whole.

Betjeman celebrates Barnes' life as having embodied the communal spirit of Anglicanism. This ethos he equates with other, unarguable virtues, ones he treasures equally highly: the bonds of family and friendship, a delight in English architecture and literature, a respect for nature, and the importance of human decency. The possibilities of social fragmentation are denied if we live as Barnes lived, seeing people whole (*CP* 268–69).

For now, still among the living, Betjeman found that the timeless traditions of worship helped him to sustain the sense—though perhaps it was only an appealing illusion—of an Anglican community. Corporate activities of worship were more effective in creating for him these communal bonds than were moments alone on his knees in prayer. For him, nothing could sustain the communal spirit of faith quite like bell ringing and hymn singing. He was so passionate about bell ringing—both as a musical art and as a social gathering—that he learned the skill himself and practiced it often when he lived and worshipped in Uffington and Farnborough. Monday was the usual ringing day; he would join a group of friends for change ringing followed by a convivial drink in the pub.[25] Indeed, Betjeman truthfully lived out his description of English church bell ringing as "a class-less folk art which has survived in the church despite all arguments about doctrine and the diminution of congregations."[26] Hymn singing served the same purpose for him and, he believed, for the whole community of believers. As he expressed it once with memorable simplicity, "Hymns are the poems of the people."[27] In a remarkable series of twenty-eight radio talks delivered in the 1970s, which until quite recently were almost entirely forgotten, he set out to retell the history of hymns and hymn writers.[28] What he verifies consistently throughout these talks is the power of hymns to speak to all believers, to unify them despite their tremendous divisions of belief. As Peter J. Lowe argues, to Betjeman "even doctrinal differences can be subsumed in the act of hymn singing."[29] He found common ground not only between Anglican and Nonconformist hymnodists but even with Bible-thumping American demagogues. According to Stephen Games, Betjeman "rejected nothing: even elements of Christianity that no longer appeal, such as the militarism of the Victorian Church."[30] Despite being a devout Anglican of high church stamp, Betjeman had a deep appreciation of the contributions to church music of those of alternative liturgical leanings, and he held the stately measures of Sir Charles Parry and Ralph Vaughan Williams in harmonious balance with "the dance rhythms of the popular ballads of the day" found in the hymn music of the evangelical mission halls.[31] Thus, as Games puts it, "*Sweet Songs* became an object lesson in how Christianity's numerous strands—often hostile to each other in their origins—now lived together harmoniously on the hymnbook's pages."[32] This is evidence of Betjeman's true catholicity, that is, the catholicity by which Anglicanism defines itself: its ability to gather and unite diverse strands of belief, to absorb difference into community. What the architect Ninian Comper said about his eclectic approach to church design speaks to the faith of Betjeman: this is a "unity by inclusion."[33]

The uses to which Betjeman put his broadcasting career served a function similar to that of bell ringing and hymn singing. The experience of speaking to the English public from the pulpit of the BBC microphone taught him about the common bonds of Englishness. As Stephen Games writes of his career as a radio broadcaster, "John Betjeman's enthusiasms have made him one of the keystones of England's common culture. . . . Thanks to his determination, his memories and loves are now an intrinsic part of our literary heritage and have reawoken the English to their past to an extent without parallel anywhere else in Europe or America."[34] Betjeman's intellectual commitments, which he shared with the public in a half-century career at the BBC that lasted from 1929 to 1979, did not merely include his faith; these commitments of his were strictly informed by his faith, and he brought the passion of religious conviction to each of his causes. The effect was in a sense a revival of the English people's attitude toward their heritage from a general torpor to zeal. One of his strengths as a broadcaster was his ability to appeal to a wide cross-section of the public. Despite his interest in popular culture, he used the radio to vilify vulgarity if in his mind it served to weaken or contaminate culture. He was not a snob, however; he learned to identify and sympathize with his listeners, to imagine them as individuals, and to develop an inclusive relationship with them based on the idea of a bond, a commerce even, between the people and their past.[35] When he had all but exhausted his favored twin topics of the horrors of modern town-planning and the marvels of pre-twentieth-century life, there was one commitment from which his keen interest never waned: religious broadcasts. Even the BBC's parsimony did not dampen his dedication to sharing his interest in religion: "I must do it largely for the love of the thing." Once, when asked whether he would give a religious talk despite the low pay, Betjeman replied, "O Lord yes. Six guineas is jolly good for what is anyhow a duty."[36] To Stephen Games, Betjeman "seemed to spend the latter

part of his life in an extended struggle for redemption." As a consequence, "Religious broadcasts became his acts of grace."[37] Bevis Hillier
further substantiates Betjeman's gift for appealing even to nonbeliev-
ers with these religious programs. His "carefully pitched last words" in
A Passion for Churches "made concessions" to an audience that "would
include atheists and agnostics; Christians who had let their faith slip;
people who loved the Church of England as part of English life and its
churches as tabernacles of preserved history, without subscribing to
its doctrines."[38]

Betjeman's conviction of a real reciprocity between the Church of
England and a healthy English culture manifested itself most strikingly
in a series of poems he wrote for and read on the BBC as a conscious
effort to use the airwaves to create and sustain a sense of an Anglican
community. Beginning in 1953, and over the course of more than three
years, he created and read a series of poems called "Poems in the Porch."
These were part of a regular broadcast called "Faith in the West," a
religious program that included segments on prayer, on church music,
and on other devotional or theological topics.[39] He was initially quite
keen on the project, and at first the poems came easily and quickly.
He introduced the series with "Diary of a Church Mouse," a gently
satirical exploration of Christian hypocrisy, followed by "Electric Light
and Heating," a verse rendering of his irritations over the moderniza-
tion of ancient churches. Throughout the early months of 1954, he
continued the pattern of producing and reading one new poem per
month; soon, however, the pressure to produce an original poem every
month began to mount, and he was forced to take a hiatus.[40] In the
spring of that year he was approached by the publishers at the SPCK
(Society for Promoting Christian Knowledge), with a request to pub-
lish the poems. The idea of publishing a permanent volume of poems
that had been written specifically for broadcast was not appealing;
however, he was prevailed upon, and a slim volume with illustrations
by his friend John Piper was published later that year.[41] Yet Betjeman
was nervous about the reception. He had of course written the poems
specifically to be heard by listeners, not pondered over by readers; they
tend to be simpler, lighter pieces than much of his other verse, largely
characterized by orthodoxy in matters of faith. However, the public
did not share Betjeman's anxiety about the quality of the verse, and the

initial press run sold out within a month. He would return to the air-waves for more "Poems in the Porch" over the following two years, but poetic inspiration was hard for him to command on schedule; though he had exhausted his possibilities, the public's appreciation did not wane, and their requests for more were unrelenting. Though gradually and inevitably the poems petered out, the last one airing in February of 1957, the popularity of this series attests to the success of Betjeman's aim—to appeal to a national sense of an Anglican community.

The "Poems in the Porch" are serious poems in light verse. Betjeman's subjects affirm the elements of faith, celebrate the church's history and calendar, and describe the people of the church and their places of worship. He recalls the seasons of the church, moving from Advent and Christmas and Epiphany through Shrovetide, Lent, Holy Week, and even Harvest Festival. Always he alludes to the common life and experience of believers, the community of English people defined by their common Anglican heritage. The communal nature of parishes within a national church of timeless tradition is the point of "Septua-gesima" (1954), a poem named for the third Sunday before Lent, the Sunday that commences the pre-Lenten season of Shrovetide. Here Betjeman insists that it does not matter whether the vicar is high or low, nor whether everyone believes the same way; all that really matters is having, especially at the point of death, "The grace most firmly to believe." Implying the mind-set of theological opponents like Waugh, Betjeman imagines that "There may be those who like things fully / Argued out, and call you 'woolly'" for not adhering rigidly to the cate-chism, and resent those "Whose worship is what they call 'free.'" In the face of such opposition is the timeless comfort of Anglican community: "There's refuge in the C. of E." Thus he praises the lowly parishioners all over England whose strenuous efforts sustain village churches and thus by implication the established church: sextons, treasurers, organ-ists, bell ringers, and of course those dedicated few who always attend services "Throughout the year, whate'er the weather, / That they may worship God together." Betjeman's emphasis here is not the individual experience of belief but the communal act of worship. Wherever two or three are gathered, Betjeman suggests, the church survives:

> These, like a fire of glowing coals,
> Strike warmth into each other's souls,

And though they be but two or three
They keep the Church for you and me.[42]

"Churchyards" (1954) is likewise deceptive in its use of lighthearted rhythms, conveying a seriousness about death and faith. This poem affirms Betjeman's key principle that the church preserves the history not only of communities but by extension of the nation as well: "Our churches are our history shown / In wood and glass and iron and stone." The poem amuses first by recounting the churchyard's shared history with the alehouse; in the churchyard "horns of ale were handed round / For which churchwardens used to pay / On each especial vestry day." Yet it is in the traditional churchyard that Betjeman says we are likely to encounter God, "Close to the church when prayers were said / And Masses for the village dead." In these ancient burying grounds are the examples of the village faithful. Having believed unwaveringly that after death they would receive new bodies and the gift of eternal life, they are buried beneath simple tombstones of elegant craftsmanship that "Men gave in their Creator's praise." Despite the poem's jaunty tone, however, his lines ring out with a sense of disappointment in his and his culture's inability to believe with such complete security as generations past. Satirizing the modern tendency toward euphemism, where a cemetery is renamed "a garden of rest," he tells us that the simple tombstones of the past are more honest not only about the facts of death but also about faith in life eternal. In contemplating the history of English village life, he becomes aware of God's immanence in the churchyard. In this simple spot, with

> sharp spring sunlight thrown
> On all its sparkling rainwashed stone,
> . . . .
> That centuries of weather there
> Have mellowed it to twice as fair,

with its history of simple belief and communal life, he has learned to embrace the mystery of faith.[43]

If Betjeman's public and occasional poems tend to celebrate the notion of a communal spirit of Anglicanism, many poems more personal and meditative in nature take a darker look at the possibilities of communal regeneration. The anxiety that the English have lost their unity of faith preoccupies him in a variety of poems—a fear that manifests itself in an almost insistent litany that community must somehow be restored, even when churches are lost. This motif especially underscores his thinking about urban churches. In a 1954 letter to the *Times*, he reminded readers that "A living Christian community needs a place of worship where it works as well as where it sleeps and needs a place to pray in on week-days as well as on Sundays." He was well aware that urban churches were being sold off in order to raise funds for constructing new churches in far-flung suburbs, but he was insistent that the half-million workers who commuted into the City should not be forgotten. The conclusion of his letter is a thoughtful reminder that a largely economic environment requires spiritual balance and that a community of belief can still coalesce the fragmentation caused by a commuter society:

> Finally, a beautiful church is as a building a more permanent witness to the Christian faith than vicars or congregations. What mitigates the commercial atmosphere of the City and makes it pleasantly different from other parts of London is its numerous churches. To assume that because the nation is not at the moment given to church-going such will always be the state and we should therefore sell our churches is surely a denial of the Christian virtue of hope.[44]

Such hope does not underscore all of Betjeman's writing about churches, however. In "City" (1937), the poet imagines sitting in the churchyard of St. Botolph's Bishopsgate.[45] The resonating bell and the scent of incense awaken memories of his grandfather "Toddling along from the Barbican"; this very brief poem ends suddenly with this image. The physical nature of worship—the smells and bells—are experienced in the churchyard rather than inside, and the worship seems not to resurrect the dead so much as to awaken ghosts. The church is dying; the Christian has more in common with the churchyard than with the church, and its bells peal more to the dead than to the living (*CP* 29).[46]

"St. Mary Magdalen, Old Fish Street Hill" (1982) is another poem that laments a lost community, but the indictment is more severe.[47] Here the church—or more broadly this parish—is complicit with society in the loss of community. Betjeman imagines a persona who is very proud of being rector's warden, even though "our congregation is seldom more than ten." Indeed, this church is beyond help. The speaker blames aesthetics, namely the design of Sir Christopher Wren, who rebuilt the church after "the London Conflagration / Of sixteen sixty-six," for the decline: "It is just a box with a fanciful plaster ceiling / Devoid of a vestige of genuine Christian feeling." Though there may be a link between aesthetics and faith, the real cause of the decline of St. Mary Magdalen is much more complex. The implacable force of demographic change is the historical culprit: there were simply too many churches in the City; people decamped for the suburbs in the nineteenth century, and the City's population dropped dramatically.[48] The poetic culprit is implied in a little fact that the rector's warden drops, though he remains blithely oblivious to its significance: "We haven't the Charity children now to fill / Our old west gallery front. Some new committee / Has done away with them all." The decline of this church is attributable to a combination of demography, snobbery, and politics: for years the church was populated by nontithing poor children, but they weren't welcomed, being shunted to the balcony; finally a diocesan or parochial committee has recognized that fact and has simply made them disappear. The rector's warden does not know where they have gone and does not seem to understand the significance. The community of charity children was St. Mary Magdalen's community; perhaps they are not desirable to the few remaining oligarchs who yet control the parish, but now there is no community at all (*CP* 385).

Whereas some of Betjeman's poems lament the loss of community that results from the decline of the church, he reverses cause and effect in "Monody on the Death of Aldersgate Street Station" (1955), a poem whose title, together with the imagery in the first and last stanzas, seems to memorialize the end of the steam-train era.[49] Betjeman makes clear, however, that his real focus is the cultural and social blow to British society caused by the loss of City churches: "City of London! before the next desecration / Let your steepled forest of churches be my theme."[50] Here begins a litany of churches lost or threatened, churches whose names roll poetically off Betjeman's tongue; we discover them to be as syllabically metrical as they are colorfully and quaintly styled: "St. Mildred's Bread Street," "St. Michael Paternoster," and "Christ Church Newgate Street (with St. Leonard Foster)."[51] The poem is filled with images of loss; the speaker, identifying with that "lost generation" of "the steam and the gas-light," appears to be sitting in the open ruins of a former church, "Where once I heard the roll of the Prayer Book phrases." The sound of Sunday bells is only a memory; now there is only "Sunday Silence! with every street a dead street."[52] Betjeman renders this missing sound an irreparable loss as, once, "neighbouring towers and spirelets joined the ringing" of "the roaring flood of a twelve-voiced peal from Paul's." The poem's allusions to trains imply that the loss of bells is cultural, not spiritual; the bells of City churches served the same communal function as steam-trains and gaslights. Cultural progress consumes the gods of past generations, and the City, with its endless, alien "improvements," now disrupts a once-ritual community. Once, "the walled-in City of London, smelly and holy, / Had a tinkling mass house in every cavernous street," but now these churches are gone, displaced by gleaming but soulless centers of commerce and finance: "The new white cliffs of the City are built in vain."[53] The catholic image of the "tinkling mass house" further exemplifies that communal traditions have not been disrupted until the poet's lifetime. Betjeman loved this fantasy of Anglican unity, reminiscing in a 1971 essay about the delights of worshiping in prewar City churches: "What a joy it was to sit in a box pew while the gallery clock ticked and to hear the rolling seventeenth-century English of the Prayer Book alone with the verger and the pew-opener and breathe in the hassock-scented dust of Dickensian London."[54] In "Monody," Betjeman creates the ahistorical illusion of cultural cohesion, a continuity of ritual and community that survived reformation, civil war, and fire, only to be sundered by the transformation of the City from a home into a mere place to work, symbolized by the transformation of the nation's favorite image of Dover's white cliffs into the shining skyscrapers of the City. While the poem never explains what City churches and steam trains mean precisely, it insists that their loss creates an irrevocable void in the community (*CP* 216–17).[55]

What "Monody" accomplishes with a lament, "Distant View of a Provincial Town" (1935) does with wit, giving us a litany of decaying parishes that concludes with an image of a church whose "entrance [is] permanently locked,— / How Gothic, grey and sad it is / Since Mr. Grogley was unfrocked!" Like "Monody," this poem implies that trains as much as churches can take us on a spiritual journey; the humorous claim that we can be redeemed by a railway suggests that the redemption Betjeman has in mind is cultural rather than spiritual and that this can be accomplished as well by steam as by faith, by the G. W. R. or by Holy Eucharist:

> The old Great Western Railway shakes
> The old Great Western Railway spins—
> The old Great Western Railway makes
> Me very sorry for my sins.[56]

The equation between God's Wonderful Railway and the Church of England suggests that a similar fate is in store for both; as Betjeman lamented the scheme to nationalize the rails, so would he also have lamented any effort to disestablish the national church.[57] The communal nature of parishes within a national church of illusory timeless tradition is a central point of this poem, which, like "Church of England Thoughts," celebrates churches high, low, and broad. The delightfully inclusive national church embraces high St. Aidan's, "Where Auntie Maud devoutly bobs / In those enriched vermilion aisles." But it also has room for those offended by such Romanisms: "No Popish sight or sound or smell / Disturbed that gas-invaded air" in low St. George's. Amusingly, Betjeman laughs as much at the broad St. Mary's, whose rector filled his sermons with anything but the spiritual life, preaching "In such a jolly friendly way / On cricket, football, things that reached / The simple life of every day." Each manifestation of Anglicanism is treated with laughter. In Betjeman's comic vision of the Church of England there is a tolerant and bemused inclusivity and equality (*CP* 18–19).

Unfortunately, Betjeman well knows, inclusivity and equality in the church are often nothing more than fantasies. All too often the bonds of community are broken by the attitudes and actions of its own parishioners. "In Westminster Abbey" (1939), a dramatic monologue set during the early days of World War II, has for its persona a woman who enters the abbey to pray for a moment before hurrying off to "a luncheon date." She is Betjeman's representative of an entire class: glove-wearing snobs who live in the posh Chelsea neighborhood of Cadogan Square. The fact that the poem was published just prior to the Blitz may temper the satire only slightly, for this woman is not merely a chauvinist but a racist, an elitist, and a hypocrite more concerned with how the war will affect her portfolio than anything else, in the process confusing spiritual and material treasures: "So, Lord, reserve for me a crown / And do not let my shares go down." Is this woman a spiritual anomaly? I believe Betjeman presents her as a typical case; he sees the British as all too likely to use patriotic zeal to mask a host of sins. For instance, she blithely believes that doing her duty in the war effort in essence honors Christ's injunctions:

> I will labour for Thy Kingdom,
>   Help our lads to win the war,
> Send white feathers to the cowards
>   Join the Women's Army Corps.

Her nationalism leads her to ask the Lord himself to "bomb the Germans"; proud of what she perceives as humility, she says she will "pardon Thy Mistake" if God accidentally and incompetently kills a few German women in the process, and without a trace of ironic self-awareness she fervently prays, "Don't let anyone bomb me." She also believes she has in her heart the best interests of the "Gallant blacks," those subjects of the British empire all too vital for victory in this war: "Protect them Lord in all their fights, / And, even more, protect the whites." The speaker is absurd at best, perhaps even loathsome to some readers: insensitive, mercenary, racist.

Throughout the poem Betjeman's tone varies from unmitigated contempt for her ethical vacuity to mockery of the ludicrous vanity of her class snobbery. Here she enumerates "what our Nation stands for," by which of course she means the things that make her life a little better; the list is Betjeman's opportunity to reveal what makes Britain both pathetic and bathetic: "Books from Boots' and country lanes, / Free speech, free passes, class distinction, / Democracy and proper drains." Is Betjeman's satire merely social? Is he indicating simply that such cultural attitudes will further drive Britain down the drain?[58] First, that the setting is in a church indicates that the woman's social and ethical lapses are in fact a product of her spiritual state. Her moral flaws are, in short, sins. And because she speaks for Britain's dominant, ruling class, by extension it is fair to say that Betjeman believes that social problems are a direct result of a nation's spiritual sickness. The poem's setting in the nation's church, in the political epicenter of British Christianity, rather than in a small parish church, is not incidental background. This woman's narrow views are not rare or localized but are indicative of the moral and spiritual failure of the nation. This poem may satirize Britain's faithful as inveterate hypocrites, but it is satire born in a belief that the tenets of Christianity are true, however rarely practiced by its adherents. The poem does not mourn a lost faith so much as it excoriates a spiritually lazy nation truly to take up the cross (*CP* 74–75).

Despite the savagery of some of his satires, Betjeman still held out hope for his national church. However, some of his poems do suggest the church will continue its decline owing to attitudes that militate against community. Lack of tolerance as the most common form of ecclesiastical hypocrisy is the central idea in "Diary of a Church Mouse" (1954), the first of Betjeman's "Poems in the Porch." The poem's speaker is a literal mouse, proud to be a regular communicant of a struggling parish:

> Here among long-discarded cassocks,
> Damp stools, and half-split open hassocks,
> Here where the Vicar never looks
> I nibble through old service books.

Although he seems a devout and harmless creature, gradually he reveals to us a darker side. The mouse is observing his parish's annual Harvest Festival and uses the occasion to speak badly of other mice who show up only for special occasions:

> But all the same it's strange to me
> How very full the church can be
> With people I don't see at all
> Except at Harvest Festival.

In the mind of this church mouse, if you do not come every Sunday then you should not come for feast days and special services. Unbaptized and agnostic rodents certainly have no business here, and he wants them to go away. The rich mice only come to hear the music and have no interest in supporting his parish. He wishes to exclude all mice who don't measure up to his standard of Christian observance, and in a delightful bit of ironic self-exposure Betjeman turns the satire against the tendency toward snobbish exclusivity among his own high church ilk. Thus he sneers at

> A Low Church mouse, who thinks that I
> Am too papistical, and High,
> Yet somehow doesn't think it wrong
> To munch through Harvest Evensong.

Concluding the poem with ruthless irony, Betjeman has the mouse wish that rodents could be as devoutly religious as humans. Betjeman's solutions to all these complex parish problems are simple, but that is because Christ's message was simple: spend time in prayer, observe the sacraments, and demonstrate charity (*CP* 205–7).

Demonstrating just how far from devout and tolerant Anglicans could be, "Bristol and Clifton" (1940) is a poem set in church following a service of Evening Prayer.[59] The speaker is showing off a stained-glass window memorializing the recent death of his wife, but any sympathy that this situation creates in the reader evaporates quickly as we sense his vanity and hypocrisy. To the speaker, who commissioned the window, the church is an opportunity to glorify not simply his wife's memory but his own, and a parade of vanities progresses from this point to the end of the poem. The speaker praises the execution of the window rather than confessing any desire truly to honor his late wife: "You cannot see it now, but in the day / The greens and golds are truly wonderful." When his friend offers his sympathy for the loss of his wife, the widower misquotes Shakespeare ("'The glory that men do lives after them'"), a suggestion that the window is in honor of himself rather than his wife. After all, the image of his late wife is not even central in the window but merely part of a grouping. The speaker shows this window as a demonstration of what he perceives to be his virtues: his devotion to the church, his commitment to his marital vows, his aesthetic sense and his munificence. However, Betjeman's irony reveals vices deeper than these virtues in the speaker, who unwittingly betrays his vanity and incapacity for human feeling. Pointing out this window becomes moreover an occasion for the speaker to comment on how his church has resisted the rising tide of Anglo-Catholicism:

> Our only ritual here is with the Plate;
> I think we make it dignified enough.
> I take it up myself, and afterwards,
> Count the Collection on the vestry safe.

As he rattles on it becomes clear that Betjeman's point is to satirize the vanity and hypocrisy of the scions of the Church of England, particularly the mix of reverse-snobbery and greed that characterize those parishes of low church or protestant leanings. As people's warden, the speaker, who fears and loathes high church ritual, has even had new radiators installed so as to prevent any future construction of altars. He despises kneeling and genuflection, and when his interlocutor spots a lone woman still praying in the church and suggests they take the conversation outside, the speaker dismisses her as some sort of alien Catholic who needs to be hastened out since the service has ended: "She cannot / Be Loyal Church of England." The poem ends just as abruptly, and we are left with the statement that the church should be locked up and the lights turned out. A more apt symbol for the coldly hypocritical heart could not be found than the action of locking the door and extinguishing the light, which symbolizes Betjeman's continuing anxiety over the decline of the church (*CP* 56–58).[60]

Though the church and its spirit of communal inclusivity was under threat from the snobbish attitudes of its own parishioners, as well as from bishops whose imperative was fiscal rather than spiritual, he never relinquished his hope that the church would endure. The survival of parishes urban and rural delighted and surprised Betjeman, causing him to celebrate with rhetorical flourishes of unchecked emotion. It is small surprise that a remote and almost perfectly preserved rural parish church should excite Betjeman to expressions of ecstasy. As he wrote in 1948 of St. Protus and St. Hyacinth, a church in Cornwall, there was much more to its worth than its beauty: "But chiefly it is a living church whose beauty makes you gasp, whose silent peace brings you to your knees, even if you kneel on the hard stone and slate of the floor, worn smooth by generations of worshippers."[61] There was likewise more to the vitality of St. Endellion, another Cornish church, than its living faith: "Why does St Endellion seem to go on praying when there is no one in it? The Blessed Sacrament is not reserved here, yet the building is alive."[62] The point which Betjeman makes in both instances is that these churches embody a communal spirit of living English history. It was not the obvious pastoralism of St. Endellion or of St. Protus and St. Hyacinth that aroused him, however; the same passion could be aroused by an unremarkable church in an urban setting. St. Mark's, Swindon, for example, merits no mention in Betjeman's exhaustive *Collins Guide*, but he devoted an entire 1948 radio broadcast to the place. There was nothing attractive about Swindon, Betjeman confessed. St. Mark's was not its historic parish church or even an illustrative example of Victorian church building. What attracted him was that it was a living church, but how it remained so vibrant is something of a mystery to him: "I don't know why it is St Mark's parish hangs together and is a living community, full of life and spirit." Perhaps it is because St. Mark's was built for the rail workers of the Great Western; it was a church of men whose work was not "soul-destroying" but was "really worth doing and not beneath the dignity of man." Such were the men of St. Mark's, those dedicated souls of the Great Western Railway who sacrificed their rare holidays and worked without pay to build a daughter church, St. Saviour's, "entirely by voluntary labour and in spare time."[63]

Betjeman goes to great lengths to praise the unassuming parish of St. Mark's, whose church could never inspire the church crawler but could kindle the believer. The setting, he explains at length, leaves much to be desired: "Whistles and passing trains disturb the services; diesel fumes blacken the leaves and tombstones and eat into the carved stonework of the steeple. No matter, it is a great church and though it isn't much to look at, it is for me the greatest church in England." It would be hard to find a clearer (or more hyperbolic) statement of Betjeman's interest in the church as something more than a place of beauty and history, and he goes on to explain just what he means by "great": "For not carved stones nor screens and beautiful altars, nor lofty arcades, nor gilded canopies, but the priests who minister and the people who worship make a church great."[64] Indeed, it is the faith of the parish of St. Mark's that gives it its beauty as well as its communal spirit. Across England, churches are decaying, their doors shuttered. In the face of this despair, Betjeman turns to St. Mark's:

> If ever I feel England is pagan, if ever I feel the poor old C. of E. is tottering to its grave, I revisit St Mark's, Swindon. That corrects the impression

at once. A simple and definite faith is taught; St Mark's and its daughter churches are crowded. Swindon, so ugly to look at, to the eyes of the architectural student, glows golden as the New Jerusalem to eyes that look beyond the brick and stone.

What makes Swindon different? To Betjeman, "Swindon is largely a Christian town and much of the credit for that goes to the priests and people of St Mark's. It is not Sabbatarian and smug. It has its cinemas and theatres and art gallery and library and sports grounds and good old Swindon town Football Club—but its churches are part of its life. That is the unusual thing about Swindon."[65] It was the churches of Swindon, especially St. Mark's and St. Saviour's, that instilled in Betjeman the importance of a simple but vital faith. The ornate and expensive elements of Anglo-Catholicism are ultimately inessential: "I would sooner be on my knees within the wooden walls of St Saviour's than leaning elegantly forward in a cushioned pew in an Oxford college chapel—that is to say if I am to realise there is something beyond this world worth thinking about."[66]

The idea of the value of church based in its communal potency and vitality is at the heart of what is probably Betjeman's finest poem, "St. Saviour's, Aberdeen Park, Highbury, London, N." (1946). This poem is a celebration of an urban church that, like St. Saviour's, Swindon, has no obvious aesthetic or historical resonance, and yet it becomes the setting for Betjeman's plainest assertion of his Christian faith. Built in the affluent North London suburb of Highbury in 1865, St. Saviour's is a masterpiece in the decorated style of the Arts and Crafts movement and was Betjeman's parents' church. (Ernest Betjemann and Bess Dawson both grew up in Highbury and had close affiliations with St. Saviour's.) In this poem St. Saviour's is at the point of abandonment. Owing to demographic change, the parish began a slow decline after World War II; it was at last declared redundant in 1981 and the church closed.[67] Betjeman would not have been surprised to see its eventual closure, but it would have disheartened him. It is therefore appropriate that his clearest statement of religious commitment is made in a church on the verge of redundancy, since his spiritual commitment to Christ is intrinsically connected to his intellectual commitment to England's past. "St. Saviour's, Aberdeen Park" functions as so many of Betjeman's poems do: it celebrates England through the medium of its established church. Since for Betjeman Anglicanism is ultimately fundamental to being English, to abandon the Saviour is to reject England itself. As a consequence of the church's decline, English culture is in a sadly derelict state, and England's restoration demands a national commitment to its established church with the English populace kneeling alongside the poet, an image that concludes this powerful and affecting poem (*CP* 126–27).

In the first stanza Betjeman describes a return journey to Highbury, just after the end of the Second World War, to see the church once again. As he approaches the once-familiar neighborhood by trolley, he glimpses the church spire, distorted now by the view through the maze of streetcar poles and wires, but still visible, still "peculiar" as it "Bulges over the housetops, polychromatic and high." The second stanza depicts the poet alighting from the trolley in Highbury and describes his astonishment at the change that has been wrought over this once prosperous neighborhood. Now Highbury is the epicenter of "weariest worn-out London," and the neighborhood church seems to be all that is left of what once was a vital and affluent community. Yet St. Saviour's, though surrounded by vacant lots, is still afloat, the only vibrant sight on the street: "For over the waste of willow-herb, look at her, sailing clear, / A great Victorian church, tall, unbroken and bright / In a sun that's setting in Willesden and saturating us here." Despite the waste about the church, the water imagery ("sailing," "saturating") suggests the baptismal possibilities of renewal. Stanza three gives us a memory of Edwardian Highbury, prosperous, tasteful, if a bit dull:

> The brougham that crunched the gravel . . .
> Geranium-beds for the lawn . . .
> A separate tradesman's entrance, straw in the mews behind,
> . . . .
> Solid Italianate houses for the solid commercial mind.

Though the church is not mentioned in this stanza, the point is to reveal the typically unreflective Christian who worshipped at St. Saviour's at the turn of the last century. The fourth stanza more directly connects the church to its neighborhood by asserting the social function the church once offered. Then, elegantly dressed worshippers "stepped out in flounces . . . [or] in spats / To shadowy stained-glass

matins or gas-lit evensong." Now, the daily attendance of divine service
has disappeared along with the quiet opulence of Highbury; perhaps
not coincidentally, the "tall neglected houses" have now been "divided
into flats," and the shift in demography seems to have resulted in the
decline of the church. In stanza five, the poet enters the quiet church
and is at first amused at the memory of sleeping through sermons, then
quickly awestruck at the awareness that God is still here. He recalls
the stunning interior of the church and the engrained images of worshipping there: the "red-brick transept" and its "cruciform" shape, the
decoratively painted tile "encaustics" on the floor, the "coloured brick-
work," the "stencilled chancel," and the "once familiar pew." As a flood
of ancestral memory washes over him, the poet "kneel[s] in the presence of God."[68]

In the sixth and final stanza, the poet reaffirms his faith in a statement at once profound, beautiful, and mysterious:

> Wonder beyond Time's wonders, that Bread so white and small
> Veiled in golden curtains, too mighty for men to see,
> Is the Power which sends the shadows up this polychrome wall,
> Is God who created the present, the chain-smoking millions and me;
> Beyond the throb of the engines is the throbbing heart of all—
> Christ, at this Highbury altar, I offer myself To Thee.

The poet's devotion to the "Bread so white and small" is part of a larger
complex of attitudes which include filial piety, affection for the family church and neighborhood, an awareness of beauty, and a grievous
sense of the vital past now lost forever. This is not to impugn the sincerity of Betjeman's religious convictions, only to suggest that they are
intrinsically bound to his cultural convictions. For him, God may be
transcendent, "too mighty for men to see," but God is also immanent,
the "Power" sending at this moment "shadows up this polychrome wall."
What this means in practical terms is that God is culturally immanent,
integral in the Anglican and English traditions; religion being culturally significant, a healthy church is a sign of a healthy English culture. By the same token, a loss of community deals a dire blow to the
survival of the church—at least to the survival of this neighborhood
church, which suffers as faith seems to dry up around it. Of course, one
cannot help but notice Betjeman's separation of himself from "the

chain-smoking millions." Is this cultural snobbery to blame for the church's loss of significance in the lives of Highbury's newer denizens? Here, Betjeman is asserting that he feels culturally and spiritually disjointed from, if not superior to, those who live ritualistic, mindless lives. In 1961 he wrote, "Although we are all equal in the eyes of God, we are patently not equal to each other."[69] Although he distinguishes himself from the masses, he understands that God is there for the chain-smoking Highbury infidels, too, just as he is there for him; one might even argue that at this moment Betjeman's persona becomes aware that through the brotherhood of sin and the love of God he is united with all humanity. Even if his persona remains mired in social and spiritual distinctions, this does not diminish the validity of what the poem acknowledges; such implicit snobbism in fact demonstrates it. Human or institutional efforts to provide solace for sociological problems will fail because people are sinners, and Betjeman's persona confesses that he remains one too. It is the function of the "Bread so white and small" to save souls, not to solve sociological problems. The Eucharist operates not in human time but God's, and its miracle is divine rather than sublunary; this is the true "Wonder beyond Time's wonders."[70]

However, the greatest feature of this poem lies in the fact that it embodies Anglicanism in all its manifestations: it embraces the idea of community, it suggests a dialectic of faith and doubt, and it celebrates the mystery of the incarnational nature of God made present within the Eucharist. The mystery, or wonder, arises from Christ's presence in the bread. It is veiled from our eyes, which adds to its mystery and our wonder, but it is present nonetheless for us to receive, and with it the gift of salvation and eternity. God is incarnate not just in the bread, however, but in the church itself, where the poet kneels, and even beyond the church, which cannot contain God. If one listens—and the poet must grant that with the noise of modern technology it is often difficult to hear with spiritual ears—one can hear the pulsations of God's love. In a metaphor that neatly echoes and overturns Henry Adams' rejection of the Virgin as he kneels before the dynamo, Betjeman finds that no machine, no creation of man, can shut out the incarnate God from human life: "Beyond the throb of the engines is the throbbing heart of all."[71] This rediscovery of the incarnational nature of God is what explains the poem's last line, which is as clear an assessment of Christian commitment as Betjeman ever offers: "Christ, at this Highbury altar, I offer myself To Thee." Such commitment is in keeping with the Anglican spirituality of incarnational piety. Christian faith may begin with a belief in the blessed event of the nativity, but the committed believer is required to discover and to obey God's will. What Betjeman implies is nothing less than a total offering of himself.[72]

Self-sacrifice was a concept that Betjeman could embrace. The thought that the nation was sacrificing its communal faith, however, was appalling, and he understood what the loss of something so vital and irreplaceable meant. His poems are united in their appreciation of the basic sense of community that the Anglican church offers, of the social cohesion that the church attempts to create; they address the fundamental role church plays in helping society to be a community. Though at times his poetry mourns the loss of community and church, at other times it embraces a hope that the church will survive, and along with it that singular importance of community. Whether fearing its loss or celebrating its survival, his poems make clear that communal identity is a fundamental contribution of the Anglican church. This is an inherently English idea, one shared even by admittedly agnostic writers. It is the central theme of Philip Larkin's poem "Church Going," whose speaker does not understand the church and yet is surprised by being drawn to it: "It pleases me to stand in silence here; / A serious house on serious earth it is."[73] Likewise for the agnostic Simon Jenkins, churches serve

> as witness to the bonds that have brought the English people together in village and town through a thousand years of history. . . . It is through the churches of England that we learn who we were and thus who we are and might become. Lose that learning and we lose the collective memory that is the essence of human society. We must remember.[74]

For Betjeman, the remembrance of churches is equally vital to cultural identity. His poems tell us that community is threatened when the church is threatened, for the church is a spirit that breathes life into a society, and society will not endure without community. It is a social virtue that must somehow be nurtured, and this will happen, his poems insist, where churches thrive. And thus he concludes *A Passion for Churches*:

But still the faith of centuries is seen
In those who walk to church across the green.
The faith of centuries is in the sound
Of Easter bells that ring all Norfolk round;
And though for church we may not seem to care
It's deeply part of us. Thank God it's there.[75]

Notes

Introduction

1. John Betjeman, "Pugin: A Great Victorian Architect" (BBC radio, 15 September 1952), in *Coming Home: An Anthology of His Prose, 1920–1977*, ed. Candida Lycett Green (London: Vintage, 1997), 275.

2. A title he earned in part because his public image was so lovable and in part because of his eccentric propensity for appearing in public in the company of his childhood teddy bear. It is often assumed that Betjeman was dubbed the "teddy bear to the nation" by a *Times* headline, upon the announcement of his appointment to the laureateship in 1972. However, that headline, "By Appointment: Teddy Bear to the Nation," was not actually used until ten years later, when Alan Bell profiled the publication of Betjeman's *Uncollected Poems* (*Times*, 20 September 1982, 5).

3. These included a star-studded West End charity gala attended by the Prince of Wales; a Cornish birthday party and concert; a steam locomotive dedication; numerous literary events and festivals; exhibitions at the Bodleian, the British Library, and Sir John Soane's Museum; a week of dedicated Betjeman-themed programming on BBC radio 4; three new films on BBC Two; and rebroadcasts of Betjeman's own documentary films on BBC Four and ITV.

4. "1830–1930—Still Going Strong: A Guide to the Recent History of Interior Decoration," *Architectural Review* (May 1930); qtd. in Timothy Mowl, *Stylistic Cold Wars: Betjeman Versus Pevsner* (London: John Murray, 2000), 30. As Mowl notes, at the beginning of Betjeman's career as an assistant editor at the *Archie Rev*—as he jocularly referred to it—he was "a functional

modernist, though he remained, instinctively and paradoxically, a sentimental traditionalist" (32).

5   Stephen Neill, *Anglicanism* (Harmondsworth, UK: Penguin, 1958), 418. The vagueness of Anglicanism can be frustrating. According to Neill, "the non-Anglican Churches are sometimes driven to distraction and infuriation by the uncertainties of Anglican action and the indefinable quality of Anglican thought" (387). For instance, the Anglican Communion is catholic but reformed, and it is nonconfessional but creedal; its traditional sources of authority—Scripture, tradition, reason (and in moments when these three offer no security, many Anglicans rely, as did Betjeman, on the even shakier authority of personal experience)—are no less seemingly exclusionary and mutually contradictory.

6   "'Oh, to be in England . . .'" *Listener*, 11 March 1943, 295. This radio address has been retitled "Coming Home" in some collections.

7   "'Oh, to be in England . . . ,'" 296.

8   Betjeman's literary relationships have been fully explored by Bevis Hillier in three masterful and flawless volumes of biography: *Young Betjeman* (London: John Murray, 1988); *John Betjeman: New Fame, New Love* (London: John Murray, 2002); and *Betjeman: The Bonus of Laughter* (London: John Murray, 2004). It is worth noting here in brief Betjeman's personal connections with these three poets. Eliot by coincidence was one of Betjeman's teachers at the Highgate Junior School in London; much later they developed a professional and eventually a personal friendship after Eliot pursued Betjeman as an author for Faber and Faber. Through their mutual and serious commitment to their Christian faith and through their shared delight in the quirks and eccentricities of English life, their personal bond grew (see John Betjeman, *Letters, Volume One: 1926 to 1951*, ed. Candida Lycett Green [London: Methuen, 1994, 2006], 142). Auden and Betjeman had known each other since their days together at Oxford, and it was Auden who put Eliot onto Betjeman's poetry in 1936. Auden wrote an admiring preface to an American collection of Betjeman's writings, in which he asserted that he was "violently jealous" of Betjeman's poetry (introduction to *Slick but Not Streamlined: Poems and Short Pieces by John Betjeman* [Garden City, N.Y.: Doubleday, 1947], 9); he also dedicated his long poetic masterpiece, *The Age of Anxiety* (1944–1946), to Betjeman and referred to Betjeman's "The Attempt" as among the most beautiful love poems ever written (see Betjeman, *Letters, Volume One*, 371). As for Thomas, a much more retiring and secluded figure than either Eliot or Auden, Betjeman was one of his earliest proponents, writing the introduction to Thomas' *Songs at the Year's Turning: Poems, 1942–1954* (London:

Hart-Davis, 1955), 11–14. Thomas was among those who surprised Betjeman one November 1981 morning to present him in person with *A Garland for the Laureate: Poems Presented to Sir John Betjeman on His 75th Birthday* (Stratford-upon-Avon: Celandine, 1981), a volume, edited by Roger Pringle, containing poems written in his honor by more than twenty poets.

9   Qtd. in Lee Oser, *The Return of Christian Humanism: Chesterton, Eliot, Tolkien, and the Romance of History* (Columbia: University of Missouri Press, 2007), 46.

10 Qtd. in Arthur Kirsch, *Auden and Christianity* (New Haven: Yale University Press, 2005), 1–2.

11 Qtd. in William V. Davis, *R. S. Thomas: Poetry and Theology* (Waco, Tex.: Baylor University Press, 2007), 7.

12 Hillier, *Bonus of Laughter*, 618. "Betjemanesque" now appears in the *Oxford English Dictionary*.

13 John Summerson, "In the Betjeman Country," *New Statesman*, 4 October 1952, 382; qtd. in Hillier, *New Fame, New Love*, 482.

14 This is the first study of Betjeman to treat his prose and poetry together in extended analysis, a task made much easier owing to the efforts of Stephen Games, whose four recently published anthologies make a significant portion of Betjeman's prose easily accessible at last: *Trains and Buttered Toast: Selected Radio Talks* (London: John Murray, 2006); *Tennis Whites and Teacakes* (London: John Murray, 2007); *Sweet Songs of Zion: Selected Radio Talks* (London: Hodder & Stoughton, 2007); and *Betjeman's England* (London: John Murray, 2009). Moreover, reading his poetry and prose together, the possibilities of which are suggested in Games' second anthology, works to reveal how the two genres mutually reinforce and influence each other. Familiar ideas and images in his poetry are often worked out simultaneously in his prose.

15 *Daily Herald*, 19 June 1945; qtd. in Hillier, *Bonus of Laughter*, 331.

16 Osbert Lancaster, "John Betjeman," *Strand*, November 1946, 52.

17 "The Outer Suburbs," in *Mount Zion* (London: The James Press, 1931), 44.

18 "Alas, Poor London," *Strand*, November 1946, 55.

19 *Metro-land* (BBC Two, 26 February 1973, prod. Edward Mirzoeff), in *The Best of Betjeman*, ed. John Guest (London: John Murray, 1978), 220. In his introduction to *Betjeman's England*, a new anthology of Betjeman's film scripts, Stephen Games argues effectively that his writing for television was in effect an extension of his poetic imagination. He quotes Edward Mirzoeff, Betjeman's producer, about the poetic inspiration of writing for television: "Then he'd sit in the cutting room with his A4 pads, writing, for weeks and weeks, sitting in front of the editing machine, running

film sequences backwards and forwards so their rhythms would sink in, waiting for inspiration from 'the Management' [as Betjeman sometimes referred to God] up above. There were days when he'd only write two lines and you had to press him to finish because of the finance people looking over your shoulder with slide rules." (qtd. in Games, introduction to *Betjeman's England*, 25).

20 According to Bevis Hillier, *Metro-land* "was recognized not only as a high point in television history, but as a benediction on suburbia" (*Bonus of Laughter*, 352).

21 Dennis Brown, *John Betjeman*, Writers and Their Work, n.s. (Plymouth: Northcote House Publishers, 1999), 1.

22 Though Betjeman was routinely praised by critics in the better literary reviews and journals, only a few substantial critical essays have heretofore been published on Betjeman in scholarly journals, and only one of these is exclusively about his poetry; these include Leena K. Schröder, "Heterotopian Constructions of Englishness in the Work of John Betjeman," *Critical Survey* 10.2 (1998): 15–34; Kevin J. Gardner, "Anglicanism and the Poetry of John Betjeman," *Christianity and Literature* 53.3 (2004): 361–83; Mark Tewdwr-Jones, "'Oh, the planners did their best': The Planning Films of John Betjeman," *Planning Perspectives* 20 (2005): 389–411; Philip Payton, "John Betjeman and the Holy Grail: One Man's Celtic Quest," *Cornish Studies* 15 (2007): 185–208; and Peter J. Lowe, "The Church as a Building and the Church as a Community in the Work of John Betjeman," *Christianity and Literature* 57.4 (2008): 559–81. In addition to the present volume there are two other significant and newly published academic monographs: Greg Morse, *John Betjeman: Reading the Victorians* (Eastbourne, UK: Sussex Academic, 2008), and Philip Payton, *John Betjeman and Cornwall: "The Celebrated Cornish Nationalist"* (Exeter: University of Exeter Press, 2010). It is clear from the growing number of publications that Betjeman's standing in the academic community is on the rise.

Several other academic studies are worth mentioning in this context. In addition to Dennis Brown's brief but excellent monograph (see n. 21 above) and individual chapters in Geoffrey Harvey's *The Romantic Tradition in Modern English Poetry* (New York: St. Martin's, 1986; first published as "Poetry of Commitment: John Betjeman's Later Writing," *Dalhousie Review* 56 [1976]: 112–24), David Gervais' *Literary England's: Versions of "Englishness" in Modern Writing* (Cambridge: Cambridge University Press, 1993), Richard Hoffpauir's *The Art of Restraint: English Poetry from Hardy to Larkin* (London: Associated University Presses, 1991), and John Bale's *Anti-Sports Sentiments in Literature: Batting for the Opposition* (London: Routledge, 2008), several important critical books include unique and insightful evaluations of Betjeman's poetry, including John Bayley's *The Power of Delight: A Lifetime in Literature* (London: Duckworth, 2005); Michael Schmidt's *The Lives of the Poets* (New York: Knopf, 1999); Craig Raine's *Haydn and the Valve Trumpet: Literary Essays* (London: Faber, 1990); Donald Davie's *Under Briggflatts* (Chicago: University of Chicago Press, 1989); Philip Larkin's *Required Writing: Miscellaneous Pieces, 1955–1982* (London: Faber, 1983); and John Sparrow's *Independent Essays* (London: Faber, 1963; rpt. Westport, Conn.: Greenwood Press, 1977).

23 Wain's hostility to Betjeman should be placed in context. These comments are extracted from Wain's review ("A Substitute for Poetry," *Observer*, 27 November 1960) of Betjeman's verse autobiography, *Summoned by Bells* (rpt. in Wain's collection, *Essays on Literature and Ideas* [London: Macmillan, 1963], 168–71), rather than a measured and objective analysis of Betjeman's oeuvre. In an early draft (1963) of his poem "Good-Bye," Betjeman satirized "review-copy Wain" (William S. Peterson, *John Betjeman: A Bibliography* [Oxford: Clarendon, 2006], 414) as among those "prigs" whose "prods" are "harmless" (*Collected Poems* [London: John Murray, 1958, 2006], 275). However, the enmity between them did not last. Wain contributed a poem to Roger Pringle's tribute collection *A Garland for the Laureate*, and in 1983 he appeared with a group of Betjeman's friends, admirers, and fellow poets (including Kingsley Amis, Philip Larkin, Stephen Spender, R. S. Thomas, Elizabeth Jennings, and Alan Brownjohn) on a BBC television production, *Time with Betjeman*.

24 This hostility to Betjeman's success was a concern of the first full-length study of Betjeman, Derek Stanford's *John Betjeman: A Study* (London: Spearman, 1961). Stanford went to great lengths to explain the causes of the amazing popularity of Betjeman's *Collected Poems* (1958) and to position the instant hostility of critics as a kind of confusion and anxiety about a poet's mass appeal: "Is Mr Betjeman, as a poet, hindered or furthered by his sure possession of the public ear? Success is the fulfilment of the middle-brow writer; perfection, that of the high-brow artist" (10). The argument that positions Betjeman's talent in inverse relation to his popularity has been analyzed and debunked most thoroughly in Patrick Taylor-Martin's *John Betjeman: His Life and Work* (London: Lane, 1983), 10–14. In addition to sources cited above and elsewhere in this introduction, other early positive evaluations of Betjeman include the following: Auden, introduction to *Slick but Not Streamlined*; Jocelyn Brooke, *Ronald Firbank and John Betjeman*, Writers and Their Work 153 (London: Longmans, 1962); R. E. Wiehe, "Summoned by Nostalgia: John Betjeman's Poetry: An Appreciation," *Arizona Quarterly* 19.1 (1963): 37–49; Ralph J. Mills, "John Betjeman's Poetry," *Descant* (Spring 1969): 2–18; Philip Larkin,

"It Could Only Happen in England: A Study of John Betjeman's Poems for American Readers," *Cornhill Magazine* (Fall 1971): 21–36; Peter Thomas, "Reflections on the Collected Poems of John Betjeman," *Western Humanities Review* 27 (1973): 289–94; and John Press, *John Betjeman*, Writers and Their Work 237 (London: Longman, 1974).

25 A. A. Gill, "The Truth Is Out: His Poetry Had No Sole," *Sunday Times*, 20 August 2006, http://www.timesonline.co.uk/article/0,,2101231589I.html.

26 There have been, in addition to the scholarly works cited above, a handful of excellent, shorter articles on individual poems by Betjeman; these include Michael Cameron Andrews, "Betjeman's 'Senex,'" *Explicator* 43.3 (1985): 40–41; Bill Ruddick, "'Some ruin-bibber, randy for antique': Philip Larkin's Response to the Poetry of John Betjeman," *Critical Quarterly* 28.4 (1986): 63–69; Edward Wilson, "Betjeman's Riddel Posts: An Echo of Ninian Comper," *Review of English Studies* 42 (1991): 541–50; John V. McDermott, "Betjeman's 'The Arrest of Oscar Wilde at the Cadogan Hotel,'" *Explicator* 57.3 (1999): 165–66; Kevin J. Gardner, "John Betjeman's 'Bristol and Clifton': Echoes of Robert Browning's 'My Last Duchess,'" *ANQ* 19.3 (2006): 35–38; Christopher Fletcher, "John Betjeman's 'Before the Anaesthetic, or a Real Fright': A Source for Philip Larkin's 'Aubade,'" *Notes and Queries* 54.2 (2007): 179–81; Kate Macdonald, "The Travels of John Betjeman's Literary Voice in 'The Arrest of Oscar Wilde at the Cadogan Hotel': From the 1890s to the 1920s, and Back Again," *BELL: Belgian Journal of English Language and Literatures* n.s. 5 (2007): 59–66.

27 As Greg Morse has written recently in his detailed and impressive study of the powerful pull of Victorianism upon Betjeman, "The fact is that Betjeman never quite fits in anywhere. His identity depends on contrariness; hence he is always a square peg in a round hole or a round peg in a square hole—often for the sheer enjoyment, one feels, of so being" (*John Betjeman: Reading the Victorians*, 189).

28 John Sparrow, "The Poetry of John Betjeman," in *Independent Essays*, 178; rpt. of preface to Betjeman's *Selected Poems* (London: John Murray, 1948), ix–xxii.

29 Hillier argues that Betjeman was "much more tolerant towards the modernists than they were towards him. . . . What he objected to in modernism was . . . its authoritarian stance, its insistence that all should follow its diktats or be pariahs" (*Bonus of Laughter*, 605).

30 Stephen Games illustrates this surprising open-mindedness toward modernism with Betjeman's praise for the architecture of Gropius and for prefabricated American construction (introduction to *Tennis Whites and Teacakes*, 13–14).

31 Mowl, *Stylistic Cold Wars*, 153.

32 See, e.g., Ian Hamilton, "Tripping Up," *New Statesman,* 22 and 29 December 1978, 881; qtd. in Hillier, *Bonus of Laughter*, 597.

33 In his own lifetime Betjeman enjoyed praise from the pens of fellow poets Philip Larkin, W. H. Auden, Kingsley Amis, Charles Causley, Donald Davie, Craig Raine, and Elizabeth Jennings. In more recent days, poets Andrew Motion, Hugo Williams, and Anthony Thwaite have also contributed significant encomia for Betjeman's achievements as a poet.

34 Hillier's masterpiece of biographical scholarship is particularly useful to anyone wishing to trace the history of Betjemanian reception. A good overview and summation of the spectrum of critical responses to Betjeman's poetry can be found in the epilogue to Hillier's final volume (592–618). In conjunction with the centenary of Betjeman's birth, Hillier authorized the publication of a one-volume abridgment of his trilogy, *John Betjeman: The Biography* (London: John Murray, 2006). In direct competition with these volumes is a shorter and splashier biography, though it is not so well researched as Hillier's. A. N. Wilson's *Betjeman* (London: Hutchinson, 2006) is an interpretive and psychological study, with an excessive emphasis upon Betjeman's surfeit of guilt, and is in other respects heavily indebted to Hillier. While Wilson sheds some helpful light, Hillier remains the authoritative source for information on Betjeman, and I have turned to his three biographical volumes for most of the essential questions about Betjeman's life. A further volume that may be of interest is Frank Delaney's *Betjeman Country* (London: Hodder, 1983), a sort of *vade mecum* travel guide to the places of value in the life and writings of Betjeman.

35 Betjeman to Oliver Stonor, 7 August 1948, in *Letters, Volume One*, 444.

36 Evelyn Waugh to Betjeman, 19 January 1947, in *The Letters of Evelyn Waugh*, ed. Mark Amory (London: Weidenfeld, 1980), 246.

37 "Design for a New Cathedral," *Daily Telegraph*, 3 September 1951, 4.

38 See L. William Countryman, *The Poetic Imagination: An Anglican Spiritual Tradition* (London: Darton, 1999), Traditions of Christian Spirituality, ed. Philip Sheldrake. It was perhaps Alan Neame who first posited that Betjeman was not just a poet and an Anglican but in fact an Anglican poet ("Poet of Anglicanism," *Commonweal*, 4 December 1959, 282–84).

39 A. M. Allchin, "Anglican Spirituality," in *The Study of Anglicanism*, ed. Stephen Sykes and John Booty (London: SPCK, 1988), 319.

40 It was a rare topic that did not elicit some comment about churches. He even discussed the architecture of entertainment (theaters, fairs, and exhibition and music halls), for instance, with recourse to an analogy of

church building ("Pleasures and Palaces," in *Tennis Whites and Teacakes*, 249–56; originally published in *Diversion: Twenty-Two Authors on the Lively Arts*, ed. John Sutro [London: Parrish, 1950]: 17–24).

41 Owing to the immediate popularity of these readings, a collection of the first six poems was hastened to press and published as *Poems in the Porch* (London: SPCK, 1954). A complete edition following the end of the run was not published until 2008, when my edition of *Poems in the Porch: The Radio Poems of John Betjeman* (London: Continuum) was published. This is the only complete edition of this series of radio poems and publishes for the first time a number of Betjeman's poems heretofore unpublished. For more on the history of these poems, see my introduction to *Poems in the Porch* (2008), 13–31.

42 *Church Poems* was not to be the last word from Betjeman on the subject of churches. Two posthumous collections are *In Praise of Churches* (London: John Murray, 1996), a work lovingly illustrated with the watercolors of Paul Hogarth and containing both poetry and prose, and my edition of his religious poems, *Faith and Doubt of John Betjeman: An Anthology of Betjeman's Religious Verse* (London: Continuum, 2005).

43 *A Passion for Churches* (BBC Two, 7 December 1974, prod. Edward Mirzoeff), in *Betjeman's England*, 200.

44 Games, introduction to *Tennis Whites and Teacakes*, 18.

45 "Christian Architecture," *Britain Today* (February 1951), 19.

46 Betjeman to Alan Pryce-Jones, 29 July 1950, in *Letters, Volume One*, 518.

Chapter 1

1 John Betjeman, unpublished essay (written prior to 1961), qtd. in Hillier, *Bonus of Laughter*, 607–8.

2 Betjeman to William Plomer, 26 July 1947, in *Letters, Volume One*, 418.

3 Betjeman to Roy Harrod, 25 March 1939, in *Letters, Volume One*, 224.

4 Auberon Waugh, "Is Trifle Sufficient?" *Spectator*, 26 May 1984, 6.

5 Taylor-Martin, *John Betjeman*, 50. This position was also taken in Phil Edwards' highly rated television biography, "The Real John Betjeman" (*Real Lives*, Channel 4, 23 April 2000, dir. Marion Milne).

6 The first film in a two-part series called *Thank God It's Sunday* (BBC One, 10 December 1972, prod. Jonathan Stedall), in *Betjeman's England*, 165–66.

7 Payton, "John Betjeman and the Holy Grail," 185.

8 John Betjeman, *Summoned by Bells* (London: John Murray, 1960), 4.

9 *Summoned by Bells*, 4.

10 Philip Larkin, "Betjeman en Bloc," *Listen: A Review of Poetry and Criticism* 3.2 (1959): 14–23; qtd. in Fletcher, "John Betjeman's 'Before the Anaesthetic, or a Real Fright,'" 180.

11 "How to Look at a Church" (BBC radio, 31 August 1938), *Listener*, 8 September 1938, 486.

12 "The Lighting of Churches," *Country Churchman*, November 1953, 4–5; rpt. in *Tennis Whites and Teacakes*, 368.

13 Betjeman to Oliver Stonor, 7 August 1948, in *Letters, Volume One*, 444.

14 "To Uffington Ringers," in *Diversion*, ed. Hester W. Chapman and Princess Romanovsky-Pavlovsky (London: Collins, 1946), 160. The poem has never been added to Betjeman's *Collected Poems*.

15 Betjeman to Evelyn Waugh, 12 January 1947, in *Letters, Volume One*, 403.

16 "London's Least-Tasted Pleasure," *Illustrated London News* (June 1971), 25.

17 Brown, *John Betjeman*, 51.

18 Betjeman to Gerard Irvine, 30 September 1938, in *Letters, Volume One*, 214.

19 Betjeman to Ninian Comper, 12 October 1939, in *Letters, Volume One*, 243.

20 *English Cities and Small Towns* (London: Collins, 1943), 12. Excerpted as "Provincial Towns" in *Slick but Not Streamlined*, 116.

21 "Blisland," from the television film series *John Betjeman's ABC of Churches* (BBC, 15 May 1960, prod. Kenneth Savidge), in *Betjeman's England*, 90.

22 Betjeman, foreword to *The Altar Steps*, by Compton Mackenzie (London: Macdonald, 1956), viii.

23 "Billy Graham," *Spectator*, 12 March 1954, 282–83.

24 "Selling Our Churches," *Spectator*, 2 April 1954, 383–84.

25 "Pleasures and Palaces," in *Tennis Whites and Teacakes*, 250–51.

26 "Wartime Tastes in Reading" (BBC radio, 4 September 1944), in *Trains and Buttered Toast*, 150–51.

27 See chapters 4 and 5 for my discussion of the latter two poems, which, like "Christmas," were conceived during Betjeman's crucial theological crisis of 1946–1947.

28 Sermon delivered at St. Matthew's Church, Northampton, in *Five Sermons by Laymen* (Northampton: Dickens, 1946), 7–11. Apparently Betjeman hated this experience, describing his anxieties in a letter to Anthony Barnes a week later. In addition to stage fright before a congregation of six hundred, Betjeman endured the distress of having to follow his self-described "great enemy" and former tutor C. S. Lewis, who had preached the previous week (*Letters, Volume One*, 389). All emphasis is in the original unless otherwise noted.

29 "Billy Graham," 282.

30 "John Betjeman Replies," *Spectator*, 8 October 1954, 443.

31 "City and Suburban," *Spectator*, 6 July 1956, 14.

32 Foreword to *The Word Is the Seed: Meditations Starting from the Bible*, by George Appleton (London: SPCK, 1976), vii.

33 Betjeman to Evelyn Waugh, 3 February 1947, in *Letters, Volume One*, 405.

34 This letter is reprinted as "The Christian's Way," in *Tennis Whites and Teacakes*, 431–33. Quotations from this letter are from this edition. (The letter is also published in *Letters, Volume One*, 223–25.)

35 Though Betjeman was clearly not by any stretch a theologian, A. N. Wilson, author of a rather unflattering biography of Lewis (*C. S. Lewis: A Biography* [London: Collins, 1990]), asserts that he was "the best apologist for Anglicanism of his generation, far more persuasive, because far more modest, far less bossy, than his old tutor C. S. Lewis" (*Betjeman*, 310). The antipathy between Lewis and Betjeman has been well rehearsed by his primary biographer, Bevis Hillier (*Young Betjeman*, 135–38, 183–86), and much of this material has since been reiterated by Wilson (*Betjeman*, 51, 54–55, 69–72).

36 "N.W.5 & N.6," *Collected Poems*, 231; *Summoned by Bells*, 18. The church, built in 1852–1853, still stands. It is in the South Camden Deanery of the Diocese of London.

37 Though the church and parish were relatively new (the church was consecrated in 1896), it was demolished in 1939. Designed in the Arts and Crafts style, which was somewhat unusual for ecclesiastical architecture, it must have been an appealing structure to Betjeman. St. Anselm's never drew a large congregation, and for financial reasons the parish was split between two others and the last service was held there in 1938 ("Davies Street: West Side," *British History Online*, http://www.british-history.ac.uk/report.aspx?compid=42109#s8).

38 The City refers to that original square-mile that was the Roman city of Londinium and is now the financial sector of London. Anchored by St. Paul's Cathedral, it is bounded by the Inns of Court to the west, Smithfield Market and Liverpool Street Station to the north, and the Tower to the east.

39 "To Stuart Piggott, 1975." "Parker's Glossary" refers to John Henry Parker's *Glossary of Architecture* (1836), though Betjeman might also have had in mind Parker's *Introduction to the Study of Gothic Architecture* (1849). Many architectural critics have suggested that Uffington is the most nearly perfect medieval church in England; see, e.g., John Betjeman, ed., *Collins Guide to English Parish Churches Including the Isle of Man* (London: Collins, 1958); David N. Durant, *The Good Church Guide* (London: Vermilion, 1995); and Simon Jenkins, *England's Thousand Best Churches* (London: Lane, 1999).

40 Betjeman wrote amusing accounts of this experience in his letters; his greatest irritation may have been having to share his spotlight with "Mr C. S. Bloody Lewis" (Betjeman to T. S. Eliot, 9 August 1939, in *Letters, Volume One*, 233).

41 Betjeman to Evelyn Waugh, Whitmonday [26 May] 1947, in *Letters, Volume One*, 411–12.

42 "Death," *Country Churchman*, April 1958, 3.

43 *Summoned by Bells*, 6. (N.b.: "nappies" are diapers and "dummies" are pacifiers.)

44 Preface to *Hymns as Poetry*, ed. Samuel Carr (London: Batsford, 1980), 7.

45 *Summoned by Bells*, 48. He also wrote of this experience in an essay in *My Oxford*, ed. Ann Thwaite (London: Robson, 1977), 60–71; rpt. as "My Oxford" in *Coming Home*, 474–82.

46 For bibliographic information, see n. 39 of this chapter; introduction n. 43.

47 Betjeman wrote amusing accounts of his experiences on such committees and organizations. See, for instance, "City and Suburban," *Spectator*, 15 November 1957, 642.

48 "St Protus and St Hyacinth, Blisland, Cornwall" (BBC radio, 21 July 1948), in *Trains and Buttered Toast*, 236.

49 "Domine Dirige Nos," *Listener*, 9 January 1941, 37–38.

50 *Summoned by Bells*, 59–60.

51 *Summoned by Bells*, 88.

52 *Summoned by Bells*, 85.

53 *Summoned by Bells*, 96.

54 Betjeman to Gerard Irvine, 13 March 1950, in *Letters, Volume One*, 508.

55 *Summoned by Bells*, 108. Recent archival research at Oxford has revealed that Betjeman misrepresented this incident for the sake of poetic license. In fact, the university allowed him to retake the exam twice, finally passing on the third try. With Lewis' permission, he was readmitted as a "Pass degree" candidate, but eventually he left Oxford for good after passing only one of the three required exams in English literature (Judith Priestman, "The Dilettante and the Dons," *Oxford Today* 18.3 [2006]: 20–23).

56 Hillier, *Bonus of Laughter*, 577.

57 Hillier, *New Fame, New Love*, 84–85.

58 Candida Lycett Green in *Letters, Volume One*, 323, 259.

59 Hillier, *New Fame, New Love*, 84.

60 F. P. Harton, *The Elements of the Spiritual Life: A Study in Ascetical Theology* (London: SPCK, 1932), 9.

61 Betjeman to T. S. Eliot, 17 December 1936, in *Letters, Volume One*, 164.

62 Betjeman to John Sparrow, 25 December 1947, in *Letters, Volume One*, 427. Sparrow was then putting the finishing touches on his edition of Betjeman's *Selected Poems* (London: John Murray, 1948), and Betjeman was writing in response to having read a draft of Sparrow's preface to this

volume, which was perhaps the first extended, insightful analysis of Betjeman's achievement in poetry.

63 Betjeman to Anne Barnes, 13 November 1947, in *Letters, Volume One*, 421–22; "Christian Architecture," 18.

64 Betjeman to Kenneth Harrison, 19 December 1947, in *Letters, Volume One*, 425.

65 By the time the chapel at King's College was completed, much of the architecture was already old-fashioned and discredited in the rest of Europe. Just as Betjeman was disparaged by post-Eliot critics as a Victorian throwback, the chapel at King's must have appeared to be an outrageous anachronism to a continental observer familiar with St. Peter's Basilica, begun in Rome a century earlier.

66 Hillier recounts the fascinating history of Betjeman's composition of this poem in *New Fame, New Love*, 387–89. It was written in 1947 but not published until 1954. Despite his self-deprecating comments to the dean of King's about this poem, Betjeman knew otherwise and said in his Christmas letter to Jock Murray that "it is the best poem I've ever written" (Hillier, *New Fame, New Love*, 400).

67 "Christmas Nostalgia" (BBC radio, 25 December 1947) was first published as "Christmas" in *Coming Home*, 212–16.

68 "Christmas," in *Coming Home*, 213.

69 "Christmas," in *Coming Home*, 215.

70 "Christmas," in *Coming Home*, 215–16.

71 Wilson, *Betjeman*, 164.

72 Betjeman to Gerard Irvine, 20 March 1947, in *Letters, Volume One*, 408.

73 Candida Lycett Green in *Letters, Volume One*, 374.

74 Wilson cites Betjeman's friend Osbert Lancaster, who reportedly said that "for Betjeman, going to church with a woman mattered more than going to bed" (*Betjeman*, 176).

75 The poem was originally intended for publication in *A Few Late Chrysanthemums* in 1954, along with "Sunday Morning, King's Cambridge" and "Christmas." However, Betjeman's publisher Jock Murray felt that the poem was too personal and deleted it just before the volume went to press. The poem was not published until after the deaths of both John and Penelope, when their daughter, Candida Lycett Green, included it in her edition of Betjeman's letters (*Letters, Volume One*, 439–40). At the behest of Bevis Hillier, the poem was at last included in Betjeman's *Collected Poems* with the publication of the 2001 edition under the title, provided by Hillier, "The Empty Pew" (395).

76 Penelope Betjeman to John Betjeman, in *Letters, Volume One*, 462.

77 John Betjeman to Penelope Betjeman, 2 June 1949, in *Letters, Volume One*, 460.
78 John Betjeman to Penelope Betjeman, 2 June 1949, in *Letters, Volume One*, 461.
79 *Moral Problems: Questions on Christianity with Answers by Prominent Churchmen* (London: Mowbray, 1952), 106–8.
80 Evelyn Waugh to Betjeman, 2(?) April 1947, May 1947, and 9 January 1947, in *Letters of Evelyn Waugh*, 248, 250, 244.
81 The sequence of action and intention within the Waugh-Betjeman epistolary exchange becomes clear in reading Amory's edition of Waugh's letters.
82 Waugh to Penelope Betjeman, 4 June 1947 and 14 July 1947, in *Letters of Evelyn Waugh*, 253, 252, 256.
83 Candida Lycett Green in *Letters, Volume One*, 373.
84 Waugh to Penelope Betjeman, 7 March 1948, in *Letters of Evelyn Waugh*, 271–72.
85 Betjeman to Waugh, 27 May 1945, in *Letters, Volume One*, 354.
86 Betjeman to Waugh, 17 September 1946 and 30 November 1946, in *Letters, Volume One*, 398, 400, 401.
87 John Betjeman, "Evelyn Waugh" (BBC radio, 14 December 1946), in *Coming Home*, 181–85.
88 Waugh to Betjeman, April 1947, in *Letters of Evelyn Waugh*, 248.
89 "The Angry Novelist," *Strand*, March 1947, 44.
90 Betjeman to Alan Pryce-Jones, 29 July 1950, in *Letters, Volume One*, 519. The bracketed text is Candida Lycett Green's.
91 Penelope Betjeman to John Betjeman, in *Letters, Volume One*, 462. Indeed, that important book of Anglican theology, *The Elements of the Spiritual Life*, was, according to their daughter, "her favourite, which she referred to constantly" (*Letters, Volume One*, 259).
92 Hillier, *New Fame, New Love*, 300–307; much of this is reiterated in Wilson, *Betjeman*, 169–74.
93 Waugh to Betjeman, 22 December 1946, 14 January 1947, and May 1947, in *Letters of Evelyn Waugh*, 242, 247, 250.
94 Waugh to Betjeman, 22 December 1946, in *Letters of Evelyn Waugh*, 243.
95 Betjeman to Samuel Gurney, 14 May 1948, in *Letters, Volume One*, 444.
96 Betjeman to Waugh, 28 February 1948, in *Letters, Volume One*, 438. Waugh's new novel, a satire of the American funeral industry, was initially published as a single issue of *Horizon*.
97 Waugh to Penelope Betjeman, 7 January 1950, in *Letters of Evelyn Waugh*, 317–18.

98 Betjeman would continue to praise Waugh for each subsequent novel in occasional letters to him in the 1950s and 1960s (*Letters, Volume Two: 1951 to 1984*, ed. Candida Lycett Green [London: Methuen, 1995, 2006], 42, 80–81, 178–79, and 278–79.

99 Waugh's own family members tended to look on this claim as specious and eccentric; see Alexander Waugh, *Fathers and Sons: The Autobiography of a Family* (New York: Talese, 2004), 394. Even A. N. Wilson, who proved all too hasty to attribute extramarital affairs to John Betjeman (see Kevin Gardner, "John Betjeman: Centenary Publications," *Religion and the Arts* 11.1 [2007]: 107), leans toward dismissing Waugh's boasts (*Betjeman*, 168). The editor of Waugh's letters reminds us that Waugh's propensity for exaggeration often crosses the deception border into mendacity and canard: "Somewhere there is usually a molehill from which he fashions his mountain of embellishment" (Amory, preface to *Letters of Evelyn Waugh*, viii).

100 A. L. Rowse to Candida Lycett Green, September 1992, in *Letters, Volume One*, 373.

101 Betjeman to Auberon Waugh, [1966], qtd. in Alexander Waugh, *Fathers and Sons*, 415–16. Waugh omits his grandfather's treatment of Betjeman's Anglicanism in his book.

102 In fact, Betjeman grew to be much closer with Auberon Waugh than he ever was with Evelyn. According to Candida Lycett Green, the two "were great friends—they had formed a mutual admiration society" (*Letters, Volume Two*, 490).

103 Hillier, *Bonus of Laughter*, 500.

104 A. N. Wilson is right to point out that their relationship was "marked by edginess and rivalry" (*Betjeman*, 210). Though Waugh highly praised Betjeman's next major publication, *A Few Late Chrysanthemums* (1954), in the *Sunday Times* for its "voice of authentic poetry" and attributed a "consistent fertility" to Betjeman ("Mr Betjeman's Bouquet," in *The Essays, Articles and Reviews of Evelyn Waugh*, ed. Donat Gallagher [Boston: Little, Brown, 1983], 460–61), he also satirized Betjeman in his novel *The Ordeal of Gilbert Pinfold* (1957), the latest of many such burlesques, having already parodied him in *A Handful of Dust* (1934), *Brideshead Revisited* (1945), and *Scott-King's Modern Europe* (1947) (see Hillier, *New Fame, New Love*, 302, and Wilson, *Betjeman*, 209).

105 For instance, Betjeman expressed disappointment with the stained-glass windows for the new cathedral in Coventry, despite their beauty, because these windows failed to teach the faith: "The symbolism of the windows, for all the ingenuity with which it is expressed, is not very inspiring. And the teaching it represents is very vague and noncommittal, more suitable

to an inter-denominational assembly hall than a cathedral of the Church" ("True Colour in Glass for Cathedral," *Daily Telegraph*, 4 July 1956, 8).

106 Betjeman to Evelyn Waugh, 12 January 1947, in *Letters, Volume One*, 403.

107 Qtd. in John Betjeman, "Church-Building," *Times Literary Supplement*, 6 December 1947; rpt. in *Tennis Whites and Teacakes*, 360. Comper went on to explain, "There are Protestant Meeting Houses for preaching and for praying and hymn-singing in common and they are not to be despised; but if they are more than a plain room they have become a meaningless imitation of that from which set purpose they broke away" (360).

108 Betjeman to Waugh, 3 February 1947, in *Letters, Volume One*, 405.

109 Betjeman to Waugh, 12 January 1947, in *Letters, Volume One*, 403.

110 Betjeman to Waugh, 23 January 1947, in *Letters, Volume One*, 404.

111 Betjeman to Waugh, 3 February 1947, in *Letters, Volume One*, 405.

112 Betjeman to Waugh, Whitmonday [26 May] 1947, in *Letters, Volume One*, 411.

113 Betjeman to Waugh, Whitmonday [26 May] 1947, in *Letters, Volume One*, 412.

114 Wilson, *Betjeman*, 172.

115 Betjeman to Waugh, Whitmonday [26 May] 1947, *Letters, Volume One*, 412.

116 Betjeman to Mary Wilson, 26 February 1974, *Letters, Volume Two*, 475–76.

Chapter 2

1 Betjeman, "This I Believe" (CBS radio, 21 September 1953), in *Tennis Whites and Teacakes*, 440.

2 Qtd. in Hillier, *Bonus of Laughter*, 538.

3 "John Betjeman Reads a Selection of His Own Poetry" (BBC radio, 6 October 1949), in *Trains and Buttered Toast*, 339.

4 Wilson, *Betjeman*, 3.

5 Harvey, *Romantic Tradition*, 4. Harvey further stipulates that this tension in Betjeman's work is not limited to his religious poetry, "for his response to life generally is basically one of generous affirmation; but it is qualified also by a robust scepticism" (5).

6 *Summoned by Bells*, 67. The ellipsis is Betjeman's.

7 Kenneth Allsop, "The Year of the Poet," *Daily Mail*, 9 December 1960, 8; qtd. in Mills, "John Betjeman's Poetry: An Appreciation," 18.

8 Qtd. in Hillier, *Bonus of Laughter*, 547. The ellipsis is Hillier's.

9 "May-Day Song for North Oxford" (1945), in *Collected Poems*, 96.

10 Sibyl Harton to Betjeman, 25 December 1980, in *Letters, Volume Two*, 550.

11 Countryman, *Poetic Imagination*, 62.

12 See Countryman, *Poetic Imagination*, 35, 92, 89.

13 Betjeman here alludes to the familiar liturgical phrases which follow the Psalm and Canticles in the Anglican services of Morning Prayer (Matins) and Evening Prayer (Evensong) in *The Book of Common Prayer*. When the priest says, "Glory be to the Father, and to the Son, and to the Holy Ghost," the congregation responds, "As it was in the beginning, is now, and ever shall be, world without end. Amen" (*BCP*, 1662).

14 "Childhood Days" (BBC radio, 16 July 1950), in *Coming Home*, 250.

15 The church is St. Anne Brookfield, Highgate West Hill, London.

16 "Childhood Days," in *Coming Home*, 250.

17 "Childhood Days," in *Coming Home*, 253.

18 Appropriately, the advertising slogan for Persil washing powder used to be "Persil washes whiter."

19 James Fowler (1828–1892), of Louth, Lincolnshire, was an architect whose excessive restorations Betjeman loathed.

20 Qtd. in Hillier, *Bonus of Laughter*, 553.

21 Hillier, *Bonus of Laughter*, 554.

22 "John Betjeman Reads," in *Trains and Buttered Toast*, 339.

23 Neame, "Poet of Anglicanism," 283.

24 *Time with Betjeman, Part Four* (BBC Two, 6 March 1983, prod. Jonathan Stedall); qtd. in Hillier, *Bonus of Laughter*, 538.

25 Hillier, *Bonus of Laughter*, 542.

26 "St Bartholomew's Hospital, EC1," *London Magazine*, December 1978–January 1979, 61.

27 *Mount Zion* (1931) opens with "Death in Leamington," while *A Nip in the Air* (1974) closes with "The Last Laugh."

28 Wilson, *Betjeman*, 211.

29 T. W. Rolleston (1857–1920) was an Irish poet most famous for his poem "The Dead at Clonmacnois."

30 Sir Henry Newbolt (1862–1938) was an English poet and historian known for his poetry about the sea.

31 "Clay and Spirit," in *A Few Late Chrysanthemums*, 62–63. "Clay and Spirit" was not included in Betjeman's *Collected Poems*.

32 Ernest Betjeman, with whom John had had a very poor relationship, died in 1934.

33 Introduction to *Sweet Songs of Zion*, 15–16.

34 The Sandemanians, also known as Glasites, were a sect that blossomed in the nineteenth century. They adhered to a literal reading of the Scripture and so minimized contact with the secular world that they did not even actively pursue new converts to their faith. The typical Sunday service

lasted all day, being divided by a "Love Feast" to which Betjeman alludes in his poem.

35 A poem similar in tone is "Competition," published in *Mount Zion* in 1931 but not included in the *Collected Poems*. Betjeman considered it "absolutely valueless" (qtd. in Peterson, *John Betjeman: A Bibliography*, 401), but it does have value in its exhibition of Betjeman's obsession with nonconformity. See also his articles "Nonconformist Architecture," *Architectural Review*, December 1940), 161–74; and "Men and Buildings: An Architecture of the People," *Daily Telegraph*, 20 April 1964, 19; rpt. in *Coming Home*, 403–6.

36 "Augustus Toplady" (BBC radio, 23 June 1946), in *Trains and Buttered Toast*, 196.

37 "City and Suburban," *Spectator*, 22 November 1957, 684.

38 Betjeman to H. S. Goodhart-Rendel, 7 August 1959, in *Letters, Volume One*, 483. Two unpublished poems on the Agapemonites further show his interest in this sect: manuscripts are located in the Sir John Betjeman Collection, McPherson Library Special Collections, University of Victoria (MS PUF104); and the Betjeman Archive, the British Library (Add. MS 71936, fol. 180).

39 See Betjeman's children's book, *Archie and the Strict Baptists* (London: John Murray, 1977), for a fuller account of the bear's life and religious observance. Even more of his personality is revealed in Betjeman's letters, where Archie occasionally appears, and is even the putative "author" of some them (see, e.g., *Letters, Volume One*, 77, 87, 117, 171). Further illustrating his interest in Protestant nonconformity, Betjeman also once signed a letter to his publisher Jock Murray, "From John Calvin, *John Betjeman*, John Wesley, John Knox" (*Letters, Volume One*, 246).

40 Hymns, given by their tune titles, associated with the evangelical movement.

41 "John Betjeman Reads," in *Trains and Buttered Toast*, 330–31.

42 The extent of Betjeman's disgust for the mutilating restorations of Victorian church architects can be found in his 1938 radio talk, "How to Look at a Church." Betjeman insisted, however, that while the Victorians were horrible at church restoration, they were ingenious when building new churches; see, for instance, "The Fabric of our Faith," *Punch*, 23 December 1953, 744; and "In Praise of the Victorians," *West Country Churches* (London: Society of SS Peter and Paul, 1973), 14.

43 Peterson, *John Betjeman: A Bibliography*, 433.

44 T. S. Eliot, *The Waste Land* (1922). The ellipsis in the passage quoted above is Betjeman's.

45 Betjeman to John Edward Bowle, 16 March 1971, *Letters, Volume Two*, 408.

46 Betjeman to Kenneth Clark, 11 July 1971, *Letters, Volume Two*, 418.

47 The poem is in fact specifically autobiographical, and he spoke about the experience in a 1949 radio broadcast ("John Betjeman Reads," in *Trains and Buttered Toast*, 339–42).

48 The bells of St. Giles', Oxford, have long been famous for their beauty and richness and for the skill of the ringers.

49 "John Betjeman Reads," in *Trains and Buttered Toast*, 339.

50 Dennis Brown writes that in this poem "the poet expresses the essence of any honest religious feeling—the gulf between socialized forms of belief and faith-in-itself, and the unworthiness of the believer. There is surely no reason to endorse Betjeman's sense of personal inadequacy—it is those who lack such who are preposterous (and often dangerous). The poet's profound sense of limitations precisely inspires his genuine virtues—tolerance, humour, and generosity of spirit" (*John Betjeman*, 52).

51 This is the parish of St. Mary, Willesden, a medieval village now absorbed into the northwestern quadrant of Greater London.

52 When the poem was published in 1982 in his *Uncollected Poems*, the following headnote was added: "In 1955 Mrs Margaret Knight, a humanist, caused a sensation by her broadcasts on BBC radio attacking Christianity. This was composed in reply to her arguments, and it was published in *The Listener* of February 10, 1955." Betjeman read the poem on BBC radio on 25 January 1955 as part of his series, "Poems in the Porch."

53 "Billy Graham," 282.

54 Betjeman Archive, British Library (Add. MS 71645, fol. 82). Though the manuscript is undated, its position in the collection indicates a probable composition in the late 1950s or early 1960s.

55 The second film in a two-part series called *Thank God It's Sunday* (BBC One, 17 December 1972, prod. Jonathan Stedall), in *Betjeman's England*, 79.

56 Allsop, "The Year of the Poet"; qtd. in Mills, "John Betjeman's Poetry," 18.

Chapter 3

1 Betjeman, introduction to *Collins Guide to English Parish Churches*, 51.

2 *Collins Guide to English Parish Churches*, 30.

3 *A Passion for Churches*, in *Betjeman's England*, 202.

4 Neill, *Anglicanism*, 422.

5 Paul Elmer More, "The Spirit of Anglicanism," in *Anglicanism: The Thought and Practice of the Church of England, Illustrated from the Religious Literature of*

the Seventeenth Century, ed. Paul Elmer More and Frank Leslie Cross (London: SPCK, 1935, 1957), xxxvii.

6   Qtd. in Taylor-Martin, *John Betjeman,* 36–37.

7   William Temple, *Christus Veritas: An Essay* (London: Macmillan, 1924), 144, 139; qtd. in William J. Wolf, *The Spirit of Anglicanism* (Wilton, Conn.: Morehouse-Barlow, 1979), 114.

8   Published in *Poems in the Porch,* ed. Gardner (2008), 75–80. "Poems in the Porch" was a series of Anglican poems he wrote to read on BBC radio in the 1950s.

9   Broadcast in 1955 but not published until it appeared in *Uncollected Poems,* ed. Bevis Hillier (London: John Murray, 1982), 51–53.

10   Perhaps one of the rare moments of concord between Betjeman and C. S. Lewis can be found in their shared theological opinion that no effort of humanity to glorify God ever succeeds in worthily magnifying him. As Lewis wrote, "For all our offerings, whether of music or martyrdom, are like the intrinsically worthless present of a child, which a father values indeed, but values only for the intention" ("On Church Music," in *Christian Reflections* [Grand Rapids: Eerdmans, 1967], 99).

11   Sermon delivered at St. Matthew's, Northampton, 5 May 1946, in *Five Sermons by Laymen,* 7.

12   Betjeman's talk was recorded at the BBC on 21 September 1953 for broadcast in the United States on "This I Believe," a CBS radio program hosted by Edward R. Murrow from 1951 to 1955. When (or whether) the recording was actually broadcast is unknown. Quotations of this essay are from *Tennis Whites and Teacakes,* 439–40.

13   Michael Townsend, "Sir John Betjeman—Christian Poet?" *Expository Times* 97.12 (1986): 360.

14   Allchin, "Anglican Spirituality," 316.

15   A. R. Vidler, *Essays in Liberality* (London: SCM Press, 1951), 166; qtd. in Wolf, *Spirit of Anglicanism,* 151.

16   Qtd. in *Letters, Volume Two,* 443.

17   *Summoned by Bells,* 25.

18   *Summoned by Bells,* 89.

19   *Summoned by Bells,* 95.

20   *Summoned by Bells,* 95.

21   Stephen Games, introduction to *Sweet Songs of Zion,* 9.

22   *Summoned by Bells,* 17.

23   "Suicide on Junction Road Station after Abstention from Evening Communion in North London" (1937). "Jehovah Jireh," a biblical phrase that first appears in the story of Abraham and Isaac, means "the Lord will

provide." The "Mintons" are likely encaustic tiles in the church; Mintons Ltd., founded by Thomas Minton in 1793, continues to specialize in decorative ceramic tiles and statuary porcelain.

24 *Summoned by Bells*, 60.

25 "Narcissus" (1965), in *Collected Poems*, 280–81.

26 *Summoned by Bells*, 73–74.

27 *Summoned by Bells*, 67.

28 *Summoned by Bells*, 72.

29 This manuscript fragment is headed "Rochester" and has been identified by Bevis Hillier as a likely draft for the passage describing the chapel at Marlborough in *Summoned by Bells*. My thanks to Bevis Hillier for supplying me with a transcription of the verses. The ellipsis is in the original.

30 Hillier, *Young Betjeman*, 115–18, 176–81. A. N. Wilson suggests a greater complexity in Betjeman's sexual orientation but in general concurs with Hillier (*Betjeman*, 300–303).

31 Born in 1931, Anthony Barnes was the son of Betjeman's close friend and adviser George Barnes, then director of the BBC's Talks Department.

32 Betjeman to Anthony Barnes, 6 October 1949, *Letters, Volume One*, 487.

33 Betjeman to Barnes, 15 October 1949, *Letters, Volume One*, 488.

34 Betjeman to Barnes, 15 October 1949, *Letters, Volume One*, 489.

35 "Now is my heart on fire," in *The Barrier*, by Robin Maugham (London: W. H. Allen, 1973), 195. This sonnet is one of five Betjeman wrote for Maugham, who inserted them into his novel as poems written by his narrator, a married Englishwoman in India having an affair with a young Indian man. The love affair being doubly transgressive, in terms of both age and ethnicity, it serves as a fruitful translation of forbidden homosexuality.

36 The primary reason for this problematic difference is that *Summoned by Bells* describes his childhood in an essentially all-male climate of boarding schools and ends at the point he embarks upon adulthood.

37 *Summoned by Bells*, 25.

38 "The Irish Unionist's Farewell to Greta Hellstrom in 1922" (1945), in *Collected Poems*, 118–19.

39 "Blisland, Bodmin," *Oxford Outlook*, June 1927, 319. Though the poem is signed "Dorothie Harbinger," this was only a playful pseudonym of the undergraduate Betjeman. William Peterson attributes the poem to Betjeman (*John Betjeman: A Bibliography*, 395).

40 Based on a biographical context, Bevis Hillier offers a more literal reading of this poem that precludes my interpretation of the poem's sexually charged atmosphere. In *New Fame, New Love*, he argues that the poem's "Mary" is the teenaged daughter of Betjeman's friend, P. Morton Shand.

Hillier shows that Betjeman almost certainly had a "romantic and pla-
tonic" crush on Mary Shand, though his passion for her remained unrequited. Based on this, the biographer prefers a reading of the poem that
preserves both the innocence of the poem's "Mary" and the chivalry of
the poem's persona (278–79). Despite biographical evidence to the contrary, I remain unconvinced that the blanket will have been flattened only
by the picnic and not by a sexual encounter as well. It is at least evidence
of the speaker's tremendous passion for something besides churches.

41 The poem is a tribute to the writer and librettist Myfanwy Piper, née
Evans (1911–1997). Betjeman was a close friend of John and Myfanwy Piper
throughout his life. John Piper attributed his and Myfanwy's conversions
to Christianity to the example of John Betjeman (Hillier, *New Fame, New
Love*, 101).

42 Hillier, *Young Betjeman*, 135, 180.

43 Betjeman claimed that the inspiration for the poem was factual. The
poem's footnote asserts, "This is about a lady I see on Sunday mornings
in a London church" (*Collected Poems*, 311). For more details on the background, see Hillier, *Bonus of Laughter*, 384; *Letters, Volume Two*, 442–43.

44 Harvey, *Romantic Tradition*, 84.

45 This church, situated on Sloane Square in Upper Chelsea, is a bastion
of Anglo-Catholicism. Betjeman called it the "cathedral of the Arts and
Crafts movement" (*Collins Guide to English Parish Churches*, 255).

46 James Whistler lived with his mother in nearby Cadogan Square in the
1880s. Mothering Sunday, which bears no connection with the American holiday, is celebrated in Britain on the fourth Sunday of Lent. It was
established as a day for the domestic servant to be released from duties in
order to visit his or her mother.

47 Neill, *Anglicanism*, 418; cf. Countryman, *Poetic Imagination*, 34.

48 "My Oxford," in *Coming Home*, 475.

49 "Pugin: A Great Victorian Architect," in *Coming Home*, 271.

50 "Christian Architecture," 19. Betjeman especially admired the screen in
Hereford Cathedral for its ability to make the cathedral look "more mysterious" ("Hereford Screen," *Times*, 4 March 1966, 13).

51 "Design for a New Cathedral," *Daily Telegraph*, 3 September 1951, 4. Likewise he noted that a central problem with much modern church design
was that such structures were less like churches than "cinemas with
ecclesiastical trappings or lecture halls with a reredos on the wall when
normally there would be a blackboard" embellished with "devices for
turning the church into a community hall for youth discussion groups"
("Church-Building"; rpt. in *Tennis Whites and Teacakes*, 359).

52 "London's Least-Tasted Pleasure," 6.

53 "The Lighting of Churches," *Country Churchman*, November 1953; rpt. in *Tennis Whites and Teacakes*, 368. Also of interest in this context is Betjeman's review-essay "Church-Building," rpt. in *Tennis Whites and Teacakes*, 358–62.

54 The lighting of churches was a veritable obsession of Betjeman's in 1953; in addition to "The Lighting of Churches" he wrote "Glories of English Craftsmanship—Electricity and Old Churches" (*Time and Tide*, 5 December 1953, 1582–83), as well as the highly amusing poem, "Electric Light and Heating" (one of his "Poems in the Porch"), broadcast on the BBC on 10 November 1953. The subject would crop up again in his column, "City and Suburban," *Spectator*, 15 November 1957, 642.

55 Countryman, *Poetic Imagination*, 60; see also 108, 49, 124.

56 "Christmas," in *Coming Home*, 215.

57 Qtd. in Hillier, *New Fame, New Love*, 399.

58 "Polzeath" (BBC radio, 7 July 1950), in *Coming Home*, 240.

59 "Trebetherick," in *Both Sides of the Tamar: A West Country Alphabet*, ed. Michael Williams (St. Teath, Cornwall: Bossiney, 1975); rpt. in *Coming Home*, 441–42.

60 Payton, "John Betjeman and the Holy Grail," 194.

61 "Coast and Country," in *First and Last Loves* (London: John Murray, 1952), 232. Originally written for the radio: "Highworth" (BBC radio, 29 September 1950).

62 St. Barnabas, a bastion of Anglo-Catholicism, is a byzantine-style church in the Jericho section of Oxford.

63 "Essential England," *Daily Telegraph*, 29 April 1954, 6.

64 *A Passion for Churches*, in *Betjeman's England*, 196.

65 "The Church of St John the Baptist at Mildenhall, Wiltshire," in *West Country Churches*, 12. Originally written for radio: "St. John the Baptist, Mildenhall, Wiltshire" (BBC radio, 28 July 1948).

66 "Coast and Country," in *First and Last Loves*, 232.

67 "City and Suburban," *Spectator*, 28 December 1956, 930.

68 "1837–1937: A Spiritual Change Is the One Hope for Art," *Studio*, February 1937, 61.

69 "St Protus and St Hyacinth, Blisland, Cornwall" (BBC radio, 21 July 1948), in *Trains and Buttered Toast*, 235.

70 "Three Churches," in *First and Last Loves*, 180. Betjeman revised this radio address slightly for publication, and I have quoted from both broadcast and print versions. Even as a youth Betjeman was astonished with how Blisland's seemingly dead stones could nurture life. In his undergraduate

poem "Blisland, Bodmin," he describes "her tower / Of hardest surface granite stones, / Stuff'd in between with fern and flower" ("Blisland, Bodmin," 319).

71 "Three Churches," in *First and Last Loves*, 182.

72 Even an urban church could evoke connections to the natural world; as Betjeman and Osbert Lancaster described the interior of London's St. Mary-le-Strand, "it looks like a grotto inside" ("St Mary-le-Strand," *Times*, 5 November 1981, 13).

73 Betjeman's daughter Candida and her husband Rupert named one of their daughters Endellion.

74 *Summoned by Bells*, 87.

75 "St. Endellion" (BBC radio, 1 July 1949), in *The Best of Betjeman*, 149.

76 "St. Endellion," in *The Best of Betjeman*, 147.

77 "St. Endellion," in *The Best of Betjeman*, 149.

78 "St. Endellion," in *The Best of Betjeman*, 150.

79 On this passage Bevis Hillier made the following observation: "As I read this, I suddenly think, 'What would Betjeman's poetry be without religion?' What a gift to him God is!" (correspondence with the author, 26 July 2008).

80 Wolf, *Spirit of Anglicanism*, 178.

81 *The Olney Hymns* was a collection of evangelical hymns published in 1779 by the poets and hymnodists William Cowper (1731–1800) and John Newton (1725–1807). Newton was priest in the parish church of SS Peter and Paul in Olney, the Buckinghamshire village that had been home to Newton and Cowper since 1769.

82 A sixth-century Welsh priest martyred in Cornwall by Saxons while serving Mass, Cadoc is the patron saint of scrofula, deafness, cramps, and glandular disorders.

83 Payton, "John Betjeman and the Holy Grail," 203, 197.

84 *Summoned by Bells*, 87, 88.

85 "The Parson Hawker of Morwenstow" (BBC radio, 7 February 1939), in *Trains and Buttered Toast*, 163–64.

86 St. Enodoc is a chapel at Trebetherick, Cornwall, where Betjeman had a home, and is attached to the parish of St. Minver in the Diocese of Truro. Betjeman is buried in the churchyard of St. Enodoc.

87 Introduction to *Collins Guide to English Parish Churches*, 51.

88 The wandering or distracted mind of a worshipper is a favorite motif of John Betjeman's; rarely are his worshippers attentive to their services, as we can see in such other poems as "Sunday Morning, King's Cambridge," "Lenten Thoughts of a High Anglican," "Verses Turned," "St. Saviour's,

Aberdeen Park," and "The Conversion of St. Paul." Such wanderings usually lead the worshipper to an insight more profound than what the sermon or liturgy normally provides. In a television film celebrating Minstead parish church, Betjeman admitted that "when the sermon was boring, as I expect they often were, your attention wandered away from the preacher and you'd gaze idly through the window to the oaks and parks of the forest where this Church began" (*John Betjeman's ABC of Churches*, in *Betjeman's England*, 126).

89 William Shakespeare, *King Lear* (Cambridge: Cambridge University Press, 1968), 93.

90 Simon Jenkins describes the church's positioning in a hollow, surrounded by dunes planted with tamarisk hedges to prevent the encroaching sand from engulfing the chapel. Under the hedge stands a shed that was formerly employed as a sort of temporary morgue for sailors drowned in wrecks offshore (*England's Thousand Best Churches*, 82).

91 This idea finds a surprising echo in C. S. Lewis, who feared "the steady, unrelenting approach of Him whom I so earnestly desired not to meet" (*Surprised by Joy* [London: Harcourt, 1955], 228).

92 Although Betjeman's poem provides no specific identity for the church, Bevis Hillier makes a convincing case that Betjeman was in fact recreating one particular church, St. Margaret's, Huttoft, near Sutton-on-Sea (*New Fame, New Love*, 365–66, 670–71).

93 George Herbert, "Prayer (1)," in *The Temple* (1633), ed. Henry L. Carrigan (Brewster, Mass.: Paraclete Press, 2001).

94 *A Passion for Churches*, in *Betjeman's England*, 205.

Chapter 4

1 Betjeman, "How to Look at a Church," 484.

2 Jenkins, *England's Thousand Best Churches*, 82. The church, which is a chapel of the parish of St. Minver in the Diocese of Truro, also warrants entries in David N. Durant's *The Good Church Guide* and Betjeman's *Collins Guide to English Parish Churches*.

3 *Collins Guide to English Parish Churches*, 123; "A Lincolnshire Church," in *Collected Poems*, 141.

4 Hillier, *Young Betjeman*, 85; Jenkins, *England's Thousand Best Churches*, 82.

5 "The Fabric of Our Faith," 744.

6 "Not Necessarily Leeds," *Spectator*, 1 October 1954, 392; rpt. in *Poems in the Porch* (2008), 131–33. Hillier quoted a portion of the poem in *New Fame, New Love*, 532. This poem was inspired by Betjeman's battle with the archdeacon, C. O. Ellison, in the pages of the *Spectator* in 1954 over the fate of Holy Trinity. Referring to modern bishops as "the slaves of finance,"

Betjeman insisted that "They do not realize that a beautiful church is a more lasting witness to the Faith than they are" ("A Spectator's Notebook," *Spectator*, 27 August 1954, 244). The archdeacon of Leeds replied on 3 September, and a remarkable letter of support for Betjeman's position came from H. S. Williamson on 10 September. Though the battle would rage periodically in these pages for three more years, in the end the church was saved.

7   See also "Selling Our Churches," 383–84.

8   Twenty years later London's Holy Trinity, Sloane Street, came under attack, and Betjeman led a campaign to prevent the sale of a perfectly preserved church simply for the value of the land. To help with the campaign, Betjeman contributed these new verses ("Holy Trinity, Sloane Street," *Sunday Times*, 15 September 1974, 35):

>   Bishop, archdeacon, rector, wardens, mayor
>   Guardians of Chelsea's noblest house of prayer
>   You who your church's vastness so deplore
>   "Should we not sell and give it to the poor?"
>   Recall, despite your practical suggestion
>   Which the disciple was who asked that question.

9   Lowe, "The Church," 564.

10 Betjeman wrote (or lent his name as signatory to) at least eighteen letters to the *Times* alone about threatened churches over the course of his life.

11 "St. Mary Redcliffe," *Times*, 7 July 1961, 13.

12 "Hawksmoor's Churches," *Times*, 3 May 1977, 15.

13 "Fons et Origo," *Times*, 3 August 1982, 9.

14 "Essential England," *Daily Telegraph*, 29 April 1954, 6. The idea that "a civilisation is remembered by its buildings" is one he would reiterate in numerous essays and articles.

15 Hillier, *Young Betjeman*, 85.

16 Hillier, *New Fame, New Love*, 561–69, and *Bonus of Laughter*, 126–45, 163–82, 219–35, 259–74, 454–70.

17 "Royal Agricultural Hall," *Times*, 15 August 1974, 13. Betjeman was the lead author; his cosignatories were Hugh Casson, Nikolaus Pevsner, Jack Simmons, and Basil Spence.

18 "London Tower Blocks," *Times*, 9 June 1980, 15. For more on Betjeman's views on the vital beauty of a skyline, see "Outline and Skyline," *Daily Telegraph*, 24 January 1953, 6; rpt. in *Coming Home*, 282–85.

19 "Winchester Motorway," *Times*, 14 May 1971, 17.

20 Betjeman, "Topographical Verse," in *Slick but Not Streamlined*, 22; originally published as the preface to *Old Lights for New Chancels* (London: John Murray, 1940), xi–xviii.

21 W. H. Auden, *Making, Knowing and Judging: An Inaugural Lecture Delivered before the University of Oxford on 11 June 1956* (Oxford: Clarendon, 1956); qtd. in Mills, "John Betjeman's Poetry," 9.

22 Betjeman to Frank Gallagher, 16 June 1943, in *Letters, Volume One*, 318.

23 "White Horse Hill," *Times*, 26 April 1947, 5.

24 "Uffington White Horse," *Times*, 6 June 1975, 15.

25 "Southend Pier," *Times*, 22 February 1974, 15.

26 "Threat to Setting of Bury St Edmunds," *Times*, 4 October 1972, 15.

27 "A Tower opposite the Tate," *Times*, 4 February 1980, 13. Cosigned by Stephen Gardiner.

28 "St. Mark's, Swindon," *West Country Churches*, 18. Originally written for radio: "St Mark's, Swindon, Wiltshire" (BBC radio, 4 August 1948).

29 *The Englishman's Home* (BBC Two, 5 April 1969; prod. Edward Mirzoeff), in *Tennis Whites and Teacakes*, 353–54. Mark Tewdwr-Jones has effectively argued that this film helped to stem the nearly irresistible tide of modernism then sweeping the English landscape ("'Oh, the planners did their best,'" 406).

30 "A Tower opposite the Tate," 13.

31 This topic is one he addressed very early in his career: see "The Passing of the Village" (*Architectural Review*, September 1932, 89–93) and "Councillor Bloggins Is Changing the Face of England" (*Daily Express*, 15 July 1936, 10); both rpt. in *Tennis Whites and Teacakes*, 319–27.

32 "Letcombe Bassett," *Times*, 3 December 1948, 5.

33 "England's Cottages a Heritage Worth Defending," *Daily Telegraph*, 23 August 1954, 4.

34 Concrete standards were beginning to replace traditional lampposts throughout England, and Betjeman railed against them for their ugliness, their lack of proportion, and their standardization of England's variety. His antipathy to them can be found in many essays and articles through the 1950s and 1960s. The following should give a clear sense of his feelings on the subject: "Concrete standards never vary except in brutality. They lack proportion in themselves and to their surroundings. A very thick column generally of lumpy shape with a giant's match-strike at its base rears up to bend over and carry, one would expect, a very large corpse. Instead, all this effort goes into hanging a tiny bubble of light or else a thing like a carpet sweeper" ("Concrete Lamp-Standards in Old Town Settings," *Daily Telegraph*, 23 February 1952, 4). In another essay, he fulminated, "More damage has been done since the war by lighting authorities to our landscape than ever was done by German bombs or greedy commercialism" ("Lamp-Posts and Landscape," in *Light and Lighting*, November 1953; rpt. in *Coming Home*, 309–10).

35 "High Frecklesby Has a Plan," *Punch*, 27 May 1953, 624–25, rpt. as "High Frecklesby," in *Coming Home*, 246–49.

36 Lowe, "The Church," 572.

37 Betjeman railed against town clerks and local councils in his journalism. A particularly illustrative example of the causes of his contempt can be found in "Fulham Grange," *Spectator*, 16 July 1954, 75.

38 In his fascinating essay on Betjeman's films on the English landscape, Mark Tewdwr-Jones calls Betjeman an "alternative planning wizard" for his ingenious and creative responses to the accepted wisdom of modernist and professional planning experts. Ironically, as Tewdwr-Jones concludes, "by utilizing film to espouse his own views, one may argue that Betjeman was adopting a modernist practice himself by possibly convincing the audience that he too was a planning expert, albeit an expert with a perspective that went against the grain of other commentators at the time" ("'Oh, the planners did their best,'" 407).

39 The danger of driving Britain's roads—including death by car crash and even road rage—is a recurring motif in Betjeman's poems; see, e.g., "Exeter" (1937; *CP* 33–34), "Meditation on the A30" (1966; *CP* 285), "Dilton Marsh Halt" (1968; *CP* 321), and "Executive" (1972; *CP* 312–13).

40 For more on the background of "The Newest Bath Guide," see Peterson, *John Betjeman: A Bibliography*, 440.

41 "The Bressey Report," *Criterion* 18 (1938): 12. Betjeman's essay was commissioned by T. S. Eliot.

42 "'Oh, to be in England. . . ,'" 296.

43 "Lovely Bits of Old England Must Be Spared," *Daily Telegraph*, 26 July 1952, 4.

44 "I Accuse These Grey-Faced Men of Britain," *Daily Express*, 12 March 1962, 8.

45 "Face to Face with Myself," *Daily Herald,* 8 March 1961, 4.

46 "Oxford and Suburban," *Spectator*, 14 October 1955, 493.

47 "Oxford and Suburban," 493. Defending Betjeman from charges that his conservation campaigns were rooted in nostalgia and snobbery, Jocelyn Brooke insisted rightly that his "hatred of 'progress' implies no inhumanity or class-prejudice" (Brooke, *Ronald Firbank and John Betjeman*, 36). A particularly striking instance of his sensitivity to the lower economic strata is his piece "Councillor Bloggins Is Changing the Face of England," *Daily Express*, 15 July 1936, 10; rpt. in *Tennis Whites and Teacakes*, 324–27.

48 See, e.g., his humorous collection of verses, "Those Horseless Carriages," *Everybody's: The Popular Weekly*, 22 October 1955, 16–17.

49 Schröder, "Heterotopian Constructions of Englishness," 15–34.

50 See "I Accuse These Grey-Faced Men of Britain," 8; and "Men and Buildings: Heritage of the Rail Age," *Daily Telegraph*, 8 February 1960, 15; the latter rpt. in *Coming Home*, 412–15.

51 Some have argued that such surprising views were not genuine, that he was merely conforming to the modernist diktats of his employers at *The Architectural Review*; see Morse, *John Betjeman*, 30–39, and Mowl, *Stylistic Cold Wars*, 15–54. Of Betjeman's editors at the *Archie Rev*, Mowl writes, "They made him compromise his natural judgement and turn his pen to fake apologetics" (36).

52 "The Passing of the Village," in *Tennis Whites and Teacakes*, 322, 324. See also Betjeman's essays "The Ten-Storey Town" (1935), "All-Steel Homes" (1938), and "The Culture of Cities" (1939), in *Tennis Whites and Teacakes*, 293–302.

53 Games, introduction to *Trains and Buttered Toast*, 14.

54 "Christmas Nostalgia" (BBC radio, 25 December 1947), in *Trains and Buttered Toast*, 319.

55 "City and Suburban," *Spectator*, 29 October 1954, 516.

56 Harvey, *Romantic Tradition*, 74.

57 *London's Exhibition Sites* (BBC television, 28 February 1960; dir. Ken Russell), in *Betjeman's England*, 154.

58 Mowl, *Stylistic Cold Wars*, 155.

59 An excellent summary and analysis of this aspect of Betjeman's prose may be found in Press, *John Betjeman*, 9–18.

60 "1837–1937: A Spiritual Change," 56.

61 "1837–1937: A Spiritual Change," 57.

62 "1837–1937: A Spiritual Change," 57.

63 "1837–1937: A Spiritual Change," 69.

64 "1837–1937: A Spiritual Change," 72.

65 "City and Suburban," *Spectator*, 26 July 1957, 132.

66 "Wartime Tastes in Reading," in *Trains and Buttered Toast*, 148.

67 Auden, introduction to *Slick but Not Streamlined*, 9–16; Betjeman, in "Topographical Verse," in *Slick but Not Streamlined*, 17–22. See also Stanford, *John Betjeman*, 72–84; Taylor-Martin, *John Betjeman*, 75–105.

68 Sparrow, "The Poetry of John Betjeman," in *Independent Essays*, 168. Hillier similarly but more wittily noted, "the shellfish mattered as much as the shells" (*Bonus of Laughter*, 75).

69 Betjeman to John Sparrow, 25 December 1947, in *Letters, Volume One*, 427. That same Christmas Day, Betjeman wrote to his publisher Jock Murray a similar sentiment: "When I am describing Nature, it is *always* with a view to the social background or the sense of Man's impotence before the vastness of the Creator" (qtd. in Hillier, *New Fame, New Love*, 399).

70 "Winter at Home," in *First and Last Loves*, 6–7. Originally published in *Vogue* (November 1948): 42, 102.

71 "St. Petroc" (BBC radio, 11 July 1949), in *Trains and Buttered Toast*, 208.

72 "Three Churches," in *First and Last Loves*, 179–80. Originally written for radio: "St Protus and St Hyacinth."

73 "City and Suburban," *Spectator*, 4 May 1956, 615.

74 *Seaside Resorts in the South and South-West* (BBC Two, 25 December 1969; prod. Edward Mirzoeff), in *Betjeman's England*, 72. This film, originally titled *Beside the Seaside*, was part of Mirzoeff's series, *Bird's-Eye View*.

75 This idea resonates throughout twentieth-century British literature. One of the earliest instances is in the epilogue to H. G. Wells' *The Time Machine* (1895): "He . . . thought but cheerlessly of the Advancement of Mankind, and saw in the growing pile of civilization only a foolish heaping that must inevitably fall back upon and destroy its makers in the end. If that is so, it remains for us to live as though it were not so. . . . And I have by me, for my comfort, two strange white flowers—shrivelled now, and brown and flat and brittle—to witness that even when mind and strength had gone, gratitude and a mutual tenderness still lived on in the heart of man" (Whitefish, Mont.: Kessinger, 2004), 71.

76 Hillier (*New Fame, New Love*, 543) notes that Betjeman's quotation of "Unmitigated England" is from Henry James' *English Hours* (1905). What James meant by this phrase was that England was a country of mild and pleasing exteriors but of deep and painful emotions; Betjeman applies this idea specifically to the English landscape.

77 "Alas, Poor London," 51.

78 "'Oh, to be in England. . . ,'" 296.

79 "The Victorian Sunday" (BBC radio, 10 July 1951), in *Tennis Whites and Teacakes*, 289.

80 Betjeman's attitude here is undoubtedly snobbish as well as hypocritical. He (like his father before him) owned a house at the Cornish coast. He imagines the duchy "unpeopled" by all except his privileged caste.

81 Jocelyn Brooke was accurate in noting the strong undercurrent of pessimism in Betjeman's faith: "Mr. Betjeman would say that our sole hope of regeneration lies in the Christian religion . . . , but it is fairly clear from his writings that he considers the hope a forlorn one, and that our increasingly materialistic society is unlikely to undergo any such change of heart" (*Ronald Firbank and John Betjeman*, 36).

82 "Long, Long Trail," *Punch*, 9 June 1954, 682.

83 "City and Suburban," *Spectator*, 7 October 1955, 445.

84 "Childhood Days" (BBC radio, 16 July 1950), in *Coming Home*, 253; see also

"Little Hells Let Loose," *Evening Standard*, 1 August 1934, 7; rpt. in *Tennis Whites and Teacakes*, 39–42.

85 "Love Is Dead," in *First and Last Loves*, 3.

86 "'Huxley Hall,'" as Geoffrey Harvey puts it, "develops a contrapuntal opposition between traditional Christian values and those of the state; between the spiritual and the secular; and between the individual and the collective" (*Romantic Tradition*, 76). Interestingly, elsewhere Betjeman waxes lyrical about garden cities; see, e.g., his poem "The Garden City," *Mount Zion*, 54.

87 See Sarah Lyall, "A Town Trying Not to Live Up to Its Name," *The New York Times*, 21 March 2008, http://www.nytimes.com/2008/03/21/world/europe/21slough.html?ref=world.

88 Even as early as 1939 he wrote, with just perhaps a touch of irony, that one reason to fight to sustain British democracy against Hitler was "to make the world safe for Slough to go on" (Betjeman to Cyril Connolly, 19 October 1939, in *Letters, Volume One*, 244).

89 Betjeman to Mr. Percival, 9 January 1967, in *Letters, Volume Two*, 326; see also Peterson, *John Betjeman: A Bibliography*, 455.

90 Evidence that the poem's vision is religious, and that Betjeman did not relinquish this vision, can be found in his 1946 sermon delivered at St. Matthew's Church, Northampton (*Five Sermons by Laymen*, 10).

91 "Wartime Tastes in Reading," in *Trains and Buttered Toast*, 149–50.

92 "Love Is Dead,"in *First and Last Loves*, 2–3. Hillier provides a strong summary of the reaction to this publication (*New Fame, New Love*, 479–86).

93 This prayer, from the 1662 *Book of Common Prayer*, is the collect for Quinquagesima Sunday (the Sunday before Lent) and was composed by Thomas Cranmer for the first English prayer book (1549) in response to the assigned epistle, 1 Corinthians 13, which is famously about love.

94 Betjeman to Ninian Comper, 12 October 1939, in *Letters, Volume One*, 241.

95 It was widely rumored that Betjeman was involved in espionage, a dangerous engagement in an Ireland that was technically neutral but generally pro-Germany. For a time, Betjeman was even the subject of an IRA assassination plot. His actual job was more in the line of disseminating pro-British propaganda and helping to suppress anti-British sentiments. For more on this period of Betjeman's life, see Hillier, *New Fame, New Love*, 229–37; and Robert Cole, *Propaganda, Censorship and Irish Neutrality in the Second World War* (Edinburgh: Edinburgh University Press, 2006), 52–53, 69–72, 91–96, 130–37, 152–53. See also Eunan O'Halpin, *Spying on Ireland: British Intelligence and Irish Neutrality during the Second World War* (Oxford: Oxford University Press, 2008), 138–39, 210–12; and Robert Fisk, *In Time*

of War: Ireland, Ulster and the Price of Neutrality, 1939–1945 (Philadelphia: University of Pennsylvania Press, 1983), 381.

96 "'Oh, to be in England…,'" 296. See also "Some Comments in Wartime" (BBC radio, 4 July 1940), in *Trains and Buttered Toast*, 129–33.

97 Philip Larkin, "It Could Only Happen in England," 32. Larkin is quoting Betjeman's poem "Margate, 1940" (*CP*, 100).

Chapter 5

1 *A Passion for Churches* (BBC Two, 7 December 1974; prod. Edward Mirzoeff), in *Betjeman's England*, 205.

2 Taylor-Martin, *John Betjeman*, 50.

3 "Three Churches," in *First and Last Loves*, 179.

4 *A Passion for Churches*, in *Betjeman's England*, 197.

5 *A Passion for Churches*, in *Betjeman's England*, 204–5.

6 "Domine Dirige Nos," 39. St. Vedast's was lovingly restored following the war.

7 "The Church of St John," in *West Country Churches*, 13.

8 "The Church of St John," in *West Country Churches*, 11.

9 "A Ballad of the Investiture 1969" was written before Betjeman was appointed Poet Laureate.

10 Neill, *Anglicanism*, 426.

11 *A Passion for Churches*, in *Betjeman's England*, 202, 205–6.

12 According to William J. Wolf, "Anglicanism, coming from an establishment position as a national church concerned with all types and conditions of people, has always been deeply rooted in a cultural context" (*Spirit of Anglicanism*, 158).

13 See Countryman, *Poetic Imagination*, 33–35.

14 "An Ecumenical Invitation" (1982).

15 "How to Look at a Church," 486.

16 It is important to note that Betjeman's vision of community is specifically Anglican, despite his fascination with nonconformity (see chap. 2). His vision does not embrace a broader notion of a nondenominational Christian community, let alone of an English community regardless of faith. For instance, he found great fault with the fuzziness surrounding the meaning and purpose of the designs for a rebuilt cathedral in Coventry: "Among the public there is a vague feeling that there ought to be a cathedral and that it ought to be religious but it does not matter really what kind of religion so long as there is general goodwill all round." Such thinking, which ignored the fundamental fact that this was to be an Anglican cathedral and not "a Christian service centre," provoked much vituperation from

Betjeman. He was especially skeptical of the idea of Coventry's cathedral having a "Chapel of Unity" ("Christian Architecture," 16).

17 "How to Look at a Church," 484.

18 Even the poem's archaic title is meant to suggest a sense of unity in spirit across time. An occasional poem, its full title is as follows: "Verses turned in aid of *A Public Subscription* (1952) towards the restoration of the Church of St. Katherine Chiselhampton, Oxon." The parish of St. Katherine, Chiselhampton, is united with St. John the Baptist, Stadhampton, in the Diocese of Oxford. The little Georgian church (1762–1763), now preserved by the Churches Conservation Trust, holds occasional services there. It is of sufficiently singular merit to warrant entries in several significant guides, including Betjeman's *Collins Guide to English Parish Churches*; Mark Chatfield's *Churches the Victorians Forgot* (Ashbourne: Moorland, 1989), a work whose title becomes meaningful in light of Betjeman's question, "If it were an old church, would it be ruined inside by Victorian 'restoration'?" (13); Durant's *The Good Church Guide*; and Jenkins' *England's Thousand Best Churches*.

19 Betjeman's own parish history of his church in Wantage makes this point; see "Wantage," *Country Churchman*, November 1955, 4–5; rpt. in *Parish of Wantage*, online: www.wantageparish.com/aparishnote.htm.

20 "Chiselhampton Church," *Times*, 18 April 1952, 18. The signatories included the church's vicar, the bishop of Oxford, and John Piper.

21 Like "Verses Turned," this poem's archaic title is meant to create a sense of poetic and spiritual unity across time and space. Its full title is "Church of England thoughts occasioned by hearing the bells of Magdalen Tower from the Botanic Garden, Oxford on St. Mary Magdalen's Day."

22 Near Bristol, Bitton St. Mary's and Kelston St. Nicholas are both famous for their bells.

23 "Village Wedding," *New Yorker*, 11 July 1959; rpt. in *Faith and Doubt*, 105–6. Betjeman wrote this poem to celebrate the marriage of Sally Weaver, a family friend.

24 Betjeman's quotation of Psalm 131 is not from the Authorized Version of the Bible but from the Psalter in *The Book of Common Prayer*.

25 Candida Lycett Green in *Letters, Volume One*, 367–68.

26 Introduction to *Collins Guide to English Parish Churches*, 28–29.

27 "Isaac Watts" (BBC radio, 6 July 1975), in *Sweet Songs of Zion*, 21. Betjeman also contributed to Samuel Carr's anthology, *Hymns as Poetry*.

28 It was Stephen Games who recovered these forgotten broadcasts, then edited and published the entire series in *Sweet Songs of Zion*.

29 Lowe, "The Church," 578.

30 Games, introduction to *Sweet Songs of Zion*, 15.
31 "Hymns of the Mission" (BBC radio, 3 August 1975), in *Sweet Songs of Zion*, 70.
32 Games, introduction to *Sweet Songs of Zion*, 15.
33 Qtd. in John Betjeman, *A Passion for Churches*, in *Betjeman's England*, 204.
34 Games, introduction to *Trains and Buttered Toast*, 1.
35 Games, introduction to *Trains and Buttered Toast*, 2, 10–11, 13. Betjeman sometimes, however, felt he had tendencies toward class-based snobbery; see "Face to Face with Myself," 4.
36 Both quotations are in Games, introduction to *Trains and Buttered Toast*, 26.
37 Games, introduction to *Trains and Buttered Toast*, 26.
38 Hillier, *Bonus of Laughter*, 410.
39 This program, for which he was already supplying occasional talks about his visits to remote churches and about such topics as "The Victorian Sunday," was a weekly religious broadcast on the BBC's West of England Home Service. Betjeman was a regular contributor to this program from 1951 to 1957.
40 Owing to deadlines and other pressures, on a few rare occasions Betjeman read an older, previously published poem. Such was the case in December 1953 when he read the poem "Christmas" in this series. This poem had been published in *Harper's Bazaar* in 1947, but as it would not appear in a collection of his poetry until *A Few Late Chrysanthemums* was published in 1954, this was the first introduction for much of the public to what would soon become a beloved holiday classic. Few people now realize that this poem, so often recited at school and church pageants, was in fact the third of Betjeman's "Poems in the Porch."
41 See introduction, 11; introduction, n. 41.
42 *Poems in the Porch* (2008), 53–56.
43 *Poems in the Porch* (2008), 57–62. In a 1953 essay for the *Country Churchman*, Betjeman wrote essentially the same piece in prose; cf. "Country Church-yards"; rpt. in *Tennis Whites and Teacakes*, 362–64.
44 "Churches in New Towns," *Times*, 2 June 1954, 7.
45 Located in the City near Liverpool Street Station, St. Botolph's Bishop-sgate escaped the great fire but was demolished in the early eighteenth century and was rebuilt by James Gold in 1729. It is still open for occasional weekday services. In its churchyard today is a tennis court.
46 Even church ruins, however, could sustain a community. Betjeman added his support to a 1968 campaign to save the houses that had been built into the ruins of St. Edmundsbury Abbey. These eighteenth-century dwellings were now a part of the living history of the abbey and served to illustrate

that, though ruined, its architecture and culture was unique and vital ("Bury St Edmunds Abbey," *Times*, 10 August 1968, 9).

47 One of Sir Christopher Wren's City churches, St. Mary Magdalen, Old Fish Street Hill, was lost to fire in 1886, and the parish was united to St. Martin Ludgate in 1890.

48 Figures accounting for the population of the City and of greater London vary widely, but both before and after the Great Fire of 1666 it is quite possible that more than 100,000 souls resided within the walls of the City. As late as 1861, an estimated 129,128 people lived in the City out of a total population of nearly 3 million (www.victorianlondon.org/publications/raggedlondon-tables.htm). The massive migration out of the City occurred in the last three decades of the nineteenth century (Ben Weinreb and Christopher Hibbert, eds., *The London Encyclopedia* [Bethesda, Md.: Adler, 1986]). By 1951, the City could claim only 5,324 residents (Demographia, "London Political Subdivisions (Boroughs & Cities): Population & Population Density from 1951," *Demographia*, www.publicpurpose.com/dmlonpop.htm), although in the 2001 census that figured had risen to 7,185 (London Statistics Online, "Census 2001: Population Pyramids: City of London," *London Statistics Online*, www.statistics.gov.uk/census2001/pyramids/pages/00aa.asp).

49 Like many of the churches in central London, Aldersgate Street Station and its delightful buffet were destroyed by Nazi bombs. See Betjeman, "Alas, Poor London," 54; "City and Suburban," *Spectator*, 29 October 1954, 516.

50 Within the ancient walls of the City there were once 97 parish churches, but a mere 38 now survive, and many of those have been declared redundant and leased for other purposes. See Betjeman's *The City of London Churches* (London: Pitkin Pictorials, 1965) and Gerald Cobb's *London City Churches* (London: Batsford, 1977).

51 All three of these churches were designed by Wren to replace older churches lost during the great fire of 1666, which destroyed 89 of the original 97 parish churches in the historic City. Fifty-one of these were rebuilt, requiring many parishes to be united. Of the three churches that Betjeman cites, only St. Michael, Paternoster Royal, is still open for occasional weekday services. St. Mildred's Bread Street was destroyed in the Blitz, and its parish was united to St. Mary-le-Bow in 1954. Christ Church Newgate was also destroyed during the war, though its steeple survives. St. Leonard, Foster Lane, was united to Christ Church Newgate in 1670, and both were united to St. Sepulchre Holborn (a.k.a. Holy Sepulchre without Newgate) in 1954. See *GenDocs* (homepage.ntlworld.com/hitch/gendocs/city-ch.html) for histories of all the original 97 parishes.

52 Betjeman echoed this sentiment in his "Men and Buildings" series of newspaper essays: "The quietest Sunday walk today is in the heart of a big city" ("What a Town Ought to Be," *Daily Telegraph*, 24 February 1964, 15; rpt. as "The Ideal Town," in *Coming Home*.

53 Betjeman echoed the metaphor three years later in a letter to the *Times* concerning the proposed demolition of the Coal Exchange in order to widen certain roads: "We do not want to see its site as one more gap among the new cliffs of the City while the rest of the proposed new route remains uncompleted, or is abandoned altogether" ("Coal Exchange," *Times*, 25 October 1958, 7).

54 "London's Least-Tasted Pleasure," 25.

55 Betjeman makes a similar point in his *Collins Guide to English Parish Churches*. Here he laments the social and ecclesiastical changes wrought by technological development: "They have been brought about by the change in transport from steam to motor-bus and electric train. People are moving out of the crowded early Victorian industrial lanes and terraces, into little houses of their own, each with its little patch of garden at the back and front, each isolated from its neighbour by social convention, in districts where miles of pavement enlivened by the squeak of perambulators lead to a far-off bus route and parade of chain stores, and a distant vita-glass school, used as a Community Centre in the evenings. To these places, often lonely for all the people in them, is the new mission Church" (82). Though the diatribe is conservative in tone, Betjeman retains hope that the church will serve to reunite a disparate community.

56 The recurring analogy between railways and the church is not unique to Betjeman. Christopher Howse has written recently about the special feeling that Anglican clergy in particular seem to have for railways ("Dog-collars on the Footplate," *Daily Telegraph*, 9 February 2008, http://www. telegraph.co.uk/opinion/main.jhtml?xml=/opinion/2008/02/09/do0908. xml). The Reverend W. V. Awdry, creator of the Thomas the Tank Engine series of children's books, famously said, "Railways and the Church have their critics, but both are the best way of getting man to his ultimate destination" (http://www.bigg-wither.com/Obituaries_and_Eulogies/The_ Reverend_W_V_Awdry_1911_-_1987.htm).

57 Evelyn Waugh, who argued at length and in vain with Betjeman about converting to the Roman Catholic Church, excoriated him for his loyalty to the established church and his opposition to a nationalized railway. In a 1952 review of Betjeman's *First and Last Loves*, Waugh takes his friend to task: "He rants against state control, but he is a member of the Church of England. In the face of that prodigious state usurpation laments about the

colour of nationalized railway engines lose their poignancy" ("Mr Betjeman Despairs," in *The Essays, Articles and Reviews of Evelyn Waugh*, 430). Betjeman did not demand a political or institutional consistency from himself; he was also a supporter of the National Health Service ("City and Suburban," *Spectator*, 25 February 1955, 216; "Face to Face with Myself," 4).

58 Helge Nowak argues that this stanza "reads like an ironic summary of one of Churchill's war speeches, even more so as in both cases the war effort is directed towards one overall purpose: to keep or to return to the *status quo ante bellum* after having got rid of the threat posed to it by the German enemy" ("Britain, Britishness and the Blitz: Public Images, Attitudes and Visions in Times of War," in *War and the Cultural Construction of Identities in Britain*, eds. Barbara Korte and Ralf Schneider [Amsterdam: Rodopi, 2002], 252).

59 Betjeman's title emphasizes geographical specificity and historicity, for the church in question is Emmanuel Church, Clifton, in the city of Bristol (Hillier, *New Fame, New Love*, 281–82). Constructed during the great frenzy of Victorian church building, it was situated at the intersection of Guthrie Road and Pembroke Road, where the speaker now lives, a fine address (as he tells it) and a significant step up socially from his previous address in Manilla Road, only a few blocks away. Emmanuel Church was Clifton's low church, liturgically speaking, and this explains in part the speaker's deeply seated antipathy to anything that smacks of Roman ritualism. Emmanuel Church was declared redundant in 1974 and demolished to build flats for the elderly. Only the tower remains and is incorporated into the new structure. It stands within sight of Clifton College and is also very near the Bristol Zoo.

60 This poem's indebtedness to Robert Browning's "My Last Duchess" is the subject of my essay "John Betjeman's 'Bristol and Clifton': Echoes of Robert Browning's 'My Last Duchess,'" 35–38.

61 "Three Churches," in *First and Last Loves*, 182.

62 "St. Endellion," in *The Best of Betjeman*, 149.

63 "St Mark's, Swindon," in *West Country Churches*, 19. Originally written for radio: "St Mark's, Swindon, Wiltshire" (BBC radio, 4 August 1948).

64 "St Mark's, Swindon," in *West Country Churches*, 17.

65 "St Mark's, Swindon," in *West Country Churches*, 18.

66 "St Mark's, Swindon," in *West Country Churches*, 19.

67 On 24 November 1981 the parish and benefice of St. Saviour's, Highbury, was united to that of Christ Church, Highbury, with St. John, forming the new parish and benefice of Christ Church, Highbury, with St. John and St. Saviour. Still located off Highbury Road between Islington and

Stoke Newington, St. Saviour's has since 1988 been leased by the London Diocesan Fund to the Florence Trust Studios, a group which provides studio space for young artists and which occasionally sponsors shows of their work. Thanks to Mr. Paul Howlett, Team Leader of the Redundant Churches Division, the Church Commissioners for England, for this information (correspondence with the author, 4 September 2003).

68 Betjeman was always taken with St. Saviour's proportions, light, and decorations, and concluded that "the effect of the building though small is of mystery and size" (*Collins Guide to English Parish Churches*, 257).

69 "Face to Face with Myself," 4.

70 According to Derek Stanford, Betjeman's poetic vision "recognized the present inequality of men before men and their final equality *before God*. It would posit a world where men were separated by the marks of their upbringing, station, and calling; but a world where they, too, were brought together in a communion of worship *of God*" (*John Betjeman*, 58).

71 Betjeman also worked this idea into his 1946 sermon delivered at St. Matthew's Church, Northampton (*Five Sermons by Laymen*, 11).

72 Such piety, writes Wolf, "must seek to incarnate something of the deeper joy of Christ's sacrifice and the willingness to die to self for the glory of God" (*Spirit of Anglicanism*, 178).

73 Philip Larkin, *Collected Poems*, ed. Anthony Thwaite (New York: Farrar, Straus & Giroux, 2003), 59.

74 Jenkins, *England's Thousand Best Churches*, xxix.

75 *A Passion for Churches*, in *Betjeman's England*, 207.

BIBLIOGRAPHY

The following bibliography enumerates the works by and about John Betjeman as well as general background sources that I cite in my text. This is by no means an exhaustive bibliography of works by and about Betjeman, for which one should consult William S. Peterson, *John Betjeman: A Bibliography*. Those needing to locate contemporary responses to Betjeman's publications may wish to consult Margaret L. Stapleton, *Sir John Betjeman: A Bibliography of Writings by and about Him*, which is particularly strong in this regard.

Primary Sources

Books

The following list contains books written or edited by John Betjeman along with collections and anthologies of his writing edited by others. Most of the poems, essays, and radio and television broadcasts from which I quote in this book are collected in one or more of these books. Uncollected writings are listed separately below under "Individual Works."

Archie and the Strict Baptists. London: John Murray, 1977.
The Best of Betjeman. Ed. John Guest. London: John Murray, 1978.
Betjeman's England. Ed. Stephen Games. London: John Murray, 2009.
The City of London Churches. London: Pitkin Pictorials, 1965.
Collected Poems. London: John Murray, 1958, 2006.

Collins Guide to English Parish Churches Including the Isle of Man. Ed. John Betjeman. London: Collins, 1958.

Coming Home: An Anthology of His Prose, 1920–1977. Ed. Candida Lycett Green. London: Vintage, 1997.

Continual Dew: A Little Book of Bourgeois Verse. London: John Murray, 1937.

English Cities and Small Towns. London: Collins, 1943.

Faith and Doubt of John Betjeman: An Anthology of Betjeman's Religious Verse. Ed. Kevin J. Gardner. London: Continuum, 2005.

A Few Late Chrysanthemums. London: John Murray, 1954.

First and Last Loves. London: John Murray, 1952.

High and Low. London: John Murray, 1966.

Letters, Volume One: 1926 to 1951. Ed. Candida Lycett Green. London: Methuen, 1994, 2006.

Letters, Volume Two: 1951 to 1984. Ed. Candida Lycett Green. London: Methuen, 1995, 2006.

Mount Zion; or, In Touch with the Infinite. London: The James Press, 1931.

New Bats in Old Belfries: Poems. London: John Murray, 1945.

A Nip in the Air. London: John Murray, 1974.

Old Lights for New Chancels: Verses Topographical and Amatory. London: John Murray, 1940.

Poems in the Porch. London: SPCK, 1954.

Poems in the Porch: The Radio Poems of John Betjeman. Ed. Kevin J. Gardner. London: Continuum, 2008.

Selected Poems. Ed. John Sparrow. London: John Murray, 1948.

Slick but Not Streamlined: Poems and Short Pieces by John Betjeman. Ed. W. H. Auden. Garden City, N.Y.: Doubleday, 1947.

Summoned by Bells. London: John Murray, 1960.

Sweet Songs of Zion: Selected Radio Talks. Ed. Stephen Games. London: Hodder & Stoughton, 2007.

Tennis Whites and Teacakes. Ed. Stephen Games. London: John Murray, 2007.

Trains and Buttered Toast: Selected Radio Talks. Ed. Stephen Games. London: John Murray, 2006.

Uncollected Poems. Ed. Bevis Hillier. London: John Murray, 1982.

West Country Churches. London: Society of SS Peter and Paul, 1973.

Individual Works

The following list contains individual poems, essays, articles, chapters, and other uncollected writings by John Betjeman. In addition to these specifically enumerated items, I also quote extensively from the anthologies and collections cited above under "Books."

"1830–1930—Still Going Strong: A Guide to the Recent History of Interior Decoration." *Architectural Review* May 1930: 230–40.

"1837–1937: A Spiritual Change Is the One Hope for Art." *Studio* February 1937: 56–73.

"Alas, Poor London." *Strand* November 1946: 51–55.

"The Angry Novelist." *Strand* March 1947: 42–44.

"Billy Graham." *Spectator* 12 March 1954: 282–83.

"Blisland, Bodmin." *Oxford Outlook* June 1927: 319.

"The Bressey Report." *Criterion* 18 (1938): 1–12.

"Bury St Edmunds Abbey." *Times* 10 August 1968: 9.

"Chiselhampton Church." *Times* 18 April 1952: 18.

"Christian Architecture." *Britain Today* February 1951: 16–19.

"Churches in New Towns." *Times* 2 June 1954: 7.

"City and Suburban." *Spectator* 29 October 1954: 516.

"City and Suburban." *Spectator* 25 February 1955: 216.

"City and Suburban." *Spectator* 7 October 1955: 444–45.

"City and Suburban." *Spectator* 4 May 1956: 615.

"City and Suburban." *Spectator* 6 July 1956: 14.

"City and Suburban." *Spectator* 28 December 1956: 930.

"City and Suburban," *Spectator* 26 July 1957: 131–32.

"City and Suburban." *Spectator* 15 November 1957: 642.

"City and Suburban." *Spectator* 22 November 1957: 682–84.

"Clay and Spirit." *A Few Late Chrysanthemums*. London: John Murray, 1954. 62–63.

"Coal Exchange." *Times* 25 October 1958: 7.

"Competition." *Mount Zion*. London: The James Press, 1931. 30–31.

"Concrete Lamp-Standards in Old Town Settings." *Daily Telegraph* 23 February 1952: 4.

"Councillor Bloggins Is Changing the Face of England." *Daily Express* 15 July 1936: 10.

"Death." *Country Churchman* April 1958: 3.

"Design for a New Cathedral." *Daily Telegraph* 3 September 1951: 4.

"Domine Dirige Nos." *Listener* 9 January 1941: 37–39.

"England's Cottages a Heritage Worth Defending." *Daily Telegraph* 23 August 1954: 4.

"Essential England." *Daily Telegraph* 29 April 1954: 6.

"The Fabric of Our Faith." *Punch* 23 December 1953: 744.

"Face to Face with Myself." *Daily Herald* 8 March 1961: 4.

"Fons et Origo." *Times* 3 August 1982: 9.

Foreword. *The Altar Steps*. By Compton Mackenzie. London: Macdonald, 1956. vii–viii.

Foreword. *The Word Is the Seed: Meditations Starting from the Bible*. By George Appleton. London: SPCK, 1976. viii.

"Fulham Grange." *Spectator* 16 July 1954: 75.

"Glories of English Craftsmanship—Electricity and Old Churches." *Time and Tide* 5 December 1953: 1582–83.

"Hawksmoor's Churches." *Times* 3 May 1977: 15.

"Hereford Screen." *Times* 4 March 1966: 13.

"High Frecklesby Has a Plan." *Punch* 27 May 1953: 624–25.

"Holy Trinity, Sloane Street." *Sunday Times* 15 September 1974: 35.

"How to Look at a Church." *Listener* 8 September 1938: 484–86.

"I Accuse These Grey-Faced Men of Britain." *Daily Express* 12 March 1962: 8.

"I saw the light & I rejected it." Betjeman Archive. British Library Add. MS 71645, fol. 82.

Introduction. *Songs at the Year's Turning: Poems, 1942–1954*. By R. S. Thomas. London: Hart-Davis, 1955. 11–14.

"John Betjeman Replies." *Spectator* 8 October 1954: 443.

"Letcombe Bassett." *Times* 3 December 1948: 5.

"London Tower Blocks." *Times* 9 June 1980: 15.

"London's Least-Tasted Pleasure." *Illustrated London News* (June 1971): 23, 25–27.

"Long, Long Trail." *Punch* 9 June 1954: 682.

"Lovely Bits of Old England Must Be Spared." *Daily Telegraph* 26 July 1952: 4.

Moral Problems: Questions on Christianity with Answers by Prominent Churchmen. London: Mowbray, 1952. 106–8.

"Nonconformist Architecture." *Architectural Review* December 1940: 161–74.

"Not Necessarily Leeds." *Spectator* 1 October 1954: 392.

"Now is my heart on fire." *The Barrier*. By Robin Maugham. London: W. H. Allen, 1973. 195.

"'Oh, to be in England . . .'." *Listener* 11 March 1943: 295–96.

"The Outer Suburbs." *Mount Zion*. London: The James Press, 1931. 44.

"Oxford and Suburban." *Spectator* 14 October 1955: 493.

Preface. *Hymns as Poetry*. Ed. Samuel Carr. London: Batsford, 1980. 7–8.

"Royal Agricultural Hall." *Times* 15 August 1974: 13.

"Selling Our Churches." *Spectator* 2 April 1954: 383–84.

Sermon. 5 May 1946. St. Matthew's Church, Northampton. *Five Sermons by Laymen*. Northampton: Dickens, 1946. 7–11.

"Southend Pier." *Times* 22 February 1974: 15.

"A Spectator's Notebook." *Spectator* 27 August 1954: 244.

"St Bartholomew's Hospital, EC1." *London Magazine* (December 1978–January 1979): 61.

"St Mary-le-Strand." *Times* 5 November 1981: 13.

"St. Mary Redcliffe." *Times* 7 July 1961: 13.

"Those Horseless Carriages." *Everybody's: The Popular Weekly* 22 October 1955: 16–17.

"Threat to Setting of Bury St Edmunds." *Times* 4 October 1972: 15.

"To Uffington Ringers." *Diversion*. Ed. Hester W. Chapman and Princess Romanovsky-Pavlovsky. London: Collins, 1946. 160.

"A Tower Opposite the Tate." *Times* 4 February 1980: 13.

"Trebetherick." *Both Sides of the Tamar: A West Country Alphabet*. Ed. Michael Williams. St. Teath, Cornwall: Bossiney, 1975. 441–42.

"True Colour in Glass for Cathedral." *Daily Telegraph* 4 July 1956: 8.

"Uffington White Horse." *Times* 6 June 1975: 15.

"Village Wedding." *New Yorker* 11 July 1959: 30.

"Wantage." *Country Churchman* November 1955: 4-5; rpt. as *Parish of Wantage*. www.wantageparish.com/aparishnote.htm.

"White Horse Hill." *Times* 26 April 1947: 5.

"Winchester Motorway." *Times* 14 May 1971: 17.

Secondary Sources

Books about John Betjeman

Brooke, Jocelyn. *Ronald Firbank and John Betjeman.* Writers and Their Work 153. London: Longmans (in association with the British Council), 1962.

Brown, Dennis. *John Betjeman.* Writers and Their Work n.s. Plymouth: Northcote House (in association with the British Council), 1999.

Delaney, Frank. *Betjeman Country.* London: Hodder & Stoughton, 1983.

Hillier, Bevis. *Betjeman: The Bonus of Laughter.* London: John Murray, 2004.

———. *John Betjeman: New Fame, New Love.* London: John Murray, 2002.

———. *Young Betjeman.* London: John Murray, 1988.

Morse, Greg. *John Betjeman: Reading the Victorians.* Eastbourne, UK: Sussex Academic Press, 2008.

Mowl, Timothy. *Stylistic Cold Wars: Betjeman Versus Pevsner.* London: John Murray, 2000.

Payton, Philip. *John Betjeman and Cornwall: "The Celebrated Cornish Nationalist."* Exeter: University of Exeter Press, 2010.

Peterson, William S. *John Betjeman: A Bibliography.* Oxford: Clarendon, 2006.

Press, John. *John Betjeman.* Writers and Their Work 237. London: Longman (in association with the British Council), 1974.

Pringle, Roger, ed. *A Garland for the Laureate: Poems Presented to Sir John Betjeman on His 75th Birthday.* Stratford-upon-Avon: Celandine Press, 1981.

Stanford, Derek. *John Betjeman: A Study.* London: Spearman, 1961.

Stapleton, Margaret L. *Sir John Betjeman: A Bibliography of Writings by and about Him.* Metuchen, N.J.: Scarecrow Press, 1974.

Taylor-Martin, Patrick. *John Betjeman: His Life and Work.* London: Lane, 1983.

Wilson, A. N. *Betjeman.* London: Hutchinson, 2006.

Articles, Essays, and Book Chapters about John Betjeman

Allsop, Kenneth. "The Year of the Poet." *Daily Mail* 9 December 1960: 8.

Andrews, Michael Cameron. "Betjeman's 'Senex.'" *Explicator* 43.3 (1985): 40–41.

Auden, W. H. Introduction. *Slick but Not Streamlined: Poems and Short Pieces by John Betjeman.* Garden City, N.Y.: Doubleday, 1947. 9–16.

Bale, John. "John Betjeman." *Anti-Sports Sentiments in Literature: Batting for the Opposition.* London: Routledge, 2008. 77–95.

Bayley, John. "The Best of Betjeman." *The Power of Delight: A Lifetime in Literature.* London: Duckworth, 2005. 184–95.

Bell, Alan. "By Appointment: Teddy Bear to the Nation." *Times* 20 September 1982: 5.

Davie, Donald. "Philip Larkin and John Betjeman." *Under Briggflatts.* Chicago: University of Chicago Press, 1989. 113–19.

Fletcher, Christopher. "John Betjeman's 'Before the Anaesthetic, or a Real Fright': A Source for Philip Larkin's 'Aubade.'" *Notes and Queries* 54.2 (2007): 179–81.

Games, Stephen. Introduction. *Betjeman's England.* London: John Murray, 2009. 1–29.

———. Introduction. *Sweet Songs of Zion: Selected Radio Talks.* London: Hodder & Stoughton, 2007. 1–19.

———. Introduction. *Tennis Whites and Teacakes.* London: John Murray, 2007. 1–18.

———. Introduction. *Trains and Buttered Toast: Selected Radio Talks.* London: John Murray, 2006. 1–29.

Gardner, Kevin J. "Anglicanism and the Poetry of John Betjeman." *Christianity and Literature* 53.3 (2004): 361–83.

———. "John Betjeman: Centenary Publications." *Religion and the Arts* 11.1 (2007): 98–117.

———. "John Betjeman's 'Bristol and Clifton': Echoes of Robert Browning's 'My Last Duchess.'" *ANQ* 19.3 (2006): 35–38.

Gervais, David. "Larkin, Betjeman and the Aftermath of 'England.'" *Literary Englands: Versions of "Englishness" in Modern Writing.* Cambridge: Cambridge University Press, 1993. 185–219.

Gill, A. A. "The Truth Is Out: His Poetry Had No Sole." *Sunday Times* 20 August 2006; online edition, http://www.timesonline.co.uk/article/0,,21012315891.html.

Hamilton, Ian. "Tripping Up." *New Statesman* 22/29 December 1978: 881.

Harvey, Geoffrey. "John Betjeman: An Odeon Flashes Fire." *The Romantic Tradition in Modern English Poetry*. New York: St. Martin's, 1986. 71–96. Originally published as "Poetry of Commitment: John Betjeman's Later Writing." *Dalhousie Review* 56 (1976): 112–24.

Hoffpauir, Richard. "Social Consolations." *The Art of Restraint: English Poetry from Hardy to Larkin*. London: Associated University Presses, 1991. 241–63.

Lancaster, Osbert. "John Betjeman." *Strand* November 1946: 52.

Larkin, Philip. "Betjeman en Bloc." *Listen: A Review of Poetry and Criticism* 3.2 (1959): 14–23.

———. "The Blending of Betjeman." *Required Writing*. 129–33.

———. "It Could Only Happen in England: A Study of John Betjeman's Poems for American Readers." *Required Writing*. 204–18.

———. *Required Writing: Miscellaneous Pieces, 1955–1982*. London: Faber & Faber, 1983.

Lowe, Peter J. "The Church as a Building and the Church as a Community in the Work of John Betjeman." *Christianity and Literature* 57.4 (2008): 559–81.

Macdonald, Kate. "The Travels of John Betjeman's Literary Voice in 'The Arrest of Oscar Wilde at the Cadogan Hotel': From the 1890s to the 1920s, and Back Again." *BELL: Belgian Journal of English Language and Literatures* 5 (2007): 59–66.

McDermott, John V. "Betjeman's 'The Arrest of Oscar Wilde at the Cadogan Hotel.'" *Explicator* 57.3 (1999): 165–66.

Mills, Ralph J. "John Betjeman's Poetry: An Appreciation." *Descant* 13 (1969): 2–18. Rpt. in Stapleton, *Sir John Betjeman*. Metuchen, N.J.: Scarecrow, 1974. 1–23.

Motion, Andrew. "Introduction." *Collected Poems*. By John Betjeman. London: John Murray, 2006. xv–xxiv.

Neame, Alan. "Poet of Anglicanism." *Commonweal* 4 December 1959: 282–84.

Nowak, Helge. "Britain, Britishness and the Blitz: Public Images, Attitudes and Visions in Times of War." *War and the Cultural Construction of Identities in Britain.* Ed. Barbara Korte and Ralf Schneider. Amsterdam: Rodopi, 2002. 241–59.

Payton, Philip. "John Betjeman and the Holy Grail: One Man's Celtic Quest." *Cornish Studies* 15 (2007): 185–208.

Priestman, Judith. "The Dilenttante and the Dons." *Oxford Today* 18.3 (2006): 20–23.

Raine, Craig. "John Betjeman." *Haydn and the Valve Trumpet: Literary Essays.* London: Faber & Faber, 1990. 313–26.

Ruddick, Bill. "'Some ruin-bibber, randy for antique': Philip Larkin's Response to the Poetry of John Betjeman." *Critical Quarterly* 28.4 (1986): 63–69.

Schmidt, Michael. *The Lives of the Poets.* New York: Knopf, 1999. 742–43 and *passim.*

Schröder, Leena K. "Heterotopian Constructions of Englishness in the Work of John Betjeman." *Critical Survey* 10.2 (1998): 15–34.

Sparrow, John. Preface. *Selected Poems.* By John Betjeman. London: John Murray, 1948. ix–xxii. Rpt. as "The Poetry of John Betjeman." *Independent Essays.* By Sparrow. London: Faber & Faber, 1963. 166–79.

Summerson, John. "In the Betjeman Country." *New Statesman* 4 October 1952: 382.

Tewdwr-Jones, Mark. "'Oh, the planners did their best': The Planning Films of John Betjeman." *Planning Perspectives* 20 (2005): 389–411.

Thomas, Peter. "Reflections on the Collected Poems of John Betjeman." *Western Humanities Review* 27 (1973): 289–94.

Thwaite, Anthony. "Feeling His Way to Posterity." *The Guardian* 30 December 2006; online edition, http://www.guardian.co.uk/books/2006/dec/30/poetry.johnbetjeman.

Townsend, Michael. "Sir John Betjeman—Christian Poet?" *Expository Times* 97.12 (1986): 360–64.

Wain, John. "A Substitute for Poetry." *Observer* 27 November 1960. Rpt. in *Essays on Literature and Ideas.* By Wain. London: Macmillan, 1963. 168–71.

Waugh, Auberon. "Is Trifle Sufficient?" *Spectator* 26 May 1984: 6.

Wiehe, R. E. "Summoned by Nostalgia: John Betjeman's Poetry." *Arizona Quarterly* 19.1 (1963): 37–49.

Williams, Hugo. "Introduction." *John Betjeman*. By John Betjeman. Poet to Poet Series. London: Faber & Faber, 2006. ix–xvii.

Wilson, Edward. "Betjeman's Riddel Posts: An Echo of Ninian Comper." *Review of English Studies* 42 (1991): 541–50.

General Secondary Sources

Allchin, A. M. "Anglican Spirituality." *The Study of Anglicanism*. Eds. Stephen Sykes and John Booty. London: SPCK, 1988. 313–25.

Auden, W. H. *Making, Knowing and Judging: An Inaugural Lecture Delivered before the University of Oxford on 11 June 1956*. Oxford: Clarendon, 1956.

The Book of Common Prayer. 1662.

Chatfield, Mark. *Churches the Victorians Forgot*. Ashbourne: Moorland, 1989.

Cobb, Gerald. *London City Churches*. London: Batsford, 1977.

Cole, Robert. *Propaganda, Censorship and Irish Neutrality in the Second World War*. Edinburgh: Edinburgh University Press, 2006.

Countryman, L. William. *The Poetic Imagination: An Anglican Spiritual Tradition*. London: Darton, 1999.

"Davies Street: West Side." *British History Online*. http://www.british-history.ac.uk/report.aspx?compid=42109#s8.

Davis, William V. *R. S. Thomas: Poetry and Theology*. Waco, Tex.: Baylor University Press, 2007.

Demographia. "London Political Subdivisions (Boroughs & Cities): Population & Population Density From 1951." *Demographia*. www.publicpurpose.com/dmlonpop.htm.

Durant, David N. *The Good Church Guide*. London: Vermilion, 1995.

Eliot, T. S. *The Waste Land*. 1922. *The Waste Land and Other Poems*. New York: Harcourt, 1958.

Fisk, Robert. *In Time of War: Ireland, Ulster and the Price of Neutrality, 1939–45*. Philadelphia: University of Pennsylvania Press, 1983.

GenDocs. "City of London Churches: Anglican Church." *GenDocs*. homepage.ntlworld.com/hitch/gendocs/city-ch.html.

Harton, F. P. *The Elements of the Spiritual Life: A Study in Ascetical Theology*. London: SPCK; New York: Macmillan, 1932.

Herbert, George. *The Temple*. 1633. Ed. Henry L. Carrigan. Brewster, Mass.: Paraclete Press, 2001.

Hollingshead, John. *Ragged London in 1861.* London: Smith, Elder, 1861; online edition, www.victorianlondon.org/publications/ragged london-tables.htm.

Howse, Christopher. "Dog-collars on the Footplate." *Daily Telegraph* 9 February 2008; online edition, http://www.telegraph.co.uk/ opinion/main.html?xml=/opinion/2008/02/09/do0908.xml.

James, Henry. *English Hours.* London: Heinemann, 1905.

Jenkins, Simon. *England's Thousand Best Churches.* London: Lane, 1999.

Kirsch, Arthur. *Auden and Christianity.* New Haven: Yale University Press, 2005.

Larkin, Philip. *Collected Poems.* Ed. Anthony Thwaite. New York: Farrar, Straus & Giroux, 2003.

Lewis, C. S. "On Church Music." *Christian Reflections.* Grand Rapids: Eerdmans, 1967. 94–99.

———. *Surprised by Joy.* London: Harcourt, 1955.

London Statistics Online. "Census 2001: Population Pyramids: City of London." *London Statistics Online.* www.statistics.gov.uk/ census2001/pyramids/pages/00aa.asp.

Lyall, Sarah. "A Town Trying Not to Live Up to Its Name." *The New York Times* 21 March 2008; online edition, http://www.nytimes.com/2008/ 03/21/world/europe/21slough.html?ref=world.

Maugham, Robin. *The Barrier.* London: W. H. Allen, 1973.

More, Paul Elmer. "The Spirit of Anglicanism." *Anglicanism: The Thought and Practice of the Church of England, Illustrated from the Religious Literature of the Seventeenth Century.* Eds. Paul Elmer More and Frank Leslie Cross. London: SPCK, 1935, 1957. xvii–xi.

Neill, Stephen. *Anglicanism.* Harmondsworth, UK: Penguin, 1958.

O'Halpin, Eunan. *Spying on Ireland: British Intelligence and Irish Neutrality during the Second World War.* Oxford: Oxford University Press, 2008.

Oser, Lee. *The Return of Christian Humanism: Chesterton, Eliot, Tolkien, and the Romance of History.* Columbia: University of Missouri Press, 2007.

"The Reverend W. V. Awdry." *Bigg-Wither.* http://www.bigg-wither .com/Obituaries_and_Eulogies/The_Reverend_W_V_Awdry_ 1911_-_1987.htm.

Shakespeare, William. *King Lear*. 1605. Cambridge: Cambridge University Press, 1968.

Temple, William. *Christus Veritas: An Essay*. London: Macmillan, 1924.

Vidler, A. R. *Essays in Liberality*. London: SCM Press, 1951.

Wain, John. *Essays on Literature and Ideas*. London: Macmillan; New York: St. Martin's, 1963.

Waugh, Alexander. *Fathers and Sons: The Autobiography of a Family*. New York: Talese, 2004.

Waugh, Evelyn. *The Essays, Articles and Reviews of Evelyn Waugh*. Ed. Donat Gallagher. Boston: Little, Brown, 1983.

———. *The Letters of Evelyn Waugh*. Ed. Mark Amory. London: Weidenfeld & Nicolson, 1980.

Weinreb, Ben, and Christopher Hibbert, eds. *The London Encyclopedia*. Bethesda, Md.: Adler, 1986.

Wells, H. G. *The Time Machine*. 1895. Whitefish, Mont.: Kessinger, 2004.

Wilson, A. N. *C. S. Lewis: A Biography*. London: Collins, 1990.

Wolf, William J. *The Spirit of Anglicanism*. Wilton, Conn.: Morehouse-Barlow, 1979.

INDEX